BLÉRIOT
Herald of an Age

BLÉRIOT
HERALD OF AN AGE

Brian A. Elliott

TEMPUS

First published 2000

PUBLISHED IN THE UNITED KINGDOM BY:

Tempus Publishing Ltd
The Mill, Brimscombe Port
Stroud, Gloucestershire GL5 2QG

PUBLISHED IN THE UNITED STATES OF AMERICA BY:

Arcadia Publishing Inc.
A division of Tempus Publishing Inc.
2 Cumberland Street
Charleston, SC 29401
(Tel: 1-888-313-2665)

Tempus books are available in France, Germany and Belgium
from the following addresses:

Tempus Publishing Group	Tempus Publishing Group	Tempus Publishing Group
21 Avenue de la République	Gustav-Adolf-Straße 3	Place de L'Alma 4/5
37300 Joué-lès-Tours	99084 Erfurt	1200 Brussels
FRANCE	GERMANY	BELGIUM

British Library Cataloguing in Publication Data.
A catalogue record for this book is available from the British Library.

ISBN 0 7524 1739 8

Typesetting and origination by Tempus Publishing.
PRINTED AND BOUND IN GREAT BRITAIN.

Contents

Acknowledgements

Almost all of the archives of Blériot-Aéronautique were lost during the Second World War when a barge taking them to safety from the factory on the river bank at Suresnes sank in the Seine. However, I have gathered much valuable material from the family archives which Blériot's youngest son, Jean, deposited in the Musée de l'Air et de l'Espace in 1986. These include correspondence, accounts and photographs as well as the unpublished memoirs of Blériot's widow, Alicia, dictated in 1959.

I am indebted to many previous writers, notably: Michel Lhospice, whose *Match pour la Manche* gives a stirring account of the contest that took place over the English Channel in the summer of 1909; Jean Devaux and Michel Marani, whose meticulous research published in *Pégase* has resolved many mysteries about a large number of Blériot's aeroplanes; the late Jean Liron whose works on Blériot and Spad-Herbemont aeroplanes were serialized in *Aviation Magazine International*; Blériot's grandson, also Louis, whose *Blériot: l'Envol du XXe Siècle* provides the most comprehensive and authoritative account of the production of the Blériot firm; Blériot himself, who with Edouard Ramond wrote *La Gloire des Ailes* in 1927, a general history of aviation which would have been more useful to me if he had been less modest about his own role; and Ferdinand Collin, one of Blériot's mechanics from 1907 to 1910, whose *Parmi les Précurseurs du Ciel* gives interesting information, as well as some opinions which need to be treated with reserve, since Collin wrote as an admittedly unhappy ex-employee.

My grateful thanks for help and encouragement are due to Arnold Nayler and Brian Riddle, of the Royal Aeronautical Society; Clotilde Cucci, Gilbert Deloisy, Jean-Marc Lombarde, Jean-Yves Lorant, and Stéphane Nicolaou of the Musée de l'Air et de l'Espace, Le Bourget; John Binner; Jack Bruce; Jean Devaux; Ken Harman; Michel Marani; Marco Rochat; the late Bill Sayer; and William Wilson.

Translations from the French are by the author except where the source notes indicate otherwise.

B. A. E.

Photographs

Photographs are reproduced with the kind permission of the Musée de l'Air et de l'Espace, Le Bourget, except where captions show another source. Permission to reproduce photographs from the collections of the Royal Aeronautical Society and Mr K. E. Harman, and from the Flight collection at the Quadrant Picture Library is also gratefully acknowledged.

Foreword

When Brian Elliott first consulted me in Paris, many years ago, I did not imagine that I would one day have the honour of writing a foreword to his really outstanding book on my grandfather: *Blériot: Herald of an Age*.

As Blériot's grandson I obviously knew from childhood that he was a famous aviation pioneer – 'an early bird' – but since he died several years before I was born, to my eyes he remained a mythical figure. As the years went by the desire to know more about him became so acute that one day I decided to delve into my grandfather's life and achievements. On my first meeting with Brian Elliott I realized that the research would be long and that he was very much ahead of me in this field, for he told me that he had already written part of a book about Louis Blériot. Now that I have completed my research (inasmuch as it is ever possible to do so) and eventually written a book myself on the subject, I can appreciate the excellence of Brian Elliott's work (especially in the absence of the archives of the Blériot factory destroyed in June 1940).

Louis Blériot's story has no happy ending – it seldom happens otherwise in actual life – but it is the story of a man with a vision, of trial and error, of perseverance in adversity, of courage and fighting spirit to the very end.

The author tells us how Louis Blériot, an engineer who specialized in the lighting of motor cars in the last years of the nineteenth century, turned into one of the major pioneers in aviation history to become the first aeronautical industrialist (as early as 1910) and subsequently the leading French fighter manufacturer during the First World War.

Full of interesting and sometimes quite hilarious anecdotes, Brian Elliott's book gives us a lively account of the unique moment in history when man, having explored Land and Sea, decided to take to the Air.

'I do not say they cannot come, my Lords, I only say they cannot come by sea.' Lord St Vincent's humorous remark to his peers lost its significance on 25 July 1909 when Louis Blériot's flimsy monoplane overflew the mighty men-of-war berthed in the harbour of Dover.

Although the first cross-Channel flight heralded the end of British insularity – which might be considered by some as a major drawback – it also heralded the tremendous development of aviation which today enables anyone to reach any destination within a few hours.

It is of course sad that aviation also developed into a deadly weapon, but I suppose this was inevitable since it happened in the same way with all means of transportation: ships, cars, trains and balloons all promptly found military uses. On the other hand, ever since Blériot linked France and England both countries have always fought side by side in the skies, and more recently they have united their efforts to conceive and build beautiful and successful aircraft such as Concorde and Airbus. As for the former Blériot factory, now part of Aérospatiale, it contributed to the development of these splendid modern flying machines.

Louis Blériot

Introduction

Blériot did not go up in any air of trumpets. In the cold grey dawn of the morning, before the sun had warmed up things, before it had dissipated the dew drops, he was in our country. It marks a new era in the world.

Ernest Shackleton (1909)[1]

Louis Blériot was the first person to fly across the English Channel in an aeroplane. That is all that is generally remembered about him today, but it is well remembered, and as well in England where he landed as in France whence he came. If that single event in his life has not been forgotten, is it because his flight was in some way extraordinary, or because the phenomenal press coverage it provoked still echoes across the intervening ninety years, or because the age-old notion of Britain as an island fastness was irrevocably altered by his coming?

What manner of man was this, standing in the dewy grass beside Dover Castle very early on a summer Sunday morning, gently and patiently repeating his entire English vocabulary: 'Good morning' and 'Thank you', to the forerunners of a horde of well-wishers? Was he the 'Friend Invader', as one young man to whom he spoke surmised? Why was it he who had come, and not another? Why was it in France that the aeroplane had been made that was capable of this? How had Louis Blériot learned to fly, at a time when hardly anyone could, and built a practical aeroplane when few existed? How did he actually make his unforgettable journey and what became of him afterwards?

This book is the result of an exploration of those questions, and of others which arose as the story unfolded. I have paid attention to Blériot's activities and attitudes as a businessman and industrialist, and I may have found in these a key to understanding some strange inconsistencies in his aeronautical engineering which puzzled his contemporaries as much as they have perplexed historians.

Louis Blériot (1872-1936) was a professional engineer who at the age of twenty-four invented better ways of employing acetylene gas to illuminate the path in front of motor cars, making practicable their use at night, and then promptly set up the first firm in the world to specialize in the production of headlamps. He did this in time to catch the dramatic boom in car manufacture in the late 1890s, and with his substantial earnings was able, from 1900, to give free rein to his ambition to achieve mechanical flight. An arduous and protracted series of experiments in aviation followed, as he strove simultaneously to develop a practical aeroplane and to teach himself to be a pilot. The culmination of this pioneering phase came when he flew across the Straits of Dover on 25 July 1909 in his type XI monoplane, thus winning the *Daily Mail* prize of £1,000. Within months he became the largest aircraft manufacturer in the world, with the ubiquitous Blériot XI becoming in the air what the Model 'T' Ford would later be on the ground. It was a position which he maintained, with many enhancements, until the outbreak of the First World War in August 1914. As the war progressed he became a leading constructor of fighters, and by its end his 'Spads' had made him the largest producer of aeroplanes on the Allied side.

The return of peace enabled Blériot to pursue an earlier vision – civil air transport, which he had always seen as the true destiny of the aeroplane. Quickly he developed passenger carrying aircraft, embarked upon a huge diversification programme to absorb surplus production capacity, and created with others an airline which became in time a founding element of Air France, just as his aircraft company eventually became a constituent of what is now Aérospatiale. But survival as a constructor in the twenties and thirties became more and more difficult, and his one remaining factory came close to closure more than once. Nevertheless his faith in air transport flourished in adversity, and he became obsessed with transatlantic flying, investing massively in the development of a large flying boat which was technically a great success but commercially a disaster, following which he died in 1936. As *The Times* then remarked, he

> ...owed his spectacular success in the early days of flying and his disappointments in latter years to the quality of courageous impatience which drove him to seek the realization of his ideas before the world was ready to support him.[2]

Blériot was a herald of our age. The story of his life is one of triumph and much adversity, of implacable determination, high courage and bold vision. It is the story of a man for whom success was never a sure protection against disaster, for whom, despite fame and fortune, life in pursuit of his chosen star was a struggle without remission.

The Friend invader? *Louis Blériot after landing near Dover castle, having made the first aeroplane crossing of the English Channel, on 25 July 1909. (From the Flight Collection at the Quadrant Picture Library)*

1 The making of an engineer

The anguish of France after the cumulative disasters of the war with Prussia and the Commune was beginning to give way to hope in the early summer of 1872 as Clémence and Charles Blériot awaited their first-born at their home in Cambrai. In that north-eastern city they lived in an old house where Louis XVIII had stayed during his return from exile in England and in which long ago the treaty of the Paix des Dames had been signed, both reminders in their ways of France's infinite capacity to recover. The house, which stood in the rue de l'Arbre à Poires, since renamed the rue Sadi-Carnot, was destroyed during the First World War. It was large, formerly the *hôtel* of a nobleman, for Charles was an industrialist of considerable, if fluctuating, prosperity. At that time he was a linen manufacturer, producing a material called *baptiste* for use as lining in clothes. Later he became a distiller, and later still a farmer.

On the first of July, just before midnight, or perhaps just after, the baby was born. Uncertainty about his birth date followed, with the first of July finally gaining official ascendancy over the second. He was baptized Louis Charles Joseph, always to be known as Louis. Four more children were born to the Blériots, two sons and two daughters. Louis's brothers, Michel and André, became cattle breeders in Canada and his sisters, Madeleine and Martha, in due course emigrated to the USA.

At the age of ten Louis was sent as a boarder to the Institut Notre-Dame in Cambrai. A scientific bent became apparent, but he won class prizes in all subjects, more often the second prize but sometimes the first. It is worth noting, in view of curious claims made in later years, that one of the boy's early school prizes was for drawing.[1] In 1887 he moved on to the Lycée at Amiens, where he lived in the home of an aunt during the three years spent there. He obtained his baccalaureat in Science and German language. By now his sights were set on becoming an engineer and, greatly daring, he selected as his target the most prominent general engineering school in France, the celebrated Ecole Centrale des Arts et Manufactures in Paris.

The entrance examination for the Ecole Centrale was notoriously difficult. It was accepted that all candidates required special and arduous preparation, which in Blériot's case was provided by the Collège Sainte-Barbe. Founded in Paris in 1460, the venerable school numbered St Ignatius de Loyola and St Francois Xavier among its early pupils: Etienne Montgolfier also studied there. Nearer to Blériot's time, Gustave Eiffel, with whose tower Paris was beginning to come to terms, had also become a *barbiste* on his way to becoming a *centralien*. The winter Blériot spent there, 1890/91, was one of extraordinary severity in Paris. At the zoo many animals died from cold. There were shortages of vegetables and even of water, while seven hundred prisoners due for release at the end of their sentences accepted an offer to stay where they were until better weather came. Thus to the rigours of study more intense than any he had yet experienced, were added for the young Blériot the harshness and depressing effects of a long, bitter winter.

The Ecole Centrale is one of France's 'Grandes Ecoles', founded in 1829 by three academics, two of whom had been professors at the 'Ecole Polytechnique', a pre-eminent establishment then as now, and who brought with them some of its extreme rigours such as weekly examinations. But the aims of the new school were different. Where the Polytechnique aimed to produce highly numerate engineers mainly for the army and the civil service, the Ecole Centrale set out to train the new kind of business-oriented engineer who was already seen to be needed to lead the industrialization of France, then gathering speed.

By the time Blériot formed his ambitious idea of trying to get into the Ecole Centrale its reputation was enormous and an overwhelming demand for entry was regulated, in the manner traditional to the Grandes Ecoles, by an intensely competitive entrance exam. In 1892, a total of 243 applicants were successful: ranked seventy-fourth in order of merit was the name of Louis Blériot. He had done particularly well in all three kinds of drawing – architectural, mechanical and detailed workshop design. These were brilliant results, proof both of talent and enormous application. Moving into the lodgings which were to be his home for the next three years, with a Monsieur Bizet in the rue St Gilles in the 3ème arrondissement, Blériot prepared for his first year of study at the Mecca of his interests.

From the very start, in November 1892, he found himself under pressure to work harder, always harder, as exam followed exam, in an effort to retain his initial ranking. He did not achieve this, and passed into the second year in 119th position and facing still greater difficulties. His attendance suffered, bringing down formal warnings upon an already weary head, and soon authority's rebukes were extended to the quality and regularity of his work. The main cause of the trouble was probably a major change in the curriculum after a first year in which the emphasis had been on pure science subjects. Suddenly, applied science predominated and exacting engineering projects had to be carried out. These included designing a boiler, and a factory door, as well as a less prosaic *cinémathèque*, or film library. (This last is the first sign of what was to be a life-long amateur interest in ciné photography: from 1905 he would have each successive stage of his aeronautical experiments recorded on film.) Blériot's academic record at the Ecole Centrale reached its nadir at the end of that gruelling year of transition with a ranking of 190 in the group of 214 who passed into the third and final year.

His recovery came quickly in that last year, and it is clear that after a period of hesitation he had suddenly found his way. New subjects related to specific industries such as coal mining, railways and electricity supply were rapidly mastered and an impressively varied range of practical projects won high marks. An ultimate effort in the final exams, and Blériot finished 113th among the 207 students who obtained the coveted Diploma, and the right to put the designation 'ECP' after their names.[2]

What had Blériot learned in the past three years? Firstly, he had received a broad and well rounded technical education as an engineer. Although nominally his specialisation was in metallurgy, in reality no particular emphasis was placed on that subject and his marks for it carried the same weight as those for eight other subjects in the finals. Secondly, he learnt some law relating to economic and industrial affairs in that all but devastating second year, but of economics as such, or finance, or accountancy, or even

Louis Blériot as a child. (MA 6704)

commercial administration, there was nothing. No mention was made of 'management' – it was too soon for that. The business-oriented engineer produced by the Ecole Centrale in 1895 was expected to possess the intelligence and justified self-confidence to make his own way in industry, relying on instinct when necessary.

Before being free to start in that direction Blériot faced an obligation. He had to perform military service for one year, which he did as a sub-lieutenant in the 24th Artillery Regiment. Having some choice about where in France he could serve, he decided to get as far away from Cambrai and his family as possible, and so chose Tarbes in the Pyrenees. Army life in those circumstances must have seemed like heaven in contrast to the unremitting study that had been his existence since childhood. He relished the freedom of the mountains and the opportunities for every kind of physical exercise, earning a reputation for revelling in this to the point of eccentricity. While in the army he learned to ride, which would give him exercise and relaxation for a great many years. A time would come when it would amuse him, as an excellent horseman, to say that flying an aeroplane called for the same skill and address.[3]

As soon as he completed his military service in 1896 Blériot returned to Paris in search of work. Although his qualification as a *centralien* carried prestige, it does not seem to have been readily translatable into earning power, because he was obliged to accept a salary of only 150 francs a month, little more than a skilled manual worker could then command. He was employed as an engineer by the firm of Baguès, an electrical concern in the rue des Francs Bourgeois. He worked a six and a half day week, being free only on Sunday mornings.[4] Electricity was beginning to compete with coal gas as a means of lighting houses, apartments, factories and offices, but it did not take Blériot long to see that, for all its attractions, electricity was not yet an improvement over gas for that purpose. The primitive state of electrical engineering resulted in apparatus which was neither reliable nor safe. As early as 1890 the premature adoption of electric lighting in Paris had resulted in two very serious fires in crowded buildings, one at the Comédie Française and an even worse outbreak at the Grand Café.

Six years later matters had not greatly improved, and Blériot must have concluded quickly that for lighting buildings the time of electricity had not yet come. While in no doubt about its potential in the longer term, he clearly felt that for the present the way forward lay in the further development of gas lighting. This had already received a good deal of attention, but most of the systems and appliances available until then related to coal gas, which could be produced economically only on a large scale in centralized 'gas works' supplying customers through networks of pipes. Then as now, such systems of distribution tended to be available only in large centres of population, with the result that people living in smaller towns and in the countryside were still obliged to use paraffin or spirit lamps, and of course candles. The 'bottling' of gas was not yet fully practical for widespread distribution, and little attention had been devoted to kinds of gas which could be generated on a small scale. It was the potential scope for one of these, acetylene, that caught Blériot's imagination. He began to experiment with it in the evenings.

Acetylene is a hydrocarbon gas produced by adding water to calcium carbide. When mixed with the right proportion of air, almost twelve times its own volume, it burns with a brilliant but soft white light, which is a close artificial approach to sunlight. Although

Louis Blériot at school, the Institut Notre-Dame de Cambrai. He is on the extreme left of the front row. (MA 28699)

discovered and identified in 1836, acetylene was of little practical use until a method of making calcium carbide cheaply was found: an electric furnace was used to combine the two ingredients, coal and lime. That critical discovery was made in 1892, only four years before Blériot began his experiments.

He needed space to work, so moved out of his lodgings in the rue Jean-Jacques Rousseau into an apartment of his own, with two rooms, at Auteuil on the western edge of Paris. Fully occupied as he was, by day with his job and by night with his own work, Blériot nevertheless did not allow his new-found fascination with gas technology to make him oblivious to the direction in which he was heading. There was a huge unsatisfied demand for good domestic lighting from the vast rural population of France living beyond the reach of mains gas. What therefore could have been more natural than for him to enter that immense market, by producing domestic appliances for this newly practicable gas which could be made quite simply, in any place where it was needed, and at the time of its use so that no storage was required? That indeed was the obvious thing to do, but it was not what Blériot did. Instead he chose to aim at a quite different market, one which moreover did not yet exist.

Before 1896 there were signs, for those who could read them, that the making of motor cars would change from a small-scale craft activity into an industry, and that this change would take place in France. Louis Blériot was one of those who understood what was about to happen. Since he was to play some part in the development of the motor industry, and as that industry was to influence aviation, in which he was to be one of the chief pioneers, the beginnings of the motor industry deserve attention.

The situation in 1896 has been summarized by the industrial historian James M. Laux, as follows:

The automobile industry in France had begun to advance. Leaders of two well-established and profitable metalworking firms, Emile Levassor and Armand Peugeot, had the entrepreneurial skill and vision to move into the favourable situation produced by technical progress, the bicycle craze and good French roads. They seized the opportunity offered by the Daimler engine to begin making small numbers of sturdy cars and they had no trouble selling them. They were outdistancing the German pioneers, as Daimler could not agree with his financial backers on what policy his firm should follow, and Benz was slow to modernize his design.[5]

Although the first cars had been made in Germany, it was in France that the first really practical models were turned out, using to begin with the engine developed in Germany by Daimler. The potential market for cars had been stimulated by the spread of bicycles which began in the late 1880s and boomed in 1895 with the production of the English 'safety bicycle', with its two wheels the same size and a chain drive. As Laux explains:

> Among thousands of people, riding bicycles established a taste for speedy mechanical road vehicles, completely subject to the will of the driver. They whetted the desire for individual transportation, and developed in their owners some skill in understanding mechanical contrivances, and in maintaining them.[6]

The bicycle also helped technically, since many components needed for cars were developed first for bicycles. These included ball bearings and pneumatic tyres, as well as cable controls, used on bicycles for brakes but on cars for other purposes too. Some cars had wire-spoked wheels, which were perfected and made in quantity for bicycles.

While Blériot was beginning to consider ways of employing acetylene to provide powerful lamps for cars, which would enable them to be driven at night – and so vastly increase their usefulness – there occurred in Paris an engineering development of exceptional importance. This was the production of a small and reasonably light petrol engine capable of running up to five times as fast as the hitherto predominant Daimler type. The designer of the new engine was Georges Bouton, who had worked for two years to achieve this brilliant result in partnership with comte Albert de Dion. The availability of that engine, on top of everything else, made certain that the transformation of car making into an industry would happen in France. The particular innovations that made the De Dion-Bouton engine a success will be examined later, but an idea of its popularity is apparent from the numbers in which it was produced. In 1899 De Dion-Bouton made some 10,000 engines, half of which went into their own tricycles and the other half into a great variety of vehicles made by many other firms.[7]

What was in store for the motor industry in France can be revealed, with hindsight, in a few figures. From 1896 to 1907 annual motor vehicle production in the country rose from 320 units to 25,200 units. In 1907 French car exports exceeded those of the UK, USA, Italy, Germany and Belgium combined.[8]

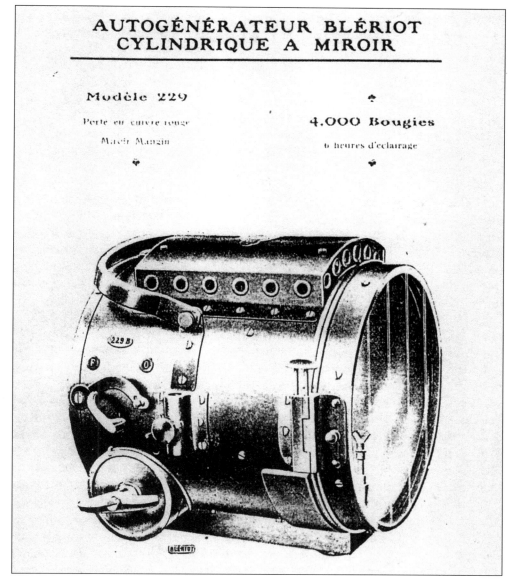

A Blériot acetylene headlamp. (Author's collection)

The experiments conducted by Blériot with acetylene at Auteuil resulted in several inventions which he protected as far as possible by registering patents. One idea was to combine a gas generator and a lamp in one compact unit, an arrangement which in several respects was superior to the system used up to that time, where a comparatively large generator fed gas to two or more lamps through lengths of tubing which were liable to break. Blériot was the originator of the use of the word *phare* (literally a lighthouse or beacon) to denote a car headlamp, a usage which continues in French to the present day.

(Unlike so many other words in the French motoring lexicon, this one never found a place in English.) It has been claimed that Blériot was actually the 'inventor' of the headlamp,[9] but that is surely an exaggeration – headlamps evolved from horse carriage lamps which burnt candles or paraffin. What is certain, however, is that Louis Blériot created the first business in the world to specialize in the manufacture of lighting systems for cars.[10]

For Blériot did decide that he must have his own business. If he was ever to have control over his life, and make any money, it would not be as an employee of Baguès. Besides, his father ran his own business so it was perfectly natural for the son to want that kind of independence too. Thus it came about that at the age of twenty-four, working with the latest technology for a market only just beginning to be perceptible, Blériot started his first business. In 1897 a showroom and offices were opened at 41 rue de Richelieu. Nearby he had a workshop which soon developed into a small factory. Financial help was provided at first by an uncle, and later by bankers who were also supporting the car makers. The new type of headlight introduced by Blériot, with its gas generator integrally mounted in the body of the lamp, was a great success. With two of these fitted - or even sometimes just one, centrally installed, a car could be driven safely on unlighted roads and streets at a reasonable speed. This marked a significant extension in the practicality of motor vehicles of all kinds, and obviously increased their attractiveness to potential buyers.

Blériot marketed his lamps as accessories to the motoring public, hence the showroom which was actually an attractive shop, but also as components to car manufacturers. In a few years he succeeded in getting the business of two of the leading firms, Panhard-Levassor and Renault. A third section of the market comprised the numerous coachbuilders, making bodies to order for the many people who bought vehicles in chassis form. For the first and the last of these categories of customer Blériot began to produce illustrated catalogues describing his ever increasing range of lamps, each made in a variety of sizes, and all systematically numbered for ease of ordering. They could be obtained in brass or, for a slight extra cost, in a nickel-plated finish. As time went by, the catalogues became sumptuous productions, the fruits of considerable effort and expense.

Blériot made it easy to change to his lamps if the motorist was dissatisfied with some other make already fitted to his car. Eager and competent staff were waiting in the showrooms (removed in 1902 to larger premises at 14-16 rue Duret), to explain the finer points and to give advice. To facilitate fitting his lamps, Blériot thoughtfully provided a simple but massive forked bracket of forged steel (the 'Fourche Blériot'), said to be 'universally' attachable to any car, which would hold the new lamp most securely in place.

The improved acetylene headlamps were adequate as long as the driver knew his route, but if he got lost, as was frequent, they were not much help. When looking all around at an isolated cross-roads on a pitch dark night in the hope of spotting some distant landmark, a movable light was needed. The opportunity thus presented was seized upon with boundless enthusiasm by the lamp makers, Blériot at the fore. The large, powerful, swivelling searchlights which resulted were promoted energetically, through the by then customary channels of motor racing, the motoring press and, of course, the catalogues. As Blériot put it in one of his:

Nowadays darkness no longer exists for the well-informed driver. He needs
only three sources of light, two headlamps at the front of the car and a swivelling
searchlight above the dashboard, which he can direct with his hand.[11]

Rather less emphasis was put on the fact that before seeing anything in the beam of his
searchlight, 'the well-informed driver' had to get it lit. As long as he had some dry
matches, carbide in the generator and water in the attached tank this would not be too
difficult, wind and rain permitting. But whether he got a good, bright and steady light
depended on other factors, because acetylene did have its drawbacks.

Although the gas is easy to generate, by dripping water onto carbide, the process is
difficult to control. Sometimes far too much gas is produced, making its pressure and flow
hard to regulate. The consumption of water can be excessive, and although this does not
matter much for searchlights which are used briefly and intermittently, it is a serious
problem for headlamps kept on for long periods which will abruptly extinguish
themselves when their tanks run dry, perhaps after only one or two hours' use. Another
inconvenience is that burning the gas leaves a messy deposit which soon dulls the reflector
and lens of the lamp, necessitating frequent and unpleasant cleaning in order to maintain
a normal output of light.

Blériot applied his technical ingenuity in sustained efforts to alleviate these problems. A
layer of carbon was introduced as a gas filter in generators, and innumerable detailed
refinements were made to gas jets, water tanks and taps, and other parts of the apparatus in
order to make the production of gas more regular. Another approach was to use two
generators for each lamp, arranged so that an excess of gas produced by the first could be
stored temporarily in the second, and there augmented for use in its turn. Yet another
method employed by Blériot, although he did not invent it, was to coat pellets of carbide
with a paste made of glucose and paraffin. Carbide thus treated produced gas very evenly.
Unlike ordinary carbide, however, this product was not widely distributed and the motorist
could have difficulty in obtaining it in the course of the ever longer journeys being
undertaken. Some improvements in gas generation, including those intended to make
refuelling and maintenance less frequent and more convenient, resulted in generators too
large or expensive to be combined with one lamp in the now classic Blériot manner, so that
central generators serving several lamps also took their place in the range offered by the
firm – in a sense a return to the system which the first Blériot innovation had replaced.

The problem of sooty reflectors and lenses was solved, with style, by fitting chimneys
of Bohemian crystal which effectively protected the optical parts. This innovation was
greeted with approval in England by *The Car Illustrated*:

> The newest type of Blériot lamp is... very attractive, among its other good
> features being the provision of a chimney of unbreakable glass which carries
> away all the fumes, and renders the polishing of the lenses rarely necessary.[12]

In addition to tackling the technical problems specifically connected with acetylene,
Blériot developed the optical qualities of his lamps with better arrangements of lenses and

reflectors intended to concentrate and guide the beam. But he also took infinite pains with the general design and construction of his lamps. So that they might better withstand the continual shaking that was their expectation in service, particular attention was given to joints of every kind. By redesigning components the number of joints in each lamp was reduced as far as possible, and he suppressed the use of brazing and solder, which he particularly distrusted. Parts were designed to be screwed together. What became a slogan of Blériot engineering first appeared in those days. This was the proud claim that 'the raw materials are of the first quality and are tested before use'.

After these developments, Blériot told his customers that in his opinion the light produced by a pair of his acetylene headlamps was sufficient for night driving at speeds of thirty to forty kilometres per hour. 'For motorists who wish to go faster than that', he added, 'we advise the fitting of an additional large lamp, either an acetylene model, or one using the New Light which I have discovered.' On the darkest night, a man standing half a mile away from the New Light could read a newspaper by it.[13] Before uncovering the secrets of the 'New Light', it is time to consider other important events in the life of Louis Blériot.

★★★★★

Shortly before setting up in business, Blériot had given up his apartment at Auteuil and gone to live with his mother, who was then living alone in Paris, separated from his father. By 1899, Blériot's affairs had prospered to the point where he could afford a car of his own. He bought a De Dion-Bouton in chassis form and had a body built for it by a coachbuilder who was a customer of his, Henri Labourdette (who later, with his 'skiff' bodies, gave cars their low, modern look.) Blériot made several long trips in this car, including one from Paris to Biarritz which was memorable not just for the distance covered, but for the number of dogs he ran over on the way – a sad total of twelve.

At home in Paris the daily round acquired a certain routine. Most days he lunched at the same restaurant, the 'Boeuf à la Mode', which was near the showroom. In the evening of one such day, in October 1900, he went home to his mother in the Avenue Kléber and declared: 'I saw a young woman today. I will marry her, or else I will marry no one.'[14]

The object of this declaration was totally unaware of the impression she had made. During lunch with her father and mother at the Boeuf à la Mode she had chatted cheerfully and unselfconsciously with them, paying no attention to the man, eleven years her elder, who sat alone at another table. As for Blériot, he 'purchased the cooperation' of a waiter to find out for him who these people were: he noticed that the father wore the ribbon of a decoration.

After a few days delay – Blériot's impatience can be imagined – the waiter was able to report back. He had accomplished his mission to perfection, having succeeded in engaging the girl's father in conversation and getting the kind of information his paymaster desired. The family were on a visit to Paris from their home in a small town in the Pyrenees, Bagnères-de-Bigorre. Their name was Védère. The daughter was seventeen years of age and her name was Alicia, although she was usually called Alice. They took a holiday every year in the autumn. Last year they had gone to Monte Carlo, and acting on a friend's advice had taken their meals at Maxim's, but Monsieur Védère's consternation at the

A publicity illustration for Blériot's acetylene headlamps and electrical internal lighting. (MA 28833)

atmosphere of that establishment, which he found unsuitable for his strictly brought up daughter, had made him enquire much more carefully about a choice of restaurant for this year's holiday. He was relieved to see that the respectability of the Boeuf à la Mode left nothing to be desired. Monsieur Ernest Védère was a retired army officer; he had been a colonel in the Artillery.

This was a stroke of luck for Blériot, and he made the most of it when he had the further good fortune of finding Monsieur Védère alone one day in the Boeuf à la Mode. Védère may not have been too enthusiastic about this intense and rather pressing young man who asked to be introduced to his cherished offspring, brought up so carefully and whom they still thought of as a child, but it was not so easy to shake off a brother officer, even if Blériot was much his junior and now only in the reserve. When that conversation was swiftly followed by an invitation from Madame Blériot to come to tea, Alice's father crustily objected, protesting that it would be a waste of time, that they had better things to do… but he went all the same. Alice was apparently still unaware that Blériot had fallen in love with her, and at the tea party she was her natural lively self, but quite indifferent to him. Blériot invited the Védères for a drive in his car the next day, which caused some excitement, as Alice had not been in one before.

Next morning he came to their hotel in the Avenue de l'Opéra, having first called at his office to pick up an important-looking bundle of letters, brought along to impress his future father-in-law. Alice enjoyed the autumn drive through the Bois de Boulogne, and on to Versailles where they had lunch. When he had brought them safely back to the Avenue de l'Opéra, Blériot enquired when they intended to return to the Pyrenees, remarking that he went there often, theoretically for short periods of training as an officer of the reserve, but actually to ride, shoot woodcock, or catch trout. He asked whether he might be allowed to call on them, in order, as he put it, to pay his respects to Madame Védère, if he happened to find himself in their district.

He arrived two days before them! From that moment events moved rapidly, and four days later he asked for Alice's hand in marriage. This does not mean he proposed – nothing so simple occurred. What happened was that a priest, Father Alexandre, who was a family friend of the Védères, told Alice's mother and father that he had been approached by a Madame Blériot whom he knew, with an earnest request for information about the religious views, and the origins, of the family into which her son wished to marry, so that she would know what risks he was running. She was fully reassured by what the priest was able to tell her, and his services as an ambassador were promptly requested by the Blériots, mother and son.

They could not have made a better choice, for not only was Father Alexandre the trusted confidant of both families, he also had two qualifications rare in a priest. He was a *polytechnicien* and he had been married, having taken holy orders after the deaths of his wife and child. Ernest Védère was no match for him. Arguments about Alice being too young, and so forth, were short-lived.

Meanwhile, Blériot seems to have been hanging about Alice's home, the Villa Jeannette, as much as he dared that week, with the complicity of her mother. During his first formal call after their return from Paris he said that he planned a day's woodcock shooting, and asked whether she would accept a gift of the bag he hoped to get, if he sent it to her.

Madame Védère replied that of course the birds would be appreciated, but it would be so much kinder if he brought them himself. He also found an opportunity to make an impression on Alice's father, a keen gardener, who was troubled by a fountain which no one had been able to make work properly until Blériot climbed to the top of its supporting statue and in a few minutes repaired the recalcitrant mechanism. As Alice recalled later 'thus was my father won over by his young comrade-in-arms.'

Alice was not at first told of the negotiations which were in progress. Thus, when Father Alexandre was expected at the house she was imperiously ordered by her father to go and supervise a workman who happened to be doing some repairs in her room, which she thought a little odd. In fact, this was the seventh time that a proposal to marry Alice had been made. On the previous six occasions she had known nothing at all about them! When she eventually found out by chance from a friend that six men had already asked to marry her, she was deeply shocked and protested to her mother, who at first was annoyed that she should wish to be informed, and even consulted, about future proposals. At length, however, her mother was convinced, perhaps by the arrival of the twentieth century, that when the seventh time came Alice would be told, and indeed that the decision would be hers to make.

This seventh suitor, needless to say, wanted an immediate answer. For her part, Alice asked for forty-eight hours to decide. This was on a Saturday, and Blériot left for Tarbes, saying he would be back on the Monday for her answer. Alice seems to have been chiefly concerned about whether she was worthy of him. To the inexperienced girl of seventeen he seemed an elite figure from another world.

He was back on Monday and that afternoon Alice gave her considered answer: she accepted. Typically in a hurry, he left at once by train for Paris, only to decide, when approaching Bordeaux, that he had to be with her at least a little longer. So at the next stop he jumped from the train, abandoning some of his luggage, and returned to the Villa Jeannette for one more evening. Next day, before he set off again, there was a discussion about when the marriage should take place. Her parents thought it should not be before her twenty-second birthday, in five years' time. Suffice it to say that the wedding took place four months later, on 21 February 1901 (before five years had passed five children would be born). As was traditional when a local person married someone from outside the district, the young people of Bagnères-de-Bigorre stretched a ribbon across the church door when the couple were coming out and presented the bride with a pair of scissors on a cushion. With these the new Madame Blériot cut the ribbon, so giving her husband the symbolic right of entry to the town.[15]

They set off in the snow in the De Dion-Bouton for a three-week honeymoon at Pau, but after a short distance the idea of driving in those conditions was abandoned and the car was put on a train. They went to see Alice's parents once a week during the honeymoon, and further frequent stays at Bagnères-de-Bigorre were a feature of their early married life. On one of those visits Blériot hired a horse for a day's riding, as he often did. But on that particular day he was very late in returning and Alice grew anxious as the evening advanced without any sign of him. At last he arrived, on foot, saying that he had only come back to pick up his wallet and that he had to go out again right away to pay the owner for his horse. It transpired that while riding in the nearby mountains Blériot had attempted to negotiate a steep and narrow path, quite unsuitable for a horse as he must well have known, and the horse had slipped off the edge, crashing to its death in the ravine far below. As for the rider, he had grabbed a bush on the way down, so saving himself. This is the earliest recorded episode showing his penchant for taking physical risks while avoiding their worst consequences.[16] Not for nothing was he to earn in coming years the reputation of 'having had more falls than any other aviator'.[17]

The newly-married couple lived in Blériot's apartment in the Avenue Kléber. He went to his office by bicycle, returning most days at four o'clock in the afternoon to share with Alice a half-bottle of champagne and some *marrons glacés*. This gave her a break from the sewing which took up a lot of her time, and in which Louis took an interest so professional as to surprise any uninformed observer. But then only he and she knew the purpose of those bands of white silk whose edges she hemstitched so carefully.[18]

★★★★★

Ever higher speeds called for lamps able to light up the road yet further ahead, but a time came when acetylene could no longer meet this requirement. As Blériot put it succinctly: 'acetylene's intensity is not sufficiently concentrated.'[19] What was needed was a light as bright as an electric arc which could be produced only by a large, and perforce stationary, installation.

Blériot solved this problem by inventing a system of burning a pre-heated mixture of oxygen and petrol, obtaining a light almost as bright as an electric arc. This terrifying cocktail of flaming gases was applied to a 'pastille of zirionia or other oxide of a rare earth metal', which instantly became incandescent with his 'New Light', as he proudly called it. The apparatus comprised a burner containing the pastille which was located in the same position as the jet in an acetylene lamp, together with a small petrol tank and 'a box made of oak containing one or two oxygen cylinders'. The device was considered simple to operate: all that was needed was to light a wick soaked in alcohol and wait for forty or fifty seconds until some petrol was vaporized and a flame appeared. Then the oxygen tap was opened and the pastille became incandescent. There was a neat little porcelain wheel which was turned to adjust the petrol supply, in order to get the most intense light possible. The customer was assured that 'La manipulation est absolument sans danger', because the originality of the system was that it dispensed with a carburettor, and thus 'no flash-back was to be feared.'

However, Blériot had reason to know how literally he was playing with fire. One Sunday, while working at home at his drawing board, a petrol tank from some of his apparatus which was standing in the room exploded in his face. His eyelashes, beard and moustache were severely singed and there were burns on his face. Alice was out and there was no one else in the house at the time. Blériot, in carpet slippers, went out into the street in search of a pharmacy where his burns could be dressed, and when Alice returned he was a sorry sight, his face shorn of its fine moustache and stained yellow with picric acid. Her first thought was that he might so easily have been blinded...[20]

The New Light was said to be twenty-eight times more intense than that given by acetylene, and to enable 'obstacles' to be seen at up to 400 metres. Blériot recommended it to customers who wished to travel fast at night, pointing out however that acetylene

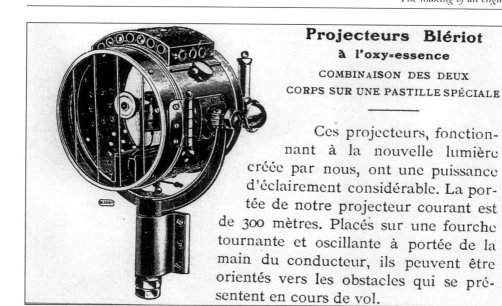

Projecteurs Blériot
à l'oxy=essence

COMBINAISON DES DEUX
CORPS SUR UNE PASTILLE SPÉCIALE

———

Ces projecteurs, fonction-
nant à la nouvelle lumière
créée par nous, ont une puissance
d'éclairement considérable. La portée de notre projecteur courant est
de 300 mètres. Placés sur une fourche
tournante et oscillante à portée de la
main du conducteur, ils peuvent être
orientés vers les obstacles qui se pré-
sentent en cours de vol.

Blériot's 'New Light' burned a pre-heated mixture of oxygen and petrol. (Author's Collection)

lamps were still needed to show up the edges of the road immediately ahead of the car. That was because the long range of the new lamp was obtained by optically concentrating its beam so that it would carry a long way ahead without dispersing to the sides. Blériot suggested that the New Light was to acetylene what the siren was to the horn: one did not replace the other, it complemented it. 'Besides, like the siren it warns from afar of the approach of a fast car and makes people get out of the way.'[21]

Despite this exciting new product, Blériot kept in close touch with technical developments which were bringing electric light nearer to cars, and his firm took part in some of them. At first, cars had not made any use of electricity, but then as the need for precisely timed ignition was understood (first by Bouton), electrical apparatus began to be employed to provide it. Car electrics took time to develop, however, and even by 1906 Blériot took a cautious view. He felt unable to recommend the dynamos available at that time. 'They add sixty or seventy kilograms to a car's weight, use up half a horsepower of the engine's output, give only a dim light, are very expensive both to buy and to run, and need frequent and troublesome maintenance.'[22]

He considered that batteries were also unsuitable as a source of energy for headlamps to be used for long periods, since they had to be recharged too often. On the other hand nothing could compare with electricity for the small lamps needed to illuminate the interior of a car, for sidelights and for tail lights. Blériot made electric lamps of all these kinds which could be run off a wet battery that he also supplied, in a fine mahogany or walnut box to be carried on the running board or under a seat.

Three years later, in May 1909, the oxygen-petrol swivelling searchlight was still being claimed by the Blériot company to be the only available practical improvement over acetylene searchlights. But the writing was on the wall, for they now felt able to offer a

Louis Blériot with his family, 1909. (Harman Collection)

dynamo to their customers 'designed to revolutionize lighting for motor vehicles, and soon no doubt to entirely replace acetylene, of which we were nevertheless the promoters.'[23] This was the 'PHI' make of dynamo, and Blériot had obtained distribution rights for France, after prolonged tests which satisfied him of its worth. The PHI differed from some other dynamos because it had been designed specially for cars, and was of moderate size and weight.

In 1905 Blériot had turned his lamp business into a private limited company, the 'Société Anonyme des Etablissements L. Blériot', with a paid up capital of 1,300,000 francs, divided into 13,000 shares of 100 francs each. In exchange for handing over most of the assets of the business, including patents, Blériot received 8,000 shares, representing just over 60% of the equity. It was made clear that henceforward the company was fully responsible – it was to meet all obligations arising from leases and commercial contracts to the letter and punctually, 'so that Monsieur Blériot would neither be troubled nor sought after.' Monsieur Blériot for his part agreed not to set up in competition with the company for a period of twelve years.[24]

These were the dispositions of a man who sought step by step to free himself from the day-to-day burdens of a business which, although growing and successful, was no longer the challenge it once had been, either technically or commercially. For some time his mind had been elsewhere, and now he had enough money to follow a new star. The S.A. des Etablissements L. Blériot could be relied upon to pay a dividend of at least 100,000 francs a year: in a really good year it could be as much as 250,000 francs.[25] He was to need it all.

2 Aviation beckons

Blériot was first attracted by the idea of flight while at the Ecole Centrale, but he told no one, 'because he did not want to be thought mad', as he said later.[1] However, he did begin to read about aeronautics. Just what literature he found, and what sense he made of the confused mixture of science and fantasy circulating in the 1890s, are matters of conjecture. As will be seen, the evidence of his first attempt to build a flying machine suggests that he did not have a great deal to go on. But there was one choice he made then from which he never afterwards deviated: the 'heavier-than-air' school of flight was the one for him. Louis Blériot never ballooned except socially. In rejecting the 'lighter-than-air' approach, which already had a long and in some respects depressing history, Blériot may perhaps have been influenced by the widely available writings of a certain Nadar.

He was a brilliant and successful photographer, in whose former fashionable studio at the corner of the Boulevard des Capucines and the rue Daunou the first Impressionist Exhibition was held in 1874, in the midst of the kind of violent controversy he thrived on. Nadar, whose real name was Félix Tournachon, was an experienced balloonist who became disenchanted with that mode of flight and made his views known by a campaign of pamphleteering whose virulent language won it an audience.

As far back as the 1860s Nadar had reached the conclusion that no way would be found of controlling the direction of a balloon's flight, that 'dirigibility' was a cruel illusion, and that no craft that was lighter than air would master the skies. He promoted the 'International Society for the Encouragement of Aerial Locomotion by means of Apparatus heavier than Air'. The ponderous term 'aerial locomotion' was chosen with the aim of giving some dignity and solemnity to a subject usually treated as a joke, for Nadar took himself seriously, or at least pretended to. 'The Divine solution of this great Problem', he thundered, 'will suppress frontiers, render war impossible…'

With a venom rarely equalled in aeronautical literature, Nadar ridiculed the Académie des Sciences in 1865 for allegedly maintaining that the reason birds could rise into the air was that they had hot air in their bodies. Believing in such absurdities, the Academy had misled people, said Nadar, by encouraging research into 'dirigibility'. Nadar, for his part, argued that an object must be heavier than the air…'to exercise an action upon the air – in the same way as, in every order of things, it is indispensable to be the strongest in order not to be beaten.' He related an incident witnessed by one of his sympathizers while walking in the street. A workman aloft on a ladder asks another, who is standing on the ground, to throw him a sponge. The man below first dips the sponge in water from the gutter, in order to make it heavy enough to carry through the air. Gleefully, Nadar boasts that thus he has proved his case.

Nadar's criticisms extended to balloonists themselves including, with fine detachment, himself. Their efforts had been altogether deplorable, he confessed, and the time had

Nadar in 1900 at the age of 80. Scourge of the scientific establishment and promoter, in the 1860s, of the International Society for the Encouragement of Aerial Locomotion by means of Apparatus heavier than Air. *(MA 33379)*

come 'to destroy the balloons which have caused us to waste effort upon a false scent these last eighty years…' He went on to propose a scheme for exacting revenge on the balloon. Having noted, in a fleeting moment of realism, that progress in heavier-than-air flight would require many practical experiments which would cost a great deal of money, he suggested that this be provided from enormous profits to be made by launching a public subscription for the construction of an exceedingly large and spectacular…balloon.[2]

In these literary antics Blériot would have found entertainment and enthusiasm but nothing else. More purposeful inspiration came early in 1900, at the Paris 'Exposition Universelle' where he was exhibiting lamps. One day he and an engineer on his staff named Bimbenet toured the exhibition. They paused before a winged flying machine built by Clément Ader, and Blériot said to Bimbenet: 'I want to take up flying'. He felt that flight had become almost feasible, and that the moment had come to declare his intentions and get to work.[3]

Clément Ader, before whose Avion III Blériot stood, is a sad and controversial figure in aviation history, in part because of the inherent difficulty in differentiating between a short, but true, flight and a mere jump or hop. (While it is widely accepted that Ader on 9 October 1890 made the first piloted powered take-off in history from level ground in his first aeroplane, the Eole, the controversy, which need not be gone into here, is about the validity of claims that a later machine, the Avion III which Blériot saw, flew 300 metres in 1897.)

There was much about Ader's machine to impress Blériot as an engineer. Amazing originality of design and execution were shown by its bat-wing framework, an extremely complex web of hollowed-out wooden struts, and by the two ultra-lightweight steam engines which drove two tractor propellers. It is not difficult to believe that the sight of it made him feel that mechanical flight was now within reach. Nevertheless, in the first of many abrupt swerves he was to make along the way of his aeronautical progress, Blériot did not follow his admiring inspection of the Avion III by emulating Ader and building an aeroplane. History might have been very different if he had.

The aeroplane did not have the field to itself. It was only one of three types of apparatus then being considered as candidates for the 'conquest of the air', the others being the helicopter and the ornithopter. The last of these, strictly speaking a device to simulate mechanically the flight of birds or bats, already had a long and unsuccessful history, in the course of which ideas were drawn from some marine creatures as well as from those of the air. Unaccountably, it was such a machine that Blériot decided to build. He began to design it in 1900, and construction was completed in 1902.[4]

Impenetrable mystery hides the truth about Blériot's ornithopter. Apart from the fact of its failure, almost everything else is conjecture. Yet there is a possibility, very slight it is true, that the original machine, or strictly speaking one version of it, may still exist! There is little doubt that several versions, perhaps three or four, were built, but Blériot did not subsequently differentiate between them, preferring simply to refer to them indifferently and collectively as the 'Blériot I'. The main reason for our ignorance is that none of the few people who saw it seems to have written down any adequate description at the time, and only one photograph of it survives. The solitary reference to the Blériot I that has been traced in the press is not very informative. In its November 1902 issue *L'Aérophile* stated that:

> M.Louis Blériot, the engineer well-known in the motoring world for his powerful acetylene lamps, is constructing a flying machine in his workshops in the rue Duret, and he expects to test it soon.[5]

The only reported dimensions clearly apply to a model rather than a full-sized apparatus. The device apparently measured 1.50m in overall width and weighed 10kg, presumably without its 'carbonic acid' motor said to develop almost 2hp. The motor was located in a central framework to two sides of which hinged frames were attached. These frames were covered with bands of silk – surely those sewn by Alice – and were arranged in some unexplained way that enabled them to act as valves that opened on the up stroke and closed on the down stroke. The flapping motion of the frames was provided by shafts driven by the motor.[6]

According to Alice Blériot's recollections dictated in 1959, the first model never left the workshop, and was not tested. But there were others, 'the motors being of carbonic acid and all exploding in one's face, the wings being flapping'.[7] Also writing many years after the event, in 1948, Gabriel Voisin recalled the first time he met Blériot, in April 1905:

> Louis Blériot led us, Ferber [Captain Ferdinand] and me, into a secret workshop where the unfinished monster revealed its inelegant skeleton. A

The ornithopter known as the Blériot I, c.1902. (MA 3692)

> piston operated by liquid air transmitted its movement to two valve frames,
> open when rising, closed when falling. This machine had the famous
> control column which would later cause so much ink to flow and unleash
> litigation without end. Conversation was difficult…[8]

It is unlikely that a machine only 1.50m across would have been remembered by Gabriel Voisin as a 'monster', but on the other hand he was mistaken about the 'liquid air', and almost certainly about the control column, as will be seen later.

Georges Houard refers to three successive 'full-size' versions with 100hp engines, all of which exploded under testing, thus forcing to a close a series of experiments which had cost, so it was said, 100,000 francs.[9] Alice Blériot also referred to the experiments as having been very expensive. As for the sole piece of photographic evidence available, it gives no conclusive evidence of scale and is difficult to interpret. The machine shown has no provision for the accommodation of a human being, in any of the bodily positions adopted by early aviators – sitting, standing or lying prone. Further reasons for considering that photograph to be of a model are that the relative proportions of several of the machine's parts suggest this, and that there is no undercarriage or other means of supporting the machine upright on the ground: it would have to be hand-held.

Most intriguing is a letter written by Alice in 1937, a few months after her husband's death. It is addressed to the Air Minister, and attached is a list of objects she was then giving to the Musée de l'Air. They include: 'A flapping wing apparatus with carbonic acid motor built in 1900.' Against this item an unknown hand has written the single word *disparu*.[10] Apparently the apparatus was stored temporarily in the basement of the residence of the then curator, Charles Dollfus (which suggests strongly that it was a model, not a full-scale aircraft). From that basement it was stolen. It has never been recovered.[11]

★★★★★

Although Gabriel Voisin had found conversation difficult when they first met, Blériot had made a powerful impression. Voisin felt himself being looked straight in the eye by a man whose manner was confident, with a touch of distinction, but whose attitude at the same time was surly and disobliging. This was very much how Blériot seemed to others who encountered him in those years. For example, Charles Dollfus, who met him first in June 1907, found him austere and withdrawn:

> Blériot was a man of average height. Once seen he was not forgotten. He was easily recognizable in a crowd, with his large aquiline nose, bright eyes and rather stiff bearing. He didn't look particularly congenial, and he wasn't. He was a man of natural authority and he wasn't easy to get on with. In the course of my career I met him several times, either for the Musée de l'Air or for the magazine *L'Aéronautique*, and the time spent with him was well worthwhile. He was always very friendly to me, taking a keen interest in the Musée de l'Air. Knowing that I was writing the history of aviation he was, I believe, well disposed towards me.[12]

The day of their first meeting, Dollfus recalled, Blériot was having his first trip in a balloon. He was in an excellent mood and was actually smiling, 'contrary to his custom'.

Such was the unsuccessful builder of flap-valve ornithopters in whose forbidding presence Voisin could think of little to say. He nevertheless took what turned out to be a momentous step – he invited Blériot to the workshop at Billancourt where he was building a glider. According to Voisin this return visit took place the very next day, and there is no doubt that Blériot, always in a hurry, would have lost no time in seeing for himself what Voisin was doing. He was to find it quite different from anything he had done himself, and a great deal more promising.

Five years had passed without Blériot obtaining the slightest result in aviation. While he had been spending time and money in ill-conceived experiments with ornithopters, Voisin had followed another course: he had learned a little about how to make gliders and how to make short flights on them. A trainee architect from near Lyons, Gabriel Voisin, born in 1880, was engaged in 1903, or 1904, to test a glider which a wealthy Parisian of British descent, Ernest Archdeacon, had had built at his own expense in the military balloon workshops at Meudon. This was a biplane glider, on the lower wing of which the pilot lay prone, operating a forward-mounted elevator which was the only movable control surface. It bore an apparent resemblance to gliders built earlier in America by Octave Chanute and by Wilbur and Orville Wright, although there were important differences. Voisin tested it from sand dunes at Berck-sur-Mer in April 1904. Although flights of no more than a few seconds were achieved, Archdeacon was sufficiently encouraged to decide to have a second glider built. He was also pleased with his young assistant, who apparently made valuable suggestions for improving the design. Archdeacon got four of his friends together and with them set up the 'Syndicat d'Aviation' with Voisin as its engineer on a salary of 190 francs a month. The second glider, which had a tailplane, was towed by a motor car but crashed when tested on 26 March 1905. Fortunately there was no pilot on board.[13]

Archdeacon then commissioned a glider with floats, to be towed into the air by a motor boat. This time Voisin did not merely influence the design, he determined it, so much so that this is generally regarded as the first 'Voisin'. By then the Syndicat d'Aviation had been taken over by Edouard Surcouf, a maker of balloons and dirigibles at Billancourt, and Voisin with his cumbersome and perhaps threatening apparatus had been squeezed out into an adjacent shed, or *hangar*, to use the original and prophetic French term, at No.4 rue de la Ferme.

Blériot could have driven there in ten minutes from his office in the rue Duret. This time Voisin thought him to be 'intelligence personified', such was the rapidity of his grasp of the essential features of the glider Voisin had almost completed for Archdeacon. Blériot stayed for three hours, and after he had gone Voisin thought the place felt empty.

But not for long. The next day Blériot was back! Without any preamble he asked brusquely whether Surcouf would take an order for a glider along the lines of the one that was there. Voisin sent him across to see Monsieur Surcouf in person. Blériot returned after a few minutes saying that he had placed the order, and demanded to see drawings right away. There followed several weeks of working together on the design of the glider that was to be the Blériot II. According to Voisin's perhaps fanciful later recollections, Blériot at this time found difficulty in expressing his thoughts on the design because his drawing was so poor. Voisin thought that for years Blériot had neglected to practise technical drawing, and that all the work on lamps had made him too concerned with detail, too gadget-minded, at the expense of a broader view of design problems. So Voisin told him this, and set up a second drawing board beside his own. There Blériot meekly took his place each day for a few hours – as many as he could spare – beside the twenty-four year old for whom drawing was a way of life. When in his nineties Gabriel was to look back and say that his life-long love of drawing was responsible above all else for his successes as an engineer.

Through the spring and early summer of 1905 the two men got to know one another, as people do who share a creative task. To Voisin, eight years his junior, Blériot seemed a sophisticated and altogether dazzling figure, even if there were a few technical points that he seemed unaccountably slow to grasp. Blériot, learning from his early mistakes, had already begun a systematic study of all the literature available on the design of wings, and was preoccupied by questions of aerofoil sections, centres of pressure and the like. There was an argument about the form of the wing section of the glider Voisin was to build for him. Blériot wanted the wing to be more cambered than Voisin considered safe following experiments he had made. He argued that a camber of one thirteenth (or one tenth according to a later account) would deprive the glider of the lateral stability they wanted it to have. (The amount of camber was expressed by Voisin as the proportion which the height of the arch of the wing bore to its chord – the distance between its leading and trailing edges.)

Yet Blériot maintained that as light-weight engines would soon be available, it was important to test wings giving as much lift as possible, which then would be fit to carry the combined weight of an engine and a pilot. He was adamant, and Voisin had to yield on this point, although he felt sure the design was dangerous. During these discussions Voisin was amused to see that Blériot's cross expression was adopted as a defence when he was unsure of his ground in an argument.

One evening something happened that Voisin claimed he had been dreading. Blériot's chauffeur arrived in front of 4 rue de la Ferme to take him home, as was the custom, but this time Voisin saw that the driver was not alone: there was a second person in the car – Madame Blériot. 'So it is you who have taken away my husband', she said to Voisin, 'from now on I am going to bring him home myself each evening, otherwise he'll end up sleeping here.' Her spontaneous, unaffected way of speaking seemed to bring light and warmth to the bare and primitive office in the shed where the two men had their drawing boards. Alice then knew that 'Aviation had taken my husband body and soul. He had found his way to the aeroplane and now would never change his course.'[14]

She made the best of the situation, saying cheerfully that aviation was his mistress, 'everything he earns is spent on her'. Voisin saw that she radiated confidence. She was not the kind of woman to say merely that her husband had high hopes of his new machine: she would state boldly that 'Louis is building a new aeroplane which will do 100 kilometres an hour'. Dollfus remarked that she never got involved in Blériot's work, 'but she was always there'.

On 8 June 1905 Voisin tested the second Archdeacon glider on the Seine between the Billancourt and Sèvres bridges. The weather was superb and the glider, towed thirty metres behind a motor boat, rose easily into a slight head wind until Voisin levelled off at the height of the top of the row of poplars lining the bank, almost twenty metres. The flight continued for 600 metres, an appreciable distance, until Voisin brought the glider down gently to rest on its floats. Although a second attempt to take off failed, all concerned were jubilant, especially Archdeacon who was beside himself. As for Blériot, 'he adopted the solemn and dignified expression reserved for great occasions.'

At eight o'clock the next morning he was in Voisin's office. 'My dear Voisin', he declared, 'your efforts will be crowned with success if you are given support. Become my partner, let's work together; I've got some money I'm prepared to risk – we should succeed'. Voisin was troubled by this proposal. He was reluctant to break his links with the Syndicat d'Aviation which had given him his start, and with Surcouf who had treated him with great kindness. On the other hand, Blériot was Blériot, and Voisin so looked up to him that he decided this undreamed of chance was an offer he could not refuse. He accepted, and Blériot paid Surcouf something for the goodwill of the fledgling aircraft business. A signboard went up outside 4 rue de la Ferme: 'Blériot-Voisin', it read, and so began in June 1905 the first firm in the world formed specifically to produce aeroplanes.

The glider built for Blériot was completed a few weeks afterwards. Known as the Blériot II, it was a biplane, with the peculiarity that the lower wing was substantially shorter than the top one, which had a span of some seven metres. Between the wings were two pairs of side curtains, the outer pair placed at a dihedral angle because of the different wing spans. The tail was of the box-kite type with vertical side curtains. There was a forward elevator, and the pilot sat on the lower wing. The whole structure rested on two long canoe-like floats.

When the time came to try it there was no question about who was going to be the pilot. Blériot in 1905 had never been higher than a horse could jump, whereas Voisin had accumulated several seconds of invaluable gliding experience in several free glides and in the towed flight already described. They both knew that a moment's hesitation, or heavy-handedness with the ultra-sensitive elevator in front, would cause disaster. Moreover, the test was to be a towed flight over the river, a procedure in which Voisin had excelled only five weeks before. Almost alone among successful pioneers, Gabriel Voisin at that time favoured this method because he considered it gave good opportunities to judge the stability of the apparatus and its behaviour at take-off and touchdown. It also, he maintained, enabled an assessment to be made of the power which would be needed if an engine were to be installed in a model of otherwise similar design. However, after the trials which will now be described he never used towing again.

Official authorization was needed for such operations on the Seine, a busy commercial waterway, and was difficult to obtain. Voisin complained of having to spend hours at a time in the Préfecture of Police pleading with uncomprehending officials, so having in the end been given permission for trials to be held on 18 July he decided to make the most of it and test both gliders that day.

The weather was bad, with a strong westerly wind making the surface of the water very rough. Worse, this was exactly across the direction of flight, which was to be from north to south. Between the Sèvres and Billancourt bridges the river flows almost due north, and the tests were to be made against the current. The Archdeacon glider was the first to be used. Voisin got off well but received such a buffeting that he touched down after about 300m of unsteady, up and down flight. Instead of then suspending operations for the day, they went ahead with preparations to fly the Blériot because of the problem of getting a new authorization for another date.

Voisin took his place on the trailing edge of the lower wing with his legs dangling through an aperture in the fabric. The towing boat was stationed ahead at the end of the towing line, too far away for Voisin to shout to the driver, so he had to communicate by signalling with his arms. A sign which he made was misinterpreted and the boat shot off at high speed before he was ready. The glider took off well, and for a moment all looked promising, but then it swerved violently down to the right, then to the left, and plunged into the water wing tips first. A great deal of it went under water, including the central part where Voisin sat, surrounded by wings, side curtains and masses of piano wire. He was trapped 'like a rat in a cage', and his right thumb was caught in something. Try as he might he could not dislodge it. A broken piano wire had pierced his left thigh. The tow rope had broken but those in the boat did not at first appreciate the seriousness of the situation. Voisin held his breath as best he could but 'began to think of giving up hope'. At length a man who had come out from the bank in a rowing boat, Albert Decarme, a foreman, freed him and took him ashore. As Voisin landed he heard applause from the crowd assembled on the road above. At first he did not understand

The Blériot II, a glider on floats, has just been launched on the Seine on 18 July 1905. (MC 1189)

why the people were clapping and cheering. But when he got close enough to see their faces, he knew.

Blériot came to him and, devastated, took his hand. 'You were right' he said 'the wings had too much camber'. The next morning he came to Voisin and asked if he might give him a present which would remind him, Blériot, of his own stubbornness. Voisin lived at a long distance from the rue de la Ferme and had difficulty in making the journey by public transport, so he said he would like a bicycle. A 'millionaire's machine' promptly arrived and Voisin was delighted.[15]

When the partners reviewed the results of the test that had so nearly cost Voisin his life, they felt that part of the problem had been caused by the towing boat itself, not just by the faulty signalling, the wind and the incorrect design of the glider. It was not the same boat as had been used for the trial in June. That motor boat had been *La Rapière*, equipped with a Panhard engine transmitting power to the propeller through a clutch which enabled the boat to accelerate away from rest very smoothly. Its driver, Tellier, was highly skilled. For the trial just concluded, however, *La Rapière* had not been available and they were obliged to use another craft, the *Antoinette*. The driver was inexperienced and, according to Voisin who was a well-placed if not impartial observer, totally unaware of the finer points of manoeuvring a speed boat. But in any case the *Antoinette* had no alternative to starting off as if from a catapult, since according to Voisin it had no clutch, and its engine could only with difficulty be made to run slowly. The running speed could be varied to some extent by advancing or retarding the ignition, but not by a throttle because there was none. It was a novel engine in other ways too, but at that moment Blériot and Voisin must have wished they had never heard of it. Yet almost at once it was to become indispensable to them. Without it the achievement of powered flight in Europe would have been delayed for years. The time has come to tell the tale of Antoinette.

3 Antoinette

For the child waking up on 15 August 1902 the day began like any other during her holiday at the seaside, but this would be a day to remember. She was in her father's house, Les Tamaris, near Etretat on the Normandy coast; her elder brother Robert was there too. Their father, Jules Gastambide, announced a walk to the beach, saying that a new business friend of his, recently arrived from Paris, would go with them. She looked shyly at the stranger, and if she failed to notice that they were being stared at by others on the beach her brother did not. Their companion cut a strange figure.

He was short and stout, and wore a heavy, unseasonable, black overcoat. The children expected the top hat tilted confidently on the back of his head to fall off at any moment, so excited were his gestures. But a more startling thing was the contrast between his full red beard and the jet-black hair of his head. The head seemed large, and from it shone two very bright eyes which flashed as he spoke. He exhorted his host to share in his latest vision, which was of a new world.

Although the present world suited Gastambide well enough, he listened politely. After all, he had good reason to be grateful to the man. Gastambide had had an anxious time with an electricity supply company he owned in Algeria. Inexplicable breakdowns of the generators had occurred on several occasions. His own technical staff had been baffled and, desperate, Gastambide had called in a new engineer who was beginning to make a name for himself. This was Léon Levavasseur, the guest of today. Quickly and with apparent ease Levavasseur had solved the problem: the generators ran as they should and their owner could relax for a while.[1]

Tactfully Gastambide led his son and daughter, followed by the still gesticulating engineer, away from the unwanted audience on the beach. They took the winding path that leads to the summit of the Falaise d'Aval, the southerly member of the imposing pair of cliffs which enclose the sumptuous bay of Etretat. Levavasseur was at home in these surroundings. He had been born not far away at Cherbourg, in 1873, the son of a naval officer. He too had wanted a nautical career but had failed the medical examination. After attending school at Angoulême he left for Paris at the age of seventeen, bent upon becoming an artist. However at that time electricity was beginning to be used for practical purposes, and he saw the potential of the new technology and fell under its spell. Giving up his artistic studies Levavasseur developed an improved arc lamp, among other things, and worked as an engineer in the Ferranti-Patin factory. There he designed new types of transformers and alternators, and set up at Orléansville the world's first electrified tramway system using alternating current. In a frenzy of engineering enthusiasm he began to investigate petrol engines, dismantling as many as he could lay hands on. In 1901 he left Ferranti-Patin to start his own business. Although still having to spend most of his time on electrical engineering – he had a wife and five children to support – Levavasseur became convinced that he could improve greatly on the current designs of petrol engines, if only he could find the money. He had come to Etretat to try to get backing from the wealthy and well-disposed Gastambide.

Pausing on their approach to the summit, they watched a flock of cormorants swooping and diving from the cliff into the sea below. In a strange tone of indignation Levavasseur said abruptly 'A man ought to be able to fly better than a bird'. Disconcerted, Gastambide would have preferred to ignore the remark as he could not think how to respond, but Levavasseur was not to be put off. Men would fly over that sea on wings he would make for them – he had worked out in his head, he said, how the whole problem of flight was to be solved. First he would provide the 'muscle'. It would be an engine with eight cylinders in the shape of a V, with the dramatically low weight of under one kilogram per horsepower. If Gastambide would help him they would 'conquer the air' together, he said, then turning to the little girl he smiled and said 'We will call the engine Antoinette'.[2]* After further explanations by Levavasseur, accompanied by excited demonstrations of paper aeroplanes in the salon of Les Tamaris, Gastambide realized that it was by then out of the question to refuse to help. So he agreed to finance Levavasseur, on condition that the engine would be built first, followed by the aeroplane.

Léon Levavasseur lost no time. Returning to Paris the next day, he rented an empty workshop at Puteaux in the western suburbs where he installed two lathes and a milling machine. He brought in his brother-in-law Charles Wachter to help and he recruited four mechanics who were all brothers, the Welferings. By the ninth day these things had been done, by the thirteenth day a patent had been applied for, and on the nineteenth day the engine was running on the bench. When tested early in 1904 by the army aeronautical establishment at Chalais-Meudon it produced over 50hp for a total weight including radiator and water of 156kg. (Levavasseur contested this result, contending that it had been arrived at unscientifically.)

What Levavasseur did needs to be seen in context. By 1902, when he first became actively involved, solutions had been found to most of the basic problems of the internal combustion engine, but they were precarious solutions. The vital systems for carburation, ignition, lubrication and cooling functioned uncertainly. Improving any one of them would generally provoke failure of another. Such problems made themselves obvious, but there were others, like the importance of the shape of combustion chambers, which would not be recognized for a long time.

Borrowing piston and cylinder technology from the steam engines of the eighteenth and early nineteenth centuries, the first internal combustion engines served mainly as static sources of power for industry and ran on gas, often coal gas from town supplies. Between 1807 and 1885 isolated attempts were made, in Austria, England and France, to use gas

---

Two years earlier a radical new car launched by Daimlers had been named after the daughter of Emile Jellinek, an Austrian banker who was their representative among the wealthier inhabitants of the Côte d'Azur. He had thought the name Daimler too Germanic for the French market, and as he was prepared to place a large order for the new model his wishes carried weight at the factory. Thus the car was called Mercedes.[3]

Léon Levavasseur, left, with Gabriel Voisin. (MA 16614)

engines for road vehicles. In 1876 there was a crucial development in Germany when Nicolaus August Otto built and successfully ran an engine on the four-stroke principle, which had been proposed but not applied by Beau de Rochas in France in 1862. Otto's engine used town gas and ran at 250rpm. One of Otto's staff who had helped to build it was Gottlieb Daimler, who after 1882 set up his own firm to concentrate on designing and building a small air-cooled engine. This was faster than Otto's, running at 800rpm, and lighter. Daimler's new engine could use either petrol or gas as fuel. Being easily portable, unlike coal gas, petrol opened up the possibility of employing the engine in a vehicle, and in 1886 Daimler used it to power the first motorcycle not to have a steam engine. This was ridden by his assistant Wilhelm Maybach, who later designed the Mercedes car, but who first, in 1897, invented the jet or spray carburettor. This replaced Daimler's surface-vaporiser and gave the accurate mixture strength which was needed for efficient running.

Daimler's engine had an 'automatic' inlet valve, opened by induction pressure and closed by a return spring, and a mechanically operated exhaust valve. It was air-cooled, assisted by a fan. Ignition was by a heated element whose temperature was kept up continuously by petrol burned outside the cylinder. This was the dangerous device known as a hot tube. Such was the historic Daimler engine, upon which were based all future piston engines for motorcycles, cars and eventually aircraft.

In the following decade, until 1895, that basic design was developed further by engineers of many nationalities, but it was in France that the crucial step forward was taken. There, comte Albert de Dion and Georges Bouton recognised that there was scope for increasing the speed and power of the petrol engine, and they decided that the key to this would be the ability to choose with great precision the best moment in the cycle at which to ignite the compressed mixture of fuel and air. Timed ignition was impossible using the hot tube system, and was provided only approximately by the first electrical systems which, from battery and Ruhmkorff coil, produced a shower of sparks across a contact breaker placed inside the cylinder. The required precision of timing was obtained by De Dion-Bouton with a system in which the internal contact-breaker was replaced by a sparking plug, and an improved battery and coil were employed, with an external contact-breaker opened by a cam driven by the engine. Their engine could run as fast as 4,000rpm without apparent ill effects and its normal operating speed was 1,800rpm. By 1895, Daimler's engines were still running at only about 800rpm and Benz's at 750rpm. Another but unrelated technical innovation by De Dion-Bouton was the use of aluminium alloy to make light crankcases.

Léon Levavasseur, in further developing the petrol engine, substituted a system of direct fuel admission for normal carburation, developed a sophisticated cooling system, and designed for lightness in countless ingenious ways. However, the evolution of the Antoinette series of engines was much influenced by the ways in which they were used, so it is well to consider their uses before looking in any detail at the technical innovations of Levavasseur's masterpieces. For that, let there be no doubt, is what they were. Dollfus has described his influence in these words:

> Léon Levavasseur created the Antoinette engine. He thus had a decisive influence on the beginnings of aviation; from 1906 to 1908 all the important performances, other than those by the Wrights, were achieved by Antoinette engines, the first in the world to be produced industrially for aviation. An engineer who remained an artist, because that was what he first trained to be, Levavasseur always knew how to give his work an astonishing *cachet d'élégance.*[4]

Jules Gastambide, financier and president of the Antoinette company. (MA 3804)

Elegant they were, but reliable they were not. The early British aviator Moore-Brabazon recalled:

> As a power unit it was lighter than anything ever dreamed of, but it was thirty years ahead of its day and as a reliable power plant was very unsatisfactory. If you could run it for five minutes you had done well. I know as I had one.[5]

The first use of one of the engines was to be abortive. In the summer of 1903 Levavasseur built an aeroplane, with a secrecy perhaps explainable by the unorthodox way the project was financed. Gastambide had convinced himself from the start that aviation could become commercially viable only if orders could be obtained from government, but an attempt to sell Levavasseur's first engine to the French army had collapsed in a furious dispute over the measurement of its power output. Although no money could be extracted from the authorities through normal channels the Minister of War, General André, was so impressed that during an interview he took twenty 1,000 franc notes from a safe in his room and handed them over to Levavasseur and Gastambide.[6]

The aeroplane was taken by night to the Château de Villotran in the Oise department where friends of Gastambide had offered facilities. The machine, a monoplane, was assembled on the lawn over a period of six weeks, and left out in the open air without protection. Wind and rain did damage which removed any chance it might have had of flying. There was a simple lesson here, but it was one which Levavasseur strangely failed to learn. The single engine drove two propellers, one in front and one behind, and take-off was to be from a rail laid out on the ground, in the manner of the Wrights. With Charles Wachter at the controls, the monoplane succeeded in rising but fell to the ground immediately, breaking a wing. Further tests were no more satisfactory and in September 1903 Levavasseur took out the engine and burnt the rest of his premature aeroplane. Gastambide continued to feel that aviation would remain unattractive to private capital until such time as the government began ordering aeroplanes. Therefore he declined to pay for any more flying experiments, but he did remain loyal to Levavasseur and agreed to support him in his next project.

In order to demonstrate the qualities of his engines, and perhaps also to develop their reliability, Levavasseur then decided to put one in a racing motor boat. This may possibly have been one of his intentions from the very beginning, and may have been suggested by Gastambide. In any event, it was an excellent move, and with the engine installed in a light-weight hull eight metres long brilliant performances were soon achieved. It was for this boat that the name 'Antoinette' was first used, and it was only afterwards given to the engines. She swept all before her in the new and spectacular sport which attracted wealthy people as spectators and as participants. The latter included a well known racing cyclist and car racing driver, Henry Farman. At Monaco, at Evian on Lake Geneva, and on Lake Garda formidable and well-established competitors such as Fiat, Mercedes, Panhard and Renault were outpaced by the Antoinette. Several versions were built, including one with two engines in tandem. Endurance races requiring four hours running at full power at sea, as well as short sprints from a standing start, fell to the all-conquering Antoinettes. In 1905 an Antoinette speed-boat held the world records for all distances from one to 150 miles. They were sometimes driven by a cousin of Jules Gastambide, a dashing young sportsman called Hubert Latham, a Frenchman of partly English descent, who was just twenty-three years old when he went faster on water than anyone had done before. It was not he who had towed Gabriel Voisin so clumsily on the Seine, but more will be heard of Latham later.

★★★★★

The series of aero engines which Levavasseur went on to design showed the nautical part of their pedigree in three ways. Firstly, connecting flanges were fitted at both ends of the crankshaft so that a pair of engines could be coupled in tandem for use in a boat. Apparently Jules Gastambide specified this as a commercial precaution, in case sales for aviation were insufficient and it became necessary to re-enter the marine market. Secondly, the direction of rotation was reversible, by means of a control which moved the camshaft along its axis to bring a second set of cams into play. While this facility had no application in aeroplanes, it was claimed by Captain Ferber, a director of the Antoinette company, to be valuable for dirigible balloons when docking. Thirdly, the water jacket of an Antoinette was of very small volume (about 1.8 litres for the V8's) because in boats a free-flow system of cooling was used. With an infinite supply of cold water available there was no need for a larger capacity.

Cooling when in the air was a different matter. For the pioneers this was a major problem, a principal cause of curtailed flights and sometimes worse, and it beset them whether their engines were cooled by water or by air. Levavasseur produced a sophisticated cooling system of unusual design. Water was boiled in the cylinder jackets, condensed in a large aluminium condenser attached to the sides of the fuselage and then returned to the engine by a belt-driven steam pump. There was also a water pump. It was designed as a full-recovery system, although in practice there was some loss of steam. The system was effective, but complicated and fragile. However it was not until 1908 that he developed this system for the Antoinette monoplane, and even then it was not made available to those who bought engines alone. Levavasseur's cooling system was an ace which he kept to himself! Customers were left to their own devices. From 1908 they could try to emulate his system, but before then they were even more in the dark. When on 13 January 1908 Henry Farman on his Voisin flew the first officially recorded circle in history, at Issy-les-Moulineaux, no radiator was fitted to save weight and Farman cooled his Antoinette with just a header tank filled at the last moment with crushed ice. He got off as quickly as possible, and when he landed one and a half minutes later, having accomplished the historic *boucle*, the remaining water was boiling.

To an onlooker the most conspicuous parts of the Antoinette engines were their water jackets, made initially of brass and later of copper. They were the basis of the reputation for elegance. The use of jackets fabricated separately from the cylinders enabled the exterior of the latter to be machined in the interests of lightness and more even expansion and contraction – the Antoinette's cylinder walls were only 1mm thick! Until 1907 Levavasseur made jackets of spun brass, cutting off the cones at each end which resulted from the spinning process. Then he changed to a radically different procedure in which

Antoinette Gastambide (MA 3796)

the cylinders were covered with a wax mould upon which a thin and even coating of copper was deposited electrostatically. The wax was then melted out, leaving a perfectly fitting water jacket which could be bolted to the cylinder block. It is difficult to say whether Levavasseur was the first to use this process, since some car makers were also using it at around the same time. The process was difficult to control, as lumps could form and the copper skin could be of different thicknesses in different places, with the result that there were many rejects in manufacture. This apart, it was a good method, not least because it was a way of making separate water jackets which made a watertight joint with the cylinder block. Others, using silver solder, had failed to achieve satisfactory joints when fabricating separate jackets from sheet material.

All Antoinette engines had a 'V' layout of their cylinders because this enabled their crankshafts to be shorter and therefore lighter than if an in-line arrangement had been chosen. With one exception they were of either eight or sixteen cylinders. A monster of thirty-two cylinders was once made but its life was short because it promptly went through the bottom of the boat it was put into. With large numbers of cylinders a turbine-like effect was achieved and, provided an air-propeller was fitted, the engine would run without a flywheel, thus saving much weight. Ferber claimed that a further factor in favour of having many cylinders was that key components were evenly stressed and could be made lighter than if subjected to the more intermittent stresses of an engine with fewer cylinders.

The inlet valves were of the 'automatic', or atmospheric variety, as used by Daimler, which opened and closed in response to changes of pressure in the inlet manifold. The exhaust valves, placed directly below the inlet valves, were mechanically operated by push-rods actuated by one central camshaft serving both banks of cylinders. The compression ratio was about 4:1, normal in days when 5:1 was considered quite extraordinary. Ignition was by sparking plugs, battery and a single trembler coil in continuous operation, and a distributor.

The term 'fuel injection' has sometimes been used to describe the system Levavasseur employed in place of carburettors. That is claiming too much for what was nevertheless an ingenious scheme, which may be fairly regarded as a precursor of fuel injection. Fuel was held in a small chamber above each cylinder, to the inlet port of which it was connected by a capillary tube. When the atmospheric inlet valve opened, the consequent depression in the capillary tube drew fuel from the chamber down into the port. 'Direct fuel admission' might be a more suitable term for this process. Some regulation of the fuel flow by the pilot was provided for, but in practice the engine's response to this control was limited. Advancing or retarding the admission had more influence on running speed, but even so it was difficult to get an Antoinette to run slowly, which helps to explain why Blériot, as will be seen, had so much trouble in maintaining control over several of his early aeroplanes while they were on the ground. Levavasseur's system of fuel admission was vulnerable to foreign bodies in petrol, more common then than now, causing blockages in filters and jets. The system was unreliable, and many customers, including Santos-Dumont, replaced it with carburettors.

Lubrication was elementary, pressurised by a belt-driven oil pump. There was a spray gallery in the crankcase, with return gullies sloping slightly downward towards the rear, where oil was collected and drawn away by the pump: not quite a dry sump system. The valves were not included in it – they got an occasional squirt of the oil can, and were in any event bathed in oil mist drawn up from the crankcase since the piston rings were not oil-tight.

Above and beyond all these individual features, some traditional and others innovative, stood a design procedure which is now the norm but was then revolutionary. This was the secret of the Antoinettes, if secret there was – the engine was precisely stressed. All parts were made to a predetermined necessary strength, no more and no less.[7]

The replacement of guesswork by calculation produced dramatic results, especially when combined with precision workmanship, in a shop which claimed to work in

Un cachet d'élégance: *Alberto Santos-Dumont takes pride in his new 24hp Antoinette V8, intended for his planned helicopter in 1906. (MA 39069)*

tolerances of 1/100th of a millimetre. No one before Levavasseur had ever extracted so much power from so little weight – 1hp from 1 to 2kg of engine. (The Wrights were content with 1hp from 6kg, but they were more concerned with reliability, and more successful in obtaining it.[8])

The Antoinette's exceptional performances were accompanied by a prodigious amount of noise. A sixteen cylinder engine running on open exhausts makes a sound which carries for miles, and which once heard is never forgotten. This was a problem for some people when learning to fly. 'The sudden roar of an aeroplane engine', wrote Louis Blériot in 1911, 'has a very disconcerting effect upon many people until they become used to it.' Experience prompted him to add:

> I have on more than one occasion seen a man absolutely unnerved and taken aback by the din when his engine has been started up for the first time. And yet, as an indication of how one can accustom oneself to any unusual circumstances, I have noticed that a pilot becomes so completely used to the noise of his engine that he does not notice it at all. One of my pupils, I remember, a man of an original turn of mind, used to sit in his shed, with the engine running, so as to make himself thoroughly accustomed to the clatter. "I feel I must become used to the noise," he said, "otherwise I cannot remember a thing that I ought to do when actually sitting in the machine, with the engine thundering away near me." This trick of his struck me as being a sound one.[9]

4 A chapter of errors

It was probably the advent of the Antoinette engine which convinced Blériot that he should now proceed directly to a powered aeroplane. The aeroplane, like the glider, would have floats. Voisin had had success as well as failure in attempting to fly from water and, despite his dramatic accident, the partners probably thought it a safer surface to come down on than solid ground. From the Seine, however, they had learned that a rather narrow river was unsuitable because the direction of intended flight could not be altered to take account of the wind. A broad, but still sheltered, stretch of water was what they needed. Just north of Paris lies the small Lac d'Enghien, whose proximity made it a natural choice because of the difficulty of transporting an aeroplane any great distance. But the lake is so very small as to prompt the speculation that with more room at their disposal they might have done better. For they did not do well at the Lac d'Enghien, not well at all.

It began badly. Soon after giving Voisin the bicycle, Blériot horrified him by announcing that four days of tests with models had shown him that the only way to make an aeroplane was with two cylindrical wings of the same size arranged in tandem. After eight days of furious argument, the partners compromised unhappily on two pairs of wings in the shape of ellipses.[1] Before dismissing Blériot's idea as absurd, it should be recognized that inherent stability was then his goal, and that he was not to be the only engineer to seek it in that way. Four years and several generations of designs later, a machine along the lines Blériot had proposed was designed by a Monsieur Givaudan, an engineer in the Vermorel company which had made cars.[2] When tested at Villefranche-sur-Saône, near Lyon, in April 1909 the cylindrical-winged machine did not fly, but it earned the perhaps over-optimistic comment from Fred T. Jane that 'the advantage of this system is that side gusts of wind have no effect whatever, and that heeling over when turning is impossible.'[3]

Although he had obtained the 'flattening' of the cylinders, Voisin still had a fight on his hands. Blériot wanted to drive two tractor propellers by flexible transmission cables from a single 24hp Antoinette mounted transversely. These flexible drives, which incorporated reduction gearing to bring the engine speed of 1,800rpm down to a propeller speed of 600rpm, weighed 110kg. As the total weight of the aeroplane was 400kg Voisin's strong objections to such an arrangement seem all too understandable, but Blériot was immovable.[4] On 7 January 1906 he and Levavasseur signed an option agreement for the purchase, for 4,000 francs, of an Antoinette engine of 20-24hp, in which it was specified that the cylinder bore (800mm) would measure the same as the stroke: in other words, a 'square' engine, then most unusual.[5] From the moment Voisin accepted that he had lost the argument over the transmission, their partnership was doomed, although its actual dissolution lay some months in the future. Throughout the winter of 1905-1906 work continued as before and Voisin loyally completed the construction of the machine, the Blériot III.

At the end of May 1906 the Blériot III was taken to the lake where an assistant of

The Blériot III on the Lac d'Enghien in May 1906. (BL 248)

Blériot's, Louis Peyret, drove it about on the surface of the water which it refused obstinately to leave. Faced with another total failure, Blériot agreed to extensive modifications, which presumably were instigated by Voisin. Chief among them was the replacement of the ellipsoidal front wing by a biplane, box-kite type of wing, with two of the side curtains that were to become a Voisin hallmark. Small ailerons were attached to the rear struts of the new wings. The biplane elevator, which had been mounted just behind the tractor propellers, was replaced by a larger one placed well forward of the front wings in the Wright manner. There were now two pusher propellers of triple laminated mahogany, each driven by a 24hp Antoinette. The controversial flexible drives had gone, but reduction gearing to the same extent as before was provided. Of the original machine little remained except the rear wings or tail, which now contained a rudder. This redesigned and rebuilt aeroplane was designated No.IV.

Apparently, it was a great improvement. The lifting surface, already very large for the time at 60sq.m, was increased to 78sq.m. It was a huge aeroplane for its day. Power was doubled, while the total weight had increased by only 80kg to 480kg. Nonetheless, the Blériot IV failed to rise when tried on the Lac d'Enghien on 12 and 18 October 1906. A stiff and steady breeze was considered necessary for a take-off, but none was forthcoming on either day. Even the supplementary efforts of a high-speed winch on shore made no difference. But this time a thoughtful observer detected some grounds for optimism. The aeroplane was able to travel across the surface at the commendable speed of 28 to 30kph and it could be steered accurately in any direction.[6]

More important in a way were certain details of construction which showed a great deal of practical sense. Ease of transport and repair counted for much in the design. The two engines, with their equipment and propellers, were mounted in a separate chassis, a sort of power pack which could be installed or removed very quickly, a great help when making the journey by road between Billancourt and the Lac d'Enghien with the aeroplane partly dismantled. Vertical

The Blériot IV on the Lac d'Enghien in October 1906. (P 21688)

and transverse struts were of white pine, rounded to reduce wind resistance, and joined to the pine longerons by aluminium brackets. These latter permitted the replacement of any individual strut without the large scale dismantling of the surrounding structure that was required when the customary mortise and tenon joints were used. Last but not least, the construction connecting the two pairs of wings is clearly an embryonic version of the distinctive fuselage that would be a unifying theme running through many future Blériot types.[7]

These public trials were not at all to the liking of Levavasseur. On 17 October a four-page letter, couched in very strong terms, urged Blériot to postpone the tests announced for the next day and requested the return of the two engines to Puteaux for checking, on the grounds that the ignition systems were not working properly.[8] Somehow, the problem was resolved, presumably by repairs made at the lakeside, but the incident suggests tension in the relations between Levavasseur and Blériot. Together with Ferber and Santos-Dumont, Blériot had been one of the first purchasers of an Antoinette engine, and at an early stage he had become a substantial minority shareholder, as well as a director from May 1906, in the Société Anonyme Antoinette.

In the next three weeks Blériot and Voisin replaced the floats with wheels, apparently because they felt that they would be less at the mercy of wind force and direction if attempts were made from the ground, which provided some lateral resistance. These trials, of the Blériot IV bis, as it had become, took place on the lawn at Bagatelle in the Bois de Boulogne on 12 November 1906 and were unsuccessful. On its final run the Blériot IV hit an obstruction on the ground and was extensively damaged. Although soon afterwards there was a report that it was being rebuilt, with a single Antoinette engine of 50hp, that work was never completed, if indeed it ever began.[9]

The last straw for Blériot, as far as the type IV was concerned, was no doubt the unhappy coincidence that on the day of its demise, and at the very same place, he saw Alberto Santos-Dumont, standing up in his bizarre *canard* biplane, make a sensational flight of 220m, the longest achieved by anyone other than the Wrights up to that time.

Gabriel Voisin was justified in expecting a torrent of criticism. Eighteen months and a vast sum of money had been spent on the Blériots III and IV, and there was not even the briefest of hop-flights to claim as a result. It was inconceivable to Voisin that this occasion could pass without hard words from his partner. Blériot astonished him. In the friendliest way he took Voisin's arm and found the right words to console him. Voisin was amazed by Blériot's ability to rise above failure. 'It was as if a divinity had revealed to him the success which awaited him at the end of his troubles', recalled Voisin years later.[10] Face to face with failure Blériot believed more than ever in success.

Mutual esteem and friendship would continue always, but the Blériot-Voisin partnership was over. Gabriel Voisin took his brother Charles into partnership and the firm of 'Les Frères Voisin' went on to become a major force in aviation. Their subsequent achievements, however, did not receive quite as much recognition as was their due, in part as a consequence of their policy of giving the early productions the names of purchasers rather than the name of the makers. Thus when at the end of November 1906 the sculptor Léon Delagrange ordered a 'Voisin', and ten days later Henry Farman did the same thing, their aeroplanes when delivered were boldly labelled 'Delagrange' and 'Farman' respectively. This enabled the astute Voisin brothers to experiment simultaneously with variations of the same basic machine at customers' expense, much to their own benefit in terms of achieving a competitive edge in development. Their customers served in effect as unpaid test pilots who bought their own aeroplanes and paid for their modification and upkeep. It is likely however that the primary motivation for the Voisin's naming policy was immediate financial necessity. The appeal to the vanity of some potential customers was strong and original, and the brothers were in desperate need of business. During the first partnership Blériot had taken care of the firm's expenditure with what Gabriel Voisin described as 'the greatest liberality'. But Voisin Frères had to start again with, reputedly, no resources except small change in the petty cash, credit from the bistro on the corner and food parcels from their sister in the country.

Louis Blériot, on the other hand, could afford to resume his struggle to fly in some style. He took premises in the Boulevard Victor-Hugo at Neuilly, close to both his home and the lamp business, and had a sign put up outside which read:

L. BLERIOT, Ing. E. C. P. Recherches Aéronautiques

Equipment was bought and men were recruited, but this was not to be a traditional workshop of the period. According to Dollfus it was:

> ...A rather curious affair...He took on a large staff, in particular young engineers who brought with them designs of their own. In effect he subsidized researchers who constructed aeroplanes according to their own plans, but usually under the Blériot name. But they were absolutely free to build whatever they wanted.[11]

The form of organization adopted by Blériot for the next couple of years, whether or not it was precisely as Dollfus thought, was to help cast an obscurity, which will probably never be removed, over the role played by Blériot himself in the design of the next machines that bore his name.

After the dissolution of his partnership with Gabriel Voisin, Louis Blériot launched his own aeronautical enterprise. This illustration is from his 1909 catalogue. (MA 28878)

Blériot's way was to tell his staff what he wanted, the objective to be achieved, and to put forward concepts and general principles. Few drawings or sketches by his own hand survive, apart from fine examples done at the Ecole Centrale. His mechanic Ferdinand Collin declared that he had never seen a drawing by Blériot, implying that he could not draw. However, it is clear that Blériot was well able to draw, and if he did not do so after 1907 when Collin joined him that was because he chose not to, probably for the simple reason he had no time, amid all his many activities.

On the other hand, one change at that time of transition does stand out sharply and unambiguously. From now on Louis Blériot would be his own pilot. That decision by the thirty-four year old husband and father marked a tightening of the screw of his commitment to 'conquer the air'. From now on life and limb, as well as fortune, were offered up to Fate.

★★★★★

> The first aeroplane that I brought out in 1907 was a monoplane in the shape of a duck [*canard*]. It was not without intense emotion that I tested this machine, the sixth.[sic] If only it would rise! Very cautiously at first, I let it run about on the ground, to try it out. It worked well. Then I could no longer resist – I just had to try to fly. So I pulled at the controls. The machine gave a terrible bound upwards. There, yes, I was frightened… for myself certainly, but also for all the little ones I had left at home…With a sudden movement I wanted to get back to the ground. The controls were sensitive. In the rough landing they broke. The engine, which in this machine was at the back, turned over on a piece of wood which held firm. If it had snapped I would have been crushed.

So wrote Blériot of events that spring, adding that six months later 'I still had none of the reflexes required to pilot an aeroplane.'[12] It was not for nothing that he would become known as 'the aviator who has had the most falls.'

Blériot's new aeroplane, which gave him those first, tentative experiences of flight, could hardly have been less like its predecessor. Gone was the birdcage, here was the bird. The first product of his new workshop was extraordinary. There was not a piece of wire to be seen on the Blériot V. In place of the cumbrous kite-like surfaces joined together by monstrous scaffolding, there were the clean, curved lines of a bird. It was the first of a series of experimental Blériots which were to give a perspicacious and increasingly accurate preview of what the modern aeroplane, when finally 'discovered', was going to be like.

There was a single wing, dramatically curved and swept back in a complex, and variable, form. The wing framework was a marvel of strong but lightweight wooden construction, and to it was glued above and below a covering of white paper, varnished to give some protection against damp. There was a very definite fuselage – a term not yet in use, since one knowledgeable reporter described it as 'a much-lengthened horizontal pyramid of rectangular section'. This structure, internally braced with wire, was covered with varnished silk, and at its pointed end – the front – carried an elevator and a rudder, beneath which was a ground skid. Inside the fuselage at the forward end were stored the batteries for the ignition system. A flat radiator made up from aluminium tubing was mounted close against the underside of the fuselage in the middle. Towards the rear were a pair of reinforced bicycle wheels, set very close together. Right at the back was a 24hp Antoinette with direct drive to a pusher propeller. The engine was covered by an aluminium bonnet, resembling those of racing cars of the time. The pitch of the propeller could be varied by turning a screw, 'not of course during an experiment, but beforehand.' There was a freewheeling mechanism to enable the propeller to continue turning if and when the engine stopped in flight. The pilot sat in the fuselage immediately in front of the engine. The weight, including Blériot's 75kg, was a startling 236kg.[13]

Although so evocative of a bird, there is little doubt that the inspiration for those amazing wings came to its designer – whoever he was – not from any feathered species but from a plant, the Zanonia. This is a tropical climber which produces a seed 'that has attached to it some leaf-like material closely resembling a pair of wings'. As the seed ripens and dries out the wings curl upwards at their turned back extremities. When the seed falls, it glides away in a stable manner. The aeronautical significance of this was first appreciated by Ahlorn of Berlin. In Germany and Austria several experimenters built, or proposed, machines of 'Zanonia form'. One of those men, Etrich, patented an example in 1905, and it may have been from reports of this that the Blériot workshop picked up the idea. Corroboration of the view that the Blériot V was Zanonia inspired is to be found in a paper read to the Aeronautical Society of Great Britain in 1913 by J.W. Dunne, whose own designs from 1907 or earlier were influenced by the Zanonia. Dunne stated that: 'Various persons have attempted to embody its characteristics in full-size aero-surfaces, Blériot among the number.' Since no other Blériot resembles the Zanonia in wing shape, this reference can only be to the type V.[14]

On 21 March 1907, at Bagatelle, Louis Blériot took his place for the first time at the controls of the aeroplane. Exactly what some of those controls were is now a tantalizing uncertainty, unlikely to be resolved since the Blériot V survived for just under a month and no drawings in any detail have been discovered. However some points are fairly clear. At his right hand there was a lever which, through a universal joint and rigid linking rods, enabled him to operate the elevator and rudder which he could see clearly in front of him. As the undercarriage could not be steered, the only way of turning the machine on the ground was by applying the rudder, highly sensitive because forward mounted, through that lever. The intriguing function of a second lever, centrally placed between his knees, was to allow him 'to raise and twist as he wished the right wing or the left wing in order to assist in turning'.[15] The tips and the swept-back parts of the wings were made flexible to enable this compound alteration in shape to take place. Some photographs of the machine at rest show the left and right wings in different shapes, as if that central lever had been moved. Certain historians have been quick to suggest that Blériot may have thus attempted to adopt the Wright brothers' system of wing warping. If so he used only part of the Wrights' arrangement, which may not have been fully understood in Europe at this date. Another possibility is that he may have got the idea from the earlier work of Clément Ader.

In front of him was a spirit level 'so that he would know in which direction and to what extent to lean his body in order to keep or recover his balance.' This was felt to be some insurance against the risk of not being able to achieve the desired results with the control

Three of Louis Blériot's children in the cockpit of the original version of the Blériot V, 24hp Aintoinette V8.
(P 25162)

levers alone. A rough approximation of his engine speed could be obtained 'simply by reading' from 'a special apparatus'. The only other thing he had to remember in the cockpit, apart from the lever to advance and retard the admission – the only effective way of varying the engine speed – was a rubber bulb which had to be squeezed from time to time to maintain air pressure in the fuel tank, itself made of rubber and hidden out of the airflow inside the fuselage. The tank was at the same level as the engine cylinders.[16] These were interesting departures from the usual gravity feed from external metal tanks. All these novelties in design and construction marked the beginning of Blériot's reputation as an innovator with a distinct personal style. His 'indefatigable tenacity' was also beginning to be remarked upon.

The Blériot V was towed to Bagatelle behind his yellow Panhard. Each wing had three hinges which allowed it to be folded upwards out of the way when the aeroplane was being taken about on the streets. These tests often began at seven o'clock in the morning – partly to benefit from windless conditions but also because of restrictions on the use of a public park as a trial ground. Thus the transport and other preparations took place at a very early hour indeed. Alice took pity on one member of the team of mechanics and invited him to sleep at their home on the nights before, so that he would not have to be up quite so early. He was Louis Paragot and he was just fourteen years old. Blériot had engaged him some weeks before, on 8 January 1907, at a wage of twenty francs a fortnight. He was the first apprentice in aviation. They called him 'P'tit Louis' and he stayed with Blériot for the rest of his employer's life.

The Blériot V arriving at Bagatelle in the Bois de Boulogne with wings folded up for road transport, March 1907. (BL 244)

The first thing they tried was pushing the aeroplane along on the grass with the car, no doubt to see if Blériot could steer it, without at the same time having to worry about the engine, which was not started. Happily, this curious procedure was not persevered with. Blériot got the engine started and set off across the lawn. Alas, he did not get far before the wheels buckled and the machine swung round to the right. He tried to bring it back to a straight and even keel, but failed. The rudder and elevator were damaged, but the wings were untouched. Apparently unmoved, Blériot stepped out calmly, and said that he would reinforce the broken parts and at the same time raise the front of the fuselage in order to increase the angle of attack of the wings. Those present that morning to watch the tests included Levavasseur, Santos-Dumont, Captain Ferber, and many other prominent members of the Aéro Club.

Repaired and slightly modified, the Blériot V was tested again on 26 March, with almost identical results. This time the forks holding the wheels broke, and the consequential damage was the same as before. Quickly repaired, the aeroplane was brought back again to Bagatelle on 2 April, only for the propeller to somehow strike the ground and be twisted out of true. More important modifications were now made: a vertical fin was added at the rear, and a third undercarriage wheel.[17]

On 5 April they tried again. At nine o'clock in the morning, against a stiff breeze, Blériot succeeded in covering some 100 metres, far further than ever before, when the machine suddenly rose and travelled five or six metres with its wheels about 600mm from the

An assistant prepares to swing the pusher propeller of the Blériot V, while others hold the nose steady. Bagatelle, 27 March 1907. (MA 137)

ground. Believing himself unable to cope with the wind, he prudently switched off the ignition and came down. A strut between the undercarriage wheels buckled on landing, thus ruling out any further attempt that day.

It was not much of a 'flight', but he had taken off for the first time. As things turned out, the number V was not to do any better than that. The machine was tested again on 7 April, with its rudder temporarily removed. The intention was simply to discover how easily it could be persuaded to take off. This it did after rolling only fifty metres, and at two-thirds engine power. Blériot was encouraged: it did not matter that the hop which ensued was only of four or five metres. More tests early in the morning of 15 April showed that he did not seem to be handling the elevator correctly. The aeroplane crossed the lawn at a good speed but could only bounce off the ground intermittently. There was a marked tendency for it to rear up, like a prancing horse.

The end came on 19 April at seven o'clock in the morning. Without the rear fin, but with a larger propeller, Blériot was travelling at 50kph when he over-corrected with the elevator, bringing the rising nose abruptly downwards. It hit the ground hard and the machine somersaulted. Blériot's friends watched in horror, and some began running towards the wreckage. But before they reached him he stepped out.[18] One of the very few pieces of wood not smashed was a horizontal strut at the back of his seat, a few inches behind which was the engine. If that strut had not held he would certainly have been crushed at that moment, as he acknowledged.

Some thought that the Blériot V could be rebuilt in three weeks or so, but the work was never done. Critics, both at the time and subsequently, who reproached Blériot for lacking continuity of effort in his experiments – although none could fault him for any lack of perseverance in general terms – implicitly judged him as if he were a scientist. They forgot that he was also a businessman, who was accustomed to deciding when to cut his losses and reinvest in a new venture. The more he is thought of as a businessman, the more sense can be made of much that he did in the following years.

5 Persistence rewarded

While Blériot had been attempting flight on his *canard*, the No.V, his chief design associate at the time, Louis Peyret, had been concentrating on the construction of a completely new and different aeroplane. Peyret had been experimenting with gliders since 1896, and was thus an unusually experienced aeronautical engineer in his own right.

The Blériot VI had two pairs of wings in tandem. Each pair had a pronounced dihedral, and they were identical except that small pivoting surfaces, sometimes termed elevons, were attached to the tips of the forward pair of wings. The elevons were intended for longitudinal control. It is probable that reliance was placed entirely on wing dihedrals for lateral stability. At the rear were two vertical triangular fins, one above the fuselage and one below: a rudder was installed behind them. The tractor propeller was driven by an eight cylinder Antoinette of 24hp.[1]

The wing layout of the Blériot VI is invariably said to have been inspired by the ill-fated creation of Samuel Pierpont Langley, in the USA, which failed dramatically in its attempts to fly when tested as a full-size aeroplane in 1903 although it had done well as a flying model. While that inspiration for the latest Blériot is not in question, it is worth recalling that he had already applied the tandem wing principle in the Blériot III, but perhaps because the wings then were ellipsoidal, and so strange to behold, the possible Langley connection has not been remarked upon.

We have an impression of Blériot and his new aeroplane from a young visitor to Paris who paid a formal call on him in the afternoon of 18 June 1907. That evening Henri Fabre, who had bought a glider from Blériot-Voisin and was later to design, build and fly the first successful seaplane, wrote in his diary:

> Visit to Blériot, marvellous Blériot! The wing span of his machine seems to me too short, and the arrangement of the wings one behind the other will not I think give enough lift, but the whole thing is admirably made: strong, simple and with all the details very carefully thought out. The way of attaching the propeller is remarkable. Wind resistance is very small. The glued-on paper is very interesting. That has to be tried, although for a final version I don't think it is strong enough. It's all highly original. The engine looks well installed, and so does the radiator.
> Blériot is modest; speaks gently, reasons clearly...He is to test tomorrow at six o'clock in the morning. I'll be there. But I very much fear he will kill himself, which would be most annoying as he is so likeable...He has some chance of success because he has been working for such a long time.[2]

Strong winds the following day caused Fabre to be disappointed, and it was not until 7 July that the *libellule* (dragonfly), was pushed by hand to Issy for the first test. The best that observers could say was that it definitely appeared to become 'lighter' as it rolled along. The wing area was then enlarged by about 10%, and Blériot tried again on 11 July. After travelling for 200 metres the front wheels rose, followed by the rear wheel, and the machine climbed to two metres, at which height it continued for a distance of twenty-five to thirty metres. Then Blériot suddenly saw people in front of him, so he wisely switched off the ignition and landed safely, despite damaging the undercarriage, as usual.

'This first decisive success', wrote Ancelle, *L'Aérophile*'s indefatigable and early-rising reporter, 'rewards the ingenious and tenacious efforts of the learned engineer Blériot, whose rare merit thus shines out before the eyes of all.'[3]

It was true that Blériot began now, at last, to make rapid progress. Every few days he flew more and more, so that by 25 July he was able to stay in the air for ten seconds, in a flight of 150 metres at an altitude of four metres. Even better, he was able to begin to change direction in the air, although not yet to make a complete turn.

This progress was achieved, however, by the adoption of a retrograde procedure. From the time of the Wright's first gliding experiments of 1899, the emphasis in most efforts to develop a successful aeroplane had been on achieving control by operating movable surfaces. But now Blériot went part of the way back to Lilienthal's method of shifting his body weight about. He installed a sliding seat, like an oarsman's, and locked the elevons in a fixed position. He had found them difficult to operate satisfactorily, and on some flights did not dare to touch them at all.

It was noted that Blériot seemed quite at home with the sliding seat, and that by this means he was able to exercise more delicate control. This is borne out by the fact that he was able to land on occasion without damage. On 6 August he reached the terrifying height of twelve metres. The bad landing which followed does not seem to have been his fault. One of the blades of the metal propeller worked loose and twisted into a position where it was producing reverse thrust. This 'invalidated the results of the test and paralysed the experimenter's stabilizing manoeuvres.'[4]

Blériot felt that he needed more power. For one thing, his *libellule* invariably turned its nose up as it left the ground, and could not be prevailed upon to regain a horizontal posture while in the air. For another, its flights were always short and it could not cope with any wind at all. He therefore replaced the eight cylinder 24hp Antoinette with Levavasseur's latest creation, a sixteen cylinder motor of 50hp. This was the first sixteen cylinder Antoinette to fly.

Other modifications had been made gradually: the dihedral angle of the forward wings had been reduced, while in the rear it had been eliminated completely, so that the 'tail' was now flat. A four-bladed propeller replaced the original two-bladed one. Blériot had become accustomed progressively to the effects of those changes on the machine's handling, but the new Antoinette was another matter. He left us his account of what happened next:

> Not knowing what to do to get myself off the ground with such a complicated engine, I decided to suppress my stabilizer so that I could

The Blériot VI bis 50hp Antoinette, making one of several short flights at Issy-les Moulineaux in September 1907. Note the wing tip elevons. (MC 1234)

concentrate on controlling the engine. I thought I would be able to ascend or descend by altering the speed of the propeller. The controls were thus fixed in one position and I started the engine. The machine shot forward like an arrow. All went well at first. Very quickly I was twenty-five metres up. I was feeling greatly impressed by this height, extraordinary for that era, when all of a sudden the engine just stopped. The machine went down in a spiral nose dive. I felt helpless and, for the first time in my life, I began to tremble. It was something I will never forget. Fortunately it didn't last for more than two or three seconds.

Seeing myself finished, the idea at once came to me to climb out of my seat and throw my myself backwards towards the tail. This gambit worked more or less: the machine came back into a horizontal position, lost speed and crashed to the ground relatively slowly.[5]

This took place on 17 September 1907 before a distinguished company. Among those present were Ferber, Gabriel and Charles Voisin, Robert Esnault-Pelterie and Henry Farman. As fate would have it Alice Blériot was also standing in the field at Issy-les-Moulineaux:

It was the first time I was able to see one of his trials. Our next child was due in a few days (and was in fact born five days later). They brought my husband back to me in a car. I could see that he was covered in red stains, and I was horrified, thinking it was blood. But it was only a red liquid from the radiator [?] which had spilt over his clothes. His injuries were in fact slight. By moving his weight backwards he had saved his life.[6]

It was also reported that just before the crash Blériot had braced himself by stretching out his legs with his feet firmly on a cross strut. Broken glass from his goggles scratched his face, but that was all.

Esnault-Pelterie measured the distance flown as 184 metres, and Blériot had stayed in the air for seventeen seconds. It was the best flight of the year so far in Europe. This performance would have won a special prize offered by the Aéro Club, if it had been officially observed, but it was not. Nevertheless the Club 'happily resolved this little difficulty' by awarding him a special medal 'by acclamation'.[7] 'It was my first recompense', recalled Blériot, 'and the one which, at the bottom of my heart, I perhaps cherished most of all.'[8]

★★★★★

In 1911 Louis Blériot wrote: 'It is my firm conviction...that the air, once completely conquered, will be an extremely safe element to move about in.'

But in the autumn of 1907 the conquest was far from complete. However, despite the dreary sequence of bad landings, amounting often to crashes, to which Blériot was conspicuously and perhaps particularly prone, it was remarkable that serious injury was so rare. No one was more aware of this than he. Commenting on what he called 'the extraordinary immunity from injury usually suffered by a pilot who is involved in an aeroplane accident', he noted that amazing escapes were being reported every day:

> For myself, when determining by actual tests with experimental machines, what the most practical form of monoplane should be, I had nearly a dozen really bad falls. More than once, I fell from heights which would have made death a certain result had I descended in anything but an aeroplane. But I escaped with only cuts and bruises...This ability to come crashing to the ground without hurting oneself does not lie in any special cleverness on the part of the pilot. It lies in ...the elasticity of the aeroplane.
>
> What happens, when an aeroplane strikes the ground, is this: first some wooden rod or strut breaks, and then another, until perhaps half the machine has been either crushed or beaten in. The breaking of these parts, one after another, absorbs the shock of the impact with the ground. Thus a very bad shock is gradually 'damped', as it were, until it has lost the greater part of its violence by the time it has reached the pilot. Thus the very fragility of the aeroplane has proved its pilot's salvation. It is possible for one to feel this dampening effect in progress...One feels...as though the machine was telescoping upon itself.[9]

Sometime during the summer of 1907, the small band of young men in the workshop in the Boulevard Victor-Hugo took a notable step. They found out what the aeroplane was going to look like. In between tests of their *libellule*, something new was taking shape. And what a shape it was. The monoplane, as we would come to know it, made its first appearance.

The monoplane as we would come to know it made its first appearance. *The Blériot VII at Issy in November 1907. Lateral as well as longitudinal control was by altering the incidence of the large tail-planes.* (MC 1238)

A single pair of wings were set low, at a gentle dihedral angle, on a fully covered fuselage pointed at both ends. There was a four-bladed metal propeller in front, while elevator and rudder were placed together at the tail. Gabriel Voisin recalled: 'I saw him one day at Issy-les-Moulineaux aim towards the heavens, on a very beautiful monoplane with wings set low, and then hit the ground with a frightful shock.'[10]

On 5 October, less than three weeks after the demise of the *libellule*, the magnificent No.VII, sleek, white and streamlined, was tested at Issy. With its 50hp Antoinette it proved to be quite a handful, dashing about the military parade ground at unprecedented speeds of up to 90kph, and the ignition had to be switched off continually to prevent a take-off. For Blériot there was no question of allowing this spirited steed into the air until he had mastered it on the ground. That, paradoxically, was made more difficult by a new arrangement intended to aid control. On this model the tail wheel had been made steerable by linking it directly to the rudder. At first, the more complicated control system this required was badly set up, and in order to steer at all brute force had to be used by the pilot. Sensitive movement was impossible, and Blériot careered about in a series of wild zigzags. These proved too much for the main undercarriage, which gently subsided, causing a bent propeller.[11]

Radical action to solve the chronic problem of collapsing undercarriages was overdue, and it was now taken. Blériot made fundamental changes, and in so doing arrived at the classic system which made such a large contribution to the success of his subsequent monoplanes. The two wheels were set wide apart in a distinctive 'chassis' which protruded prominently from the front of the fuselage on both sides. The wheels were independently sprung by a clever arrangement using elastic rubber rope, but the most subtle feature was that each wheel could swivel about a vertical axis located in front of it. The idea was that when the machine landed at an oblique angle, the castor action would automatically line up the wheels in the direction of travel.

After new tests on the ground, the first flight was made on 16 November 1907, and others followed on 29 November. These were all quite short, sometimes for extraneous reasons – once a contingent of cavalry got in the way. Blériot dared not try to fly over them, and he was unable to turn away. All he could do was cut the ignition and land immediately, putting his faith in the new undercarriage, and hoping he would be able either to turn on the ground or roll to a stop. He had of course no brakes.

By 6 December he felt just as much at ease in the No.VII as he had done in its predecessor, and was ready to better his September flight of 184 metres. That morning he made two flights of 500 metres 'at the highest speed ever attained by an aeroplane' and even achieved a U-turn in the air.[12]

With those performances Blériot leapt to the forefront of European aviation. So thought one particularly astute and well-informed observer, the urbane and ubiquitous P.Y. Alexander who was in some ways an English equivalent of Captain Ferber, like him seeking to know everyone and everything in the world of aviation. The next day Patrick Alexander wrote to Major Baden-Powell, of the Aeronautical Society: 'I got back from Paris last night. I think Blériot with his new machine is now leading the way.'[13]

But it was not to last. The next tests were made on 18 December and on landing at speed after the second flight of the day, the left wheel collapsed, whereupon the left wing scraped heavily along the ground and the Blériot VII turned upside down and was instantly destroyed. That 'the valiant sportsman' emerged with only slight bruising was due in part to a side effect of a recent modification. Originally a low-wing monoplane, the Blériot VII had been altered by raising the wings to a position two-thirds of the way up the fuselage, and bracing them by wires attached to a tubular steel frame erected above the cockpit. Called a *cabane*, this structure acted as a roll-bar when the machine turned over, and probably prevented Blériot from being crushed.[14] Like the undercarriage also pioneered on the No.VII, the *cabane* then became a standard feature of Blériots.

Within a month any predictions of pre-eminence were swept away. It was Henry Farman, not Louis Blériot, who won the greatest honour of the day. Farman's disciplined persistence, supported by the flair of the Voisin brothers, earned its reward when he won the fabulous Deutsch-Archdeacon prize of 50,000 francs for his celebrated completion of the first officially observed circle ever flown, on 13 January 1908. And Blériot was there to see him do it, just as he had seen Santos-Dumont fly in 1906 when he himself could not take off.

★★★★★

A great plain called La Beauce stretches to the west and south of Paris. The wheat grown around Chartres gives way in the east to a crop harvested later in the year, announced to the traveller by a sickly-sweet, bake-house odour borne on the autumn wind. In this season there is no escape from the powerful and intrusive smell of cooking sugar beet in any part of the little town of Toury, to whose refineries the beet is gathered in from a great distance around. Even now, although the harvesting is mechanised, many people are to be

The Blériot VIII bis at Issy-les-Moulineaux on 6 July 1908. (Royal Aeronautical Society)

seen working in the fields. In 1908 there were people everywhere. Their presence would be reassuring to anyone then thinking of flying across a stretch of countryside in an aeroplane.

No one in the world had ever done this, but by the summer of 1908 Louis Blériot judged that the time had come to try. His confidence was based on the experience he had been able, at last, to acquire in the air thanks to a new machine he had moved on to after the demise of the No.VII in December 1907. First shown to the press in February 1908, his No.VIII was a failure in its first form, but after major alterations to the wings it flew well and reliably from June onwards, enabling him to make perhaps as many as forty separate flights, one of them lasting over eight minutes in a stiff breeze.

When the No.VIII crashed he rebuilt it, an accolade not bestowed on any of its predecessors, and a sure sign of its worth in his eyes. Needless to say, he took that opportunity to make changes, such as shortening the fuselage from 10m to 7.50m. Indeed the Blériot VIII was altered repeatedly throughout its life, but the most significant modifications were those intended to improve lateral control. It is uncertain whether the first version had small ailerons at the wing tips or whether it was meant to rely on the dihedral alone for lateral stability. However, the version which first flew had large flap-type ailerons, while in the final form swivelling wing-tip ailerons were used. With these, Blériot's flying took on a completely new quality. Observers marvelled at his mastery, at the speed and assurance of his turns, and at his indifference to quite strong winds.

Blériot was determined to show that an aeroplane could be a means of transport, not just a fanciful piece of experimental apparatus. Until then all flying had taken place within the confines of small, improvised flying grounds, where a forced landing could be made on any spot at any moment. To venture beyond, over the open countryside, would be by itself a great matter, but what Blériot proposed was much more. He was to go from one town to another and back again, by a route which he would announce in advance. By

The Blériot VIII ter at Toury in October 1908. (P 42023)

joining prudence to audacity in a way that was to become characteristic, he selected the scene of his planned exploit with care.

In La Beauce, it is the vastness of the sky, not the flatness of the land which stirs the imagination. It is a silent but eloquent appeal to flight. Under that inviting sky Blériot, with a few friends and some of his mechanics, criss-crossed the land in motor cars, to carry out a thorough reconnaissance. The sugar beet country was not at all as free of potentially obstructive trees as were the wheat lands of the west, but there were other advantages, especially in one particular tract.

Toury lies beside the Route Nationale which joins Paris to Orléans (N20). Fourteen kilometres further south down this wide and generally straight road stands the next small town, Artenay. The two towns are also connected by the Paris-Orléans railway line, which runs parallel to and within sight of the road, and here follows a perfectly straight line.

Although his experience of crossing open countryside by balloon was extremely limited, Blériot had done enough to appreciate the risk of becoming disorientated soon after taking off in his aeroplane. But here, with a road and a railway to follow in a landscape devoid of natural features, there was little risk of becoming lost. Also, he could readily be pursued by helpers in cars.

Blériot and his team were made welcome at Toury. The municipality devined, correctly, that a hitherto unimagined opportunity was at hand to make its mark on history. The mayor, Monsieur Lambert, who owned the sugar refinery, gave Blériot the use of a grass field of some fifteen hectares. This was situated near the railway station, and only 200 metres from the chapel dedicated to Saint Blaise, at the place named 'Champ Perdu'. A commodious shed gave shelter to the Blériot VIII.

Operations began on 21 October 1908 with an excellent flight in a strong wind lasting six minutes forty seconds at twenty metres, the greatest height he had yet attained. The following day, in a still stronger wind, a flight was brought to an end after thirty seconds

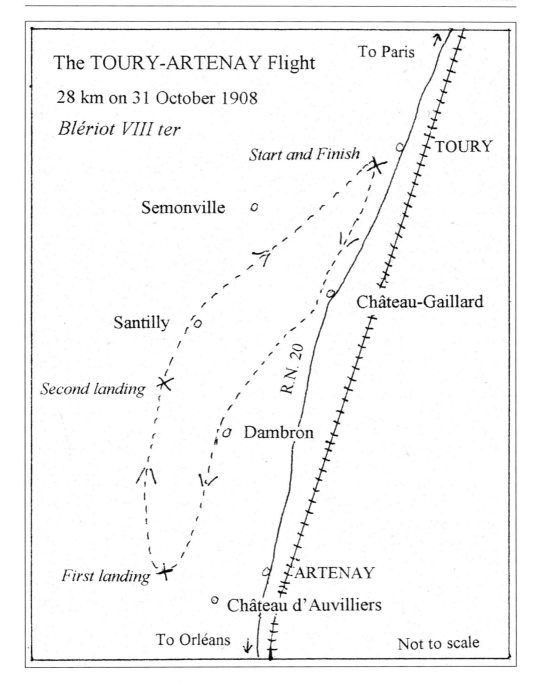

The TOURY-ARTENAY Flight

28 km on 31 October 1908

Blériot VIII ter

To Paris

Start and Finish

TOURY

Semonville

Château-Gaillard

Santilly

R.N. 20

Second landing

Dambron

First landing

ARTENAY

Château d'Auvilliers

To Orléans

Not to scale

Some key members of Blériot's workshop staff in 1908; from left to right: Louis Peyret, Louis Paragot, M. Pelletier, Alfred Bertrand and Julien Mamet. The fuselage is that of the type IX, with its 16-cylinder Antoinette. (MA 29013)

by sudden engine failure. The landing was hard and some damage resulted.[15]

At five past ten in the morning of 30 October an appalling thing happened. The cables to the elevator had been wrongly connected, thus reversing the effect of moving the control lever forward. When, after taxiing for only forty metres, Blériot pushed the lever to lift the tail, the machine reared up and fell over backwards, imprisoning him beneath. He again emerged unhurt, and surprisingly little damage was done to the machine. There had been 'culpable negligence' by one of his assistants, it was claimed, but Blériot himself can hardly have checked the operation of the elevator before starting. It was a mistake that may have cost him dearly, because in the evening came the news that Henry Farman had just flown from Bouy to Reims, a distance of twenty-seven kilometres, on his Voisin-Farman. Once again, Farman had overtaken him, this time by the narrowest of margins, seizing the glory of making the first cross-country flight, which had been within Blériot's reach that day.

In Blériot's place, many would have gone home quietly at that point. But his strength of purpose was never more awesome than when he faced failure. Time and again throughout his life he would bring off his greatest coups when apparently overwhelmed by adversity. The next morning Blériot was back at the Champ Perdu.

Friendly rivals: Henry Farman and Louis Blériot check the wind speed at a suitable altitude. Members of their entourages look on anxiously, waiting to learn if any flying will be possible. (P41198)

He was going to Artenay. He had sent men there to put up small balloons on tethered lines on the far side of the town, so that he would know where to turn round. Because he was going to return to Toury. His would be the first round trip between towns by aeroplane. In the event it was to be both less and more than that.

Just before noon on 31 October he made a short and impeccable practice flight of four or five minutes, circling near the village of Semonville, and then returning to the Champ Perdu. It was reported that he then 'added' a radiator to his Antoinette engine.

At 2.50 p.m. Blériot took off again and headed straight for Artenay. Flying on the western side of the road at a speed described as 'very rapid', and at a height of about twelve metres, he soon outdistanced his helpers following by car. Drifting slightly westwards, he passed over the villages of Château-Gaillard and Dambron. Surprised by the noise of his engine, men and women gathering beet with their horse-drawn carts stopped to look up in amazement and curiosity. Eleven minutes after take-off he was already to the south of Artenay, where he intended to turn round, when ignition failure forced him to land. This he did safely, at a spot some 800 metres from the Château d'Auvilliers. Blériot's average speed up to that point was put at 85kph., 'showing yet again that he possessed the fastest aerial automobile apparatus in the world.' This might have seemed a good moment to retire gracefully from the scene with honour intact, but if any such thought crossed his mind Blériot banished it. He at once set about making the necessary repairs, soon assisted by the mechanics who quickly found him. One and a half hours later he took off again, resuming the announced itinerary. Making for Toury on a course a little more to the west, ignition trouble struck again when he had covered half the remaining distance. He came down at the Villiers farm near Santilly, but this time was able to restart after only a few minutes. At five o'clock in the afternoon Louis Blériot landed back at the Champ Perdu with the greatest of ease, bringing a triumphant afternoon to a close.[16]

For a triumph 'Toury-Artenay' at once became.* Far from being eclipsed by Farman's great achievement of the preceding day, Blériot's round trip of 28km across country was portrayed enthusiastically as a 'first' in its own right. The fact that his two stops en route had been involuntary was conveniently overlooked. A virtue was adroitly made of necessity, by emphasising the value of 'being able' to land and take off again during a journey.

The exploits of Farman and Blériot, occurring on successive days in French aeroplanes in France, served to reinforce one another, and both contributed mightily to the renown of French aviation. Moreover, the name of Blériot now began to register for the first time in the consciousness of the general public in France.

In his *The Conquest of the Air* published the following year, Alphonse Berget had this to say about Toury-Artenay:

> Louis Blériot thus demonstrated that the French aeroplanes mounted on wheels are complete apparatuses, truly self-starting, practical, and capable of resuming their flight when it is interrupted; he showed the services that aero-locomotion would render us, [and] illustrated that aviation from that time henceforth could enter into everyday practice.'[17]

Toury has not forgotten the excitement of that day. From the principal street a narrow lane runs off obliquely to a small and quiet square. It is thus that the rue Blériot leads to the Place Blériot, in which stands a substantial granite monument, perfectly maintained and surrounded by flowers. The gilded inscription reads in translation: 'To the aviator L. Blériot the town of Toury, Eure et Loir - to commemorate the first journey by air from Toury to Artenay and back, 31 October 1908'.

6 Ask Anzani

Four days after Toury-Artenay, the No.VIII was totally destroyed when it overturned at speed on the ground. Blériot had slight bruising. Initial tests of another, rather similar monoplane which had been built at the same time, the No.IX, were never completed. Also in 1908 a large four-seater biplane on Wright lines, an aberration in the Blériot series in which it was No.X, was exhibited at the Salon but apparently never tested.

The brusque abandonment of those costly constructions is hard to understand. Perhaps Blériot simply decided, correctly as it turned out, to concentrate on the still newer fruits of the intense activity taking place in his workshop throughout the winter of 1908-1909. Another possible explanation may relate to the fact that both of the discarded aircraft had Antoinette engines. Here, there was a serious problem. Levavasseur had progressed to a point where he felt entitled to pursue again his original ambition to build an aeroplane, and this time there was no stopping him. In vain did Blériot protest to the other board members that he refused to compete with himself by remaining a director and shareholder of the S. A. Antoinette if it was going to make aeroplanes.[1] It was the parting of the ways. Blériot would never use an Antoinette engine again. Thus began a period of some difficulty.

By the middle of February 1909 Blériot began to sense that a new and very small aeroplane, the No XI, was not only his best so far, but that its performance was going to be extraordinary. However, he was never able to keep it in the air long enough to find out. After ninety seconds at most the engine, which he had borrowed from Robert Esnault-Pelterie, would begin to lose power from overheating, if it did not actually seize up, and he would have to come down. Even the very cold weather that month made no difference, or so it seemed to the increasingly frustrated pilot and his mechanics.

Ferdinand Collin has left an account of how he, exhausted one day after running repeatedly across the frozen snow to reach Blériot wherever he had been forced to land, announced in exasperation that he had had enough. He refused to start the REP engine again. After a moment of anger Blériot and Collin calmed down sufficiently to discuss what was to be done. What was needed, declared Collin, was an engine that could be counted on to continue running for an hour, and he had seen one that did. Sometimes he went to watch the cycle racing at the track called Buffalo at the Porte Maillot. In some of the races the cyclists were paced by their trainers mounted on motorcycles. These they rode in a strange, upright posture, perched over the rear wheel, to screen their charges from the air-stream. In the longer races, for *stayers*, retirements frequently occurred not because the cyclist was exhausted but because the motorcycle engine did not last the distance. One trainer, Collin had noticed, seemed unaffected by mechanical problems and usually completed the course. His name was Alexandre Anzani, and the engines he used he made himself.

Those engines, Collin told Blériot, were roughly finished and they clanked and rattled in a strange, irregular way, spurting oil from every crevice. But none of that mattered, he argued, because Anzani's engines had one supreme virtue – they could last for an hour. Therefore, he said, Blériot should go at once and ask Anzani for an engine. Blériot would certainly have heard mention of Anzani in aeronautical circles, but not in terms likely to encourage him to make his acquaintance. However, an impasse had been reached, and he accepted his mechanic's advice.[2]

Alexandre Anzani had burst into the world of aviation two years earlier with a suitably loud noise, and in a cloud of dust as he wrestled at the handlebars of one of the most infernal machines ever devised. On 11 September 1906, in the afternoon, on a tree-lined straight road through the Parc d'Achères, Anzani had tested the *aéro-motocyclette*. The originality of this device was that it was driven by a huge propeller set in front of a racing-motorcycle frame, extensively modified to accommodate the transmission and supporting structure required. Witnessed by well-known journalists, he was timed over a measured kilometre at an average speed of 79.205kph.[3] Such mastery of the machine called for colossal strength, agility and pure motorcycling skill. It is unlikely that anyone other than Anzani would have attempted to ride it. Born at Goria near Milan twenty-eight years before, he had become the champion gymnast of Europe at the age of seventeen, and a successful bicycle racer after emigrating to France. Now he was at the height of his third career, as a racing motorcyclist. That summer of 1906 he had been proclaimed 'Champion of the World', after winning a race at Ostend at 110kph.

The *aéro-motocyclette* had been built for Ernest Archdeacon, who wished to test and, for some now obscure reason to publicize, aerial propellers. The constructors were the Buchet firm, by whom Anzani had until recently been employed as an engine tuner and, of course, as a test and race rider. Apparently he went back to help his old firm with their special project, because by this time he had started a small business of his own, financed by his race winnings. At first he repaired touring motorcycles and tuned racing models, but was successful so quickly that within months he was able to treble his work-force and start producing motorcycles of his own design under his own name.[4]

His racing machines were effective from the outset, especially in track racing. Some seventy years afterwards one spectator remembered:

> The *vélodrome* at Buffalo sometimes organized motorcycle races on its oval track of 338 metres. The racers could reach 100kph. The machines were monsters weighing hundreds of kilograms. But one evening (the races always took place then) Anzani turned up with one that was almost a moped – with an engine of three cylinders. It was a tiny bike. What was most wonderful was that it won the race! That was the engine he developed later on, and introduced to aviation.[5]

Anzani's first engines, like Buchet's, were V twins. Some were cooled by air, others by water. As well as small ones, of up to 3.5hp, there were giants of 2,000cc in 1905 – a size previously unknown (this was the era of 10 to 15 litre racing cars). There is an anecdote that one day in his workshop at Asnières in the western suburbs of Paris he was visited by a well-known trainer of cyclists called Hoffman who was in search of a more powerful 'pacing' motorcycle. Eyeing a mighty V twin on the bench, he is reputed to have proposed

Alexandre Anzani in the saddle of Ernest Archdeacon's aéro-motocyclette *on 11 September 1906 when this unique machine achieved 79.205kph over a measured kilometre. (Author's Collection)*

the addition of an extra cylinder. Anzani was reluctant to attempt such a thing, and if he had been formally trained as an engineer he would surely have refused outright. But he had the open-mindedness of the self-taught, as well as self-confidence. And so the fan-shaped three cylinder engine was launched.[6] It was to make Anzani's fortune, but not yet.

In secrecy so absolute that even some of his few employees did not know of it, Anzani designed a hydroplane. It was perhaps the first in its field, and is considered by some to have been the prototype of this kind of craft. The hydroplane was tested in the sea off Monaco on 18 August 1907.[7]

Sometime in 1907 Anzani was approached to provide an engine for a biplane being constructed by Lucien Chauvière for Alfred de Pischoff. He supplied a 25hp three cylinder power unit which drove a tractor propeller through a shaft about one metre long. Apart from the engine, the most interesting feature of the de Pischoff was the propeller. It was carved from laminated walnut, superbly balanced and finished. Nothing like it had been seen before, either in conception or craftsmanship. This was the precursor of the celebrated *Intégrale* propeller which would bring fame to Chauvière when fitted to an Anzani engine, but not on the de Pischoff. When tested at Issy on 5 and 6 December 1907 the biplane, although of promising aspect, could achieve no better than a hop of seven metres.

In the aeronautical section of the Paris motor show in December 1908 there was a monoplane called the Raoul Vendôme No.2, which had an Anzani engine of 50hp. This made brief flights at Bagatelle on 16 January 1909. By December 1908 Anzani was advertising 'light motors for aviation' with three or six cylinders.[8] It seems unlikely that one of the latter had actually been built by that date.

Such were the aeronautical credentials of Alexandre Anzani when Louis Blériot set out in February 1909, driven in the yellow Panhard by his chauffeur Henri, to Asnières. For

Anzani it was unprecedented to have a caller of such magnificence. Here indeed was a *bella figura*, moreover one brimming with lively intelligence and great charm. Anzani would succumb as Voisin had done in his time.

Anzani was to be found in a small and unprepossessing shed, poorly equipped. There were very few workmen, but Blériot's rapid and expert assessment was that these were skilled Parisian craftsmen of the first rank. As for Anzani, there was little on first acquaintance to inspire confidence. According to Collin he was highly excitable, carried away alternately by rage and enthusiasm, and he seemed both unscientific and unbusinesslike. His language and manners, at that period, were of the roughest, but were best not taken too seriously. He meant no harm. This was a man intoxicated by mechanical invention.

Blériot was sufficiently impressed to place an order on the spot, and Anzani was carried away to such an extent as to accept that payment should be deferred until the engine had proved itself satisfactory, an unwise concession which he was to regret. The model ordered was to be of 25hp, and Anzani was to adapt it for installation in the Blériot XI.

A way had to be found of mounting the engine on the front supports of the fuselage. This was done by fixing a steel cradle frame, much drilled to reduce weight, to the fuselage. The engine was then bolted rigidly to the frame at four points. The propeller was to be placed directly on the end of the drive shaft, as close as possible to the crankcase. This appeared simple enough until bench running revealed overheating of the main bearings, soon traced to unaccustomed loads imposed by the propeller. This problem had not arisen with the de Pischoff because its long drive shaft ran through an additional bearing, supported separately. On the Blériot, various types of main bearing were tried before a solution was found.

The cubic capacity of the engine, which survives, is 3,377cc. The cylinder bore is 105mm and the stroke 130mm. Each cylinder is cast integrally with its head in cast iron, and there are eight cooling fins per cylinder. The three cylinders are all set in the same plane, and the dividing angle between them is 60 degrees. The pistons too are of cast iron, and they have two rings above the gudgeon pin. The connecting rods of the two outer cylinders are forked at the bottom and linked to the plain rod of the centre cylinder. All three connecting rods operate on a single crank pin. The crankshaft has disks, constituting a balanced flywheel which accounts for just over one third of the engine's total weight of 65kg. There is a split crankcase in aluminium, the two halves being joined by eight long bolts.

The two valves per cylinder are in a pocket at the back of the combustion chamber, one above the other, with the atmospherically operated inlet valve on top. The exhaust valves are opened by pushrods actuated by separate camshafts driven by the crankshaft through a train of gears. The firing order is 1, 3, 2, taking No.2 cylinder as the centre one.

There is a single carburettor of the float-feed type, without any throttle control. Ignition is by a six volt battery and one trembler coil for each cylinder, an installation provided by the Dary firm using the Ben Tayoux system. Lubrication is by a manually operated oil pump.

Overheating was a problem which Anzani tackled in robust style. His solution, while unusual, was probably not original and it was to give his engine its most notorious vice. In order to augment the work of the exhaust valves in removing hot gases, he drilled a row of holes 5 to 7mm in diameter through the cylinder walls where they would be uncovered as the piston reached the bottom of its stroke. This drastic measure seems to have been effective, but the new exhaust ports had the inconvenience that they permitted the escape into the air stream of vast quantities of castor oil from the crankcase at another moment in the cycle. After a few minutes of this the pilot's face was covered, and he could see only with difficulty, and not at all if he forgot to carry a rag to repeatedly wipe his goggles. A further but less predictable consequence was that engines 'improved' in this way would occasionally shed a cylinder, which broke off where it was weakened by the ring of perforations.

*****

While waiting for Anzani to complete the engine he had ordered, Blériot continued his trials of the number XI. Finding himself constrained by lack of space at Issy, he transferred his operations to a field used by Robert Esnault-Pelterie at Buc near Versailles. There, he succeeded immediately in making turns, and made his most impressive flight with the REP engine on 15 March, when he flew 2,500 metres in two minutes, in a strong wind.

Bounding one side of the field at Buc was a pond large enough to have a name – L'étang du Trou-Salé – which exercised a fatal fascination for aeroplanes under tentative and at best approximate control. Esnault-Pelterie had become acquainted with its happily moderate depths sufficiently often to find it worthwhile to keep a rowing boat handy. Inevitably, Louis Blériot in his turn finished up in the pond one day. According to *l'Aérophile*, while taxiing after landing on 5 April he was unable to stop and continued into its marshy edge, but little damage can have been done as he was flying the No.XI again next day. A more serious incident was not reported, but Esnault-Pelterie's watchman remembered it:

> One evening when I was alone at the aerodrome, it was after five o'clock when I saw M. Blériot coming with his machine behind his car, and his mechanic Mamet and an assistant.
>
> M. Blériot told me he had come to carry out a test at that time of day so that he could do it in peace…They attached the wings to the aeroplane and M. Blériot flew right round the aerodrome. He was above the pond when suddenly the engine spluttered and stopped, and the aeroplane No.XI came down in the middle of the Trou-Salé pond where the water is one and a half metres deep. The machine was under water and M. Blériot was standing on the fuselage, his feet in the water. I took the rowing boat with Mamet to go and get M. Blériot, who said to me 'the engine is worthless, I want to get my aeroplane out of the pond tonight. If you help me you will not be forgotten.'[9]

It was one o'clock in the morning when they finally succeeded in dragging the monoplane out, after getting ropes around it and towing it to the edge with the boat. Despite these exertions Blériot returned at 8.00 a.m. to take it away for repair.

The final and most intense phase of Blériot's personal 'conquest of the air' now began. For the first time he had two usable machines at his disposal. To his No.XI, with its Anzani engine fitted from 27 May, was added a large high-wing monoplane with an ENV engine, the No.XII, which was first brought out in public on 21 May. Ominously, however, that same day Léon Levavasseur proved that he had already become a formidable competitor:

an Antoinette monoplane flew for 13 minutes 23 seconds at an average speed of 72kph at Mourmelon-le-Grand. Blériot, at this point, had not bettered his eleven minute flight from Toury to Artenay the previous autumn. Worse was to come – ten days later he attempted to repeat that flight, but failed.

After that setback Blériot must have been cheered by finding within forty-eight hours that he was able to fly with a passenger in his No.XII. Again, he had bounced back. In later years his wife recalled that in those days he had made up his mind not to expect anything from life, and to take nothing for granted. He thus avoided disappointment, and consoled himself with philosophical reflections. When success did come it was an agreeable surprise to him.[10]

It was during the last week of June and the first week of July 1909 that Blériot once more emerged at the forefront of aviation, dramatically increasing the duration of his flights. Thus on 26 June he flew for 36 min 55 sec in the No.XI at Issy, on 3 July for 47 min 17 sec in the No.XII at Douai, and on 4 July for 50 min 8 sec at Juvisy. *L'Aérophile* declared:

> Within a few days Louis Blériot, for so long unlucky despite his rare ability, has found his genuine level. The monoplanes to whose development he has devoted so much long, ingenious and tenacious effort are now just right…but it is also important to note the progress which the pilot has made. Blériot is now in complete control, particularly of his landings which are always very gentle.[11]

The article goes on to marvel at his ability to fly with apparent indifference two aeroplanes with different systems of lateral control, and to do so from three different aerodromes. (Lateral control was by wing-warping on the type XI, and by strangely positioned ailerons on the type XII – they were on the lower fuselage longerons.)

Recognition was not confined to the aeronautical press. On 16 June an extraordinary tribute came out of the blue, from the most improbable source. On the agenda for their meeting that day, the venerable members of the Institut de France found that one important item for decision was the award of the Prix Osiris. The philanthropist whose name the prize bore had bequeathed one million francs to the Institute, to fund a prize of 100,000 francs to be given every three years to 'the Frenchman who has done most for the progress of science or who has produced the most useful work.' On previous occasions the prize had been awarded to the director of the Institut Pasteur, and to an historian who was a member of the Académie Française.

This time, there was an amazing proposal: to *consecrate* the progress made by aviation in 1908, and particularly the two performances which launched the era of 'practical utilisation', Chalons-Reims and Toury-Artenay. The proposal was presented by a member of the Académie des Sciences, Emile Picard, in a report of notable clarity. He saw Voisin and Blériot as the leading promoters in France of the biplane and the monoplane respectively. Picard noted that the Voisin aeroplane was easier to fly than the Wright, because it did not require the pilot's unremitting attention at all times, as the Wright did. This made the Voisin particularly well-suited for the training of pilots. In comparing it with the Blériot XII, he discerned the different approaches to stability and control of the two French constructors. In the case of the Voisin, 'stability is assured more or less

Louis Blériot and Alexandre Anzani, shown here with the type XI at Etampes before starting for Orléans, 13 July 1909 (P 47110)

automatically by the side-curtains in cellular structures', and control was of two kinds only: left or right and up or down. A third variable was provided on the Blériot, by wing-warping which put lateral control 'at the disposal of the driver.' (Either a reference to the type XI, or an erroneous reference to the type XII.)

The Blériot, he went on, was lighter and offered less air resistance and, in the hands of an 'attentive' pilot it could perform better. 'It is no longer the movement of an arrow: it is the more supple movement of a bird, but for the moment it is more dangerous, above all when turning, and calls for *un grand sang-froid* from the driver.'

In his peroration, Picard declined to speculate on what the future might hold for monoplanes or biplanes 'or even for triplanes'. Neither would he predict how long it would be before aeroplanes replaced railways, 'or whether this substitution would be to the greater benefit of war or peace.' Those were questions for visionaries and politicians. What he was certain of was that the true foundations of aerial navigation had been laid, and that henceforth aviation should be accorded the respect due to a science. Had not its aerodromes become genuine 'physics laboratories', and were not many of its practitioners 'learned mechanics?'[12]

Such statements were sensational, made as they were by an eminent representative of that same Académie des Sciences which all those years ago had so incensed Nadar with its theories about hot air in the bodies of birds. Happily, Nadar lived long enough to learn that they had recanted.

Finally, Picard said 'However timid the current experiments may seem one day, the history of aviation will always have a page for the flights across country that were made for the first time in 1908.'[13] He urged that the Prix Osiris be awarded jointly to Gabriel Voisin

and Louis Blériot, and so it was decided, unanimously. Word of the decision was immediately telephoned to No.4 rue de la Ferme, and Alice Blériot remembered very clearly fifty years later how Voisin had come to tell Blériot. She and her husband were at St Cloud preparing for a balloon flight. It was about seven o'clock in the evening and they were about to go up when suddenly Voisin appeared, running towards them and shouting 'The Osiris Prize is for us, for both of us!' The two men embraced 'in joy and emotion'. Excited as he was, Blériot was not to be deprived of his ballooning, and soon he and Alice set off, to descend at five o'clock the next morning at Villemontais in the Loire.[14]

Two months later a note from the secretary of the Institut invited Blériot to call to collect his half share of the prize. Was the money only then available, or was the secretary reminding him that he still had not collected what had been kept aside for him for some time? Those who believe his finances were then in crisis will dismiss the latter suggestion as unbelievable, but what cannot be disputed is that Louis Blériot had indeed been otherwise engaged between 16 June and 13 August 1909.

7 The rival beyond Sangatte

When walking in the woods Hubert Latham liked to tilt his head back so that his nostrils were horizontal. By adopting the posture of a wild animal he hoped to acquire the acute instincts and rapid reflexes he so much admired in nature. He had spent years in Africa hunting big game, observing the animal kingdom at close quarters, and drawing inspiration from it. Hereditary characteristics, or rather his perception of them, were also a powerful influence, for these he strove to bring out and combine in himself. Thus he cultivated the enterprising spirit of his English grandfather, a successful investor in indigo and other commodities, who had finally settled in France and established his base as a merchant adventurer at Le Havre. From his father he acquired the wanderlust that had led him to know and respect wild animals, while from his French mother he inherited an ability to maintain an outward calm in the most demanding circumstances, which although more apparent than real, was carried to those extreme lengths which the French like to attribute to the English.

Latham was a lightly built and languid youth, whose somewhat stooping figure belied great muscular strength and endurance. Wan and sallow of countenance, regular of feature, and with a penetrating gaze, he was highly intelligent, well-educated, and rich. He was in his time 'a man of the world' as he cheekily but daringly informed the French President when asked his occupation. Daring was Latham's outstanding quality, and he was competitive by nature.

Immediately after winning his last motor-boat race at Monaco, Latham departed for Upper Egypt. When taking leave of his cousin Robert Gastambide he made him promise to let him know as soon as Levavasseur's proposed aeroplane was ready, saying that he wanted 'to be the first to fly the Antoinette'.[1] Fortunately for Latham, that promise was not kept. No doubt Gastambide was unable to communicate with him in Africa. When eventually he did get in touch, on Latham's return to France at Christmas 1908, Levavasseur's new aeroplane was not only complete, it was actually his fourth and had been flown successfully several times since October by one of the four Welferinger brothers who had been founder members of the Antoinette workshop set up at Puteaux in 1902.

The advantage of this for Latham was incalculable. He could learn to be a pilot on an aeroplane known to be capable of flight. Not for him the struggles of Blériot, or of Santos-Dumont or of Gabriel Voisin. He was to be of the second generation of aviators, not a 'pioneer' in the strictest sense. And, in the person of a Welferinger, he had an instructor.

Latham needed all the help he could get, for his debut was far from easy. His apprenticeship began at the end of February 1909 on the flying ground at the military camp at Chalons in La Beauce. He was not nervous or lacking in confidence, but paradoxically it was his great physical strength that told against him. He seemed quite unable, just as Louis Blériot had been unable two years before, to operate the controls gently, with the sensitivity required. Day after day, without ever managing to get off the ground, he broke every part of the Antoinette IV that could be broken, the wheels, the skids, the undercarriage, then one day a wing, another day the fuselage. Competitor that he was, his frustration turned to mortification at the sight of another young man, René Demanest, much less of a sportsman than he, who on a second and similar Antoinette was making regular flights with apparent ease.

Imperturbable in public, quietly smoking a cigarette and smiling ironically, Latham was breaking down in private. By turns angry and tearful, he declared to Levavasseur and Gastambide that he would never amount to anything, and he was particularly upset about all the damage he was doing to the aeroplane. His embarrassment about that would have been greater if he had not been sharing in the repair costs, at least indirectly. Before attempting to fly the Antoinette he had persuaded his mother to invest in the company and he himself had taken a seat on the board – the one vacated by Blériot.

Happily, after a month of too strenuous effort, Latham finally succeeded in taking off and made a fine flight of 10 minutes at 20 metres altitude.[2] From then on his progress was astonishing, and it was not long before the press began to pay close attention to what was happening at Chalons. A star was about to be discovered – Latham had all the qualities the newspapers could desire. Only a record-breaking performance was lacking, and for that they did not have long to wait – and what a record it was when it came. On 5 June 1909 Hubert Latham flew for longer than anyone other than Wilbur and Orville Wright had ever done. In an uninterrupted flight of 1 hour, 7 minutes and 37 seconds he took the French record for duration in mechanical flight, and the world record for monoplanes. At a single, elegant stroke, or so it seemed, Latham stepped into a limelight which he would never leave, either in triumph or disaster, throughout the momentous summer of 1909.

Immediately, he moved to capitalise on the sensational publicity he had earned for himself and the Société Anonyme Antoinette. The next day he flew five miles across country, returning safely to his starting point, at an average speed of between 70 and 80kph. The following day he took up four passengers in succession, one of them a special correspondent of the *Daily Mail* who described his 'sensations' as follows:

> I sat directly in front of Mr Latham, with my face towards the rear, and could thus observe everything he did. Before shouting, 'Let go,' he handed me a stop-watch and lit a cigarette.
>
> After running along the ground for fifty yards, we rose in the air and headed straight for the lower end of the Chalons Camp, skirting a small wood in the centre at a height of about twenty-five feet. At that moment a strong gust of wind caught the monoplane, and the left wheel struck the ground. As we went on the machine showed a persistent tendency to work upwards, and Mr Latham finding the balance faulty, endeavoured by working the levers and shifting his seat to find out the cause.
>
> …After a magnificent sweep he steered towards a hill at the upper end of a field. Suddenly I saw a wheel running along the ground after us. Our

The rival beyond Sangatte: *Hubert Latham. (MA 5429)*

56   *M. Hubert Latham dans son Monoplan " Antoinette ". — LL*

Hubert Latham at the controls of an Antoinette in 1909 (Harman Collection)

bump during the first round had split a wire pin, and the wheel – one of the two on which the monoplane obtains its initial momentum – had gradually worked off the axle. I called Mr Latham's attention to the wheel, and he promptly cut off the ignition. We came down swiftly, but alighted without damage...My stop-watch showed that the flight had lasted 11 minutes 50 seconds, during which we had touched ground twice...[3]

Thus it was that newspaper readers in England first became aware of the existence of the astonishing Frenchman called Latham, who exemplified those very qualities the English then liked to feel were so exclusively their own. As they finished reading the article they were given, almost as an afterthought and in the lowest key possible, the intimation that 'Mr Latham is one of the entrants for the *Daily Mail* £1,000 prize for the first flight in a heavier-than-air machine across the Channel.'

That newspaper and its prize have important parts to play in this story, and so merit a digression.

★★★★★

To sell 'A penny newspaper for a half-penny' was one of the aims of Alfred Harmsworth when he launched the *Daily Mail* in May 1896 after assiduous preparations. These included leaking to his rivals in Fleet Street dummy issues containing grotesque features designed to show that the new paper posed no competitive threat to them. Great therefore was their surprise when it immediately became a huge success. Harmsworth has been credited with introducing modern journalism to Britain via the *Daily Mail*. Several amazing scoops during the Boer War consolidated its position. Harmsworth became a power in the land, disconcerting politicians by the unpredictability of his criticism. One statesman of the time described him as a 'flea', always hopping about so that you never knew where he would strike next. When repeating his strictures inside the House of Commons this was transmuted into the less offensive grasshopper, but both are aerial insects.

Harmsworth had a good understanding of motorcycles and cars. He liked to drive at high speeds, a favourite road being the Hog's Back in Surrey where he terrified many of his friends. Alert to all new developments, he was able to see the significance of aviation at a time when it was a subject of general disbelief. He was present in Paris when Santos-Dumont made his first brief hop-flight in 1906, and it was enough to trigger a memorandum to his staff criticising them for not taking the new science seriously. Did they not understand, he demanded indignantly, that the news meant that Britain was 'no longer an island'? Forthwith, an aviation correspondent – Harry Harper – was appointed on the *Daily Mail*.[4]

But Harmsworth, now Lord Northcliffe, continued to be personally involved, and showed himself capable of pungent comment, as for example when writing about the Wrights in 1907 'The air of secretiveness with which the inventors have elected to invest their machine may be justified, but must be responsible for a suspension of judgement on the subject of its merits.'[5]

Always on the look out for ways of obtaining renown and increasing its circulation, the *Daily Mail* announced on 5 October 1908 a prize of £500 for the first aeroplane flight between England and France. A note of implied jealousy was struck in the comment of a certain newspaper in Paris. The *Daily Mail's* offer, noted *Le Matin* sourly, was a clever way of getting publicity cheaply, since there would be no question of having to pay up for years and years.

Months went by with only one, highly premature and abortive, entry for the prize and it looked as if *Le Matin* might be right. At the end of 1908 the prize under its original conditions lapsed, but Harmsworth, ever hopeful, then decided to extend its availability for a further twelve months and to double the amount to £1,000. Late in the spring of 1909 signs began to appear of a possible response among aviation circles, leading for example to an announcement on 2 June that a Mr W. Arthur Seymour, who was said to have a Voisin aeroplane at Boulogne, had the previous evening telegraphed an entry for the prize to the Editor of the *Daily Mail*.

This prompted some thought to be given to the practical aspects of a possible attempt, and discussions were held with the Aero Club in London. On 17 June the paper published revised rules for the prize, which it had adopted after consulting both the Club and the International Aeronautical Federation:

> The proprietors of *The Daily Mail* hereby undertake to pay the sum of £1,000 (one thousand pounds) to the first person who shall satisfy them that he has succeeded in flying across the Channel from a point on English soil to a point on French soil or vice versa.

1. The whole flight to be made between the hours of sunrise and sunset.

2. No part of the machine shall touch the sea during the flight.

3. The flight shall be accomplished by means of a machine which is not in any manner supported by a gas lighter than air.

4. Entries for the competition can be made at any date during 1909 by giving not less than forty-eight hours' notice to the Editor of *The Daily Mail* either at Carmelite House, London E.C. or at the office of the *Continental Daily Mail*, Paris.

5. In every case notification of the first attempt to be made under these conditions shall reach the Editor of the *Daily Mail* not less than forty-eight hours prior to such attempt, and in the case of all subsequent attempts not less than twenty-four hours' notification shall be given.

6. The entrant must furnish satisfactory evidence of previous flights before making any attempt under these conditions.

7. The entrant must supply satisfactory signed evidence of the exact points of departure and arrival.

8. In accordance with the rules of the International Aeronautical Federation the entrant must be a member of, or obtain a permit from, the recognised body of the federation.

9. Should any questions arise at any time after the date of entry as to whether a competitor has properly fulfilled the above conditions, or should any other question arise in relation to them, the decision of the committee of the Aero Club in conjunction with the Editor of the *Daily Mail* shall be final.

10. Each competitor agrees to waive all claim for injury either to himself or to his apparatus, and agrees to assume all liabilities for damage to third parties or their property, and to indemnify the proprietors of the *Daily Mail* and the Aero Club against any such claims.

★★★★★

Not much more of substance was heard from Arthur Seymour whose entry had precipitated a flurry of rule-making, with the results shown above. He knew how to get his name in the paper, however, claiming: 'My ambition is for an Englishman to win the prize rather than a Frenchman'. He considerately named his unquestionably French Voisin, still in sections at Boulogne harbour, the *Britannia*; announced that he would wear 'a cork suit in case of an involuntary descent'; and in the same line of thought got a friend to arrange for a string of seventeen motor boats to be dotted across the Channel. But nothing came of all this.

Hubert Latham was evidently a much better prospect, and it was on him that the *Daily Mail* continued to lavish attention from the day he gave the 'baptism of the air' to its correspondent. Three weeks after that something happened which delighted the *Mail*, to which it was a dream come true. For the first time it looked, or at least it became possible to claim, that there was going to be a race for the prize. All of a sudden there were three entrants, and each one had some credentials to be taken seriously.

Latham was joined in the lists by Henry Farman and comte Charles de Lambert. Farman, the *Mail* informed its readers, was 'a Frenchman of English extraction', celebrated for his momentous *kilomètre bouclé* at Issy-les-Moulineaux in January 1908. There was poetic justice in the fact that the third entrant was the first pupil of Wilbur Wright who had flown a great many circles long before Farman: comte de Lambert was described by the *Mail* as 'a French gentleman'. (There is a story that Lord Northcliffe offered the Wrights £3,000 to enter, but that they refused, saying it was their principle to give demonstrations only, and not to take part in contests.[6])

Both of the new entrants were more experienced pilots than Latham, and each commanded substantial aeronautical resources, in terms of machines, competent mechanics and funds to set up temporary flying headquarters at places of their choice on either the French or the English coast. But Latham acted immediately to retain the initiative he had gained by being the first credible entrant. He took a ferry boat from Calais to Dover on 28 June, and on arrival calmly announced that he would attempt the flight within a fortnight.

He spent the morning choosing a landing place, exploring the Kent coast by car with a *Mail* reporter. (This was somewhat premature, as no base on the French coast had yet been set up by the Antoinette team: when asked about this he replied airily that he would 'choose some cliff top for the point of departure.' His aeroplane at that time had not yet left Paris.) The result of his morning in Kent was that he decided to land on the top of Shakespeare Cliff if his machine were flying 'strongly', while if his 'motor worked weakly' and he flew low he must land on the beach. In the latter case he would steer for the Admiralty Pier, then swing to the left and make for the beach below the cliff. 'No better spot could be found', he declared.

In answer to what were becoming routine questions, he said he would be wearing an inflated suit, and that French torpedo boats would be in the channel to guide his course and rescue him in case of need. The attendance of British destroyers was being sought.[7]

Latham returned to Calais that evening and went straight on to Paris for discussions with Levavasseur, reputedly about the engine. Perhaps they also considered the logistics of the attempt, but the first signs were appearing of a curiously haphazard way of making basic arrangements. The aeroplane had still not left Paris, despite earlier reports to the contrary, and no place on the coast had yet been chosen where it could be put together, sheltered from the elements and test flown.

On 30 June the *Mail* was driven to make an announcement of extraordinary obscurity: 'The exact point on the French coast near Calais from which Mr Latham will start his cross-channel flight is, for several reasons, to remain unknown until within a few days of the actual attempt.' At last, on 1 July, Levavasseur and Latham came to Calais together and began to get down to business. The *Mail* was mightily impressed by the engineer, who looked 'the very incarnation of imaginative and inventive genius, such a man as we imagine Leonardo or Alberti to have been.' Levavasseur 'had designed every part of the monoplane with which Mr Hubert Latham is going to make the great adventure.'

The two men spent an afternoon looking round the area. They settled on the country beyond Sangatte, to the west of Calais, where the ground rises behind the cliffs which go on to reach their summit in Cap Blanc Nez. There, they were attracted by the high ground, thinking it would be a great advantage to be able to begin the flight at a considerable height above the sea. The land behind the cliffs slopes down from a ridge both to the east and the west, favouring take-offs into a wind coming from either of those directions. This tract of land was however bereft of any building capable of sheltering the monoplane and serving as a base for mechanics and stores. So it was that their roving gaze fell on the derelict remains of the factory built thirty years earlier for the construction of the first seriously attempted Channel tunnel. Although this was some 500 metres away, along a very rough stony lane, they decided it would serve their purpose.

There were several delays in getting the Antoinette to Sangatte and, once there, in completing its assembly. These caused some difficulty for *Mail* reporters, who began to file what became a lengthy series of temporizing reports, embroidered with optimistic predictions of Latham's success, and accounts of the great interest aroused on the French side of the Channel by the expected attempt.

On 5 July the *Mail* said that the curiosity of visitors 'is found rather embarrassing, and a fierce black dog has been chained to Mr Latham's aeroplane.' As the aeroplane had not yet been put together, it is unclear how that was done! 'Despite the unfavourable weather, parties…have arrived from points as far distant as Lille, while all Calais seems to be talking of the approaching flight.'

On the same day the *Mail* devoted a few lines to Louis Blériot, who in the previous forty-eight hours had made two fine flights at different places on different aeroplanes. (see Chapter 6). The paper went on to give the first reported comment by Blériot on the Channel contest:

> M. Blériot stated later that if Mr Latham did not forestall him he would attempt to win the *Daily Mail* cross-Channel prize. He considers it would be imprudent to try the journey before he has succeeded in remaining in the air half a dozen times for periods longer than that he accomplished today at Juvisy [50 minutes 8 seconds]…

On 7 July the *Mail* was finally able to announce, with palpable relief, that 'Mr Latham's monoplane, all except the wings which are not yet unpacked,' had been put together in the abandoned machine shop. Furthermore, against one of the outside walls of that derelict building a great tent of red and white striped material had been erected to shelter the Antoinette when fully assembled.

Interest in Latham's approaching attempt was 'increasing hourly': visitors continued to arrive in Calais and its neighbourhood, and as for the townspeople, they were in 'a condition of extreme excitement.' So the *Mail* went on doing all it could to build up feverish suspense. The virtues of the superb looking Antoinette, notably its speed, were daily extolled. But this was insignificant by comparison with the coverage of its pilot: 'I have seen a good deal of Mr Latham during the past few days, and I like all I have seen of him. It is very hard to realize that he is a French citizen. He speaks English perfectly – that is, freely and naturally, without a trace of accent; but there is occasionally a suspicion of

A mechanic, Latham and Levavasseur with the Antoinette IV at Chalons on 5 June 1909. (MA 10847)

Gallic phrasing that gives a piquancy to his conversation…'[8]

The tempo of the Antoinette enterprise immediately quickened; Levavasseur had 'hustled' and a decisive step was taken. At 6 p.m. on 8 July Latham gave the required forty-eight hours notice of his intention to start. The flight was planned for Saturday evening, 10 July, before sunset. There would be a great welcome in England, said the *Mail*:

> Dover is thrilled with excitement at the promised coming of 'the flying man'. Everyone is talking of Mr Latham and his enterprise. Old harbour men discuss 'warping planes' (sic) and the chances of the Antoinette in a Channel breeze. Odds are freely offered on the aeronaut's success.[9]

Meanwhile at Sangatte, Levavasseur, with his 'light brown beard and eyes of a strange brightness… his indefinable look of genius and power', declared that, contrary to what was supposed, great progress had been made in preparing the monoplane. The undercarriage had been modified, chiefly by setting the wheels farther apart, thus allowing the removal of two wooden struts with balls on the ends previously used as stabilisers on or approaching the ground. However, the 'garage' of red and white striped canvas was found to be a failure. Part of it had been blown down in the night. Fortunately the Antoinette was still inside in the machine shop.

On Friday 9 July it was decided to repair the tent, and that afternoon the monoplane was rolled out of the machine shop and placed in it:

The Antoinette Company's mechanics expect to work most of the night, and the wings will be affixed before noon tomorrow. Watching the clever artisans from Paris who, with the help of half a dozen willing volunteers, rolled the exquisitely shaped machine to the garage was a crowd composed of tourists in motoring clothes, French and English journalists, artists and photographers, early holiday-makers, cyclists, and villagers, some of the last-named in the quaint costumes of Northern France.

A child, a pretty boy with brown eyes and golden hair, was lifted by his father so that he might touch the monoplane. Half a century from now perhaps he will recall the scene. Fifty years hence they will know what all this experimenting, these flights by courageous men, these gropings in what is more fearful than the dark, these adventures into unknown dangers, really mean to the world.[10]

That same day the Marconi Company began installing a wireless link across the Channel, at the suggestion of the *Daily Mail*. 'A complete sending and receiving station' was placed in a hut erected on the summit of Blanc Nez, and another on the roof of the Lord Warden Hotel at Dover. Latham was delighted. This would give him immediate news of weather conditions and prospects on the other side of the Channel.

For suddenly the weather emerged as the next cause of delay. The forecast at Calais on Friday night 9 July was wholly unfavourable to the possibility of a flight on the Saturday evening, with the prospect of freshening south-westerly winds, rain becoming general, and lower than seasonal temperatures. Worst of all, boisterous winds were expected in the Channel for some days to come.

A long and tiresome vigil now began, with the *Daily Mail* working hard, and apparently successfully, to maintain public interest, by issuing warnings to keep well clear of the aeroplane when it landed, by stories about various motor boats being available or unavailable to guide and rescue Latham, and by news of vast crowds of spectators massing on both sides of the Channel. But above all the paper relied on increasingly extravagant, if predictable, revelations about the aviator himself. Reassuringly, the *Mail* divulged that: 'Mr Latham is a splendid shot, and in *sang-froid* and general demeanour quite Anglo-Saxon.'

The weather on Saturday 10 July turned out much as forecasted, and no flight took place. The atmosphere at Dover was nevertheless festive:

On the cliffs and on the wind-swept pier there still remained late this evening a few persistent optimists who were straining their eyes in an effort to discern Mr Latham's aeroplane. The water was leaden-coloured and angry, the sky full of gloomy clouds. Rain was beginning to fall...It was evident (to us) that Mr Latham could not make his flight today... instead of trying to find a monoplane in the sky, we watched the crowd.

It was worth watching. The road to the top of Shakespeare Cliff was full of all sorts and conditions of people, all manner of vehicles. There were business-like enthusiasts with campstools, mackintoshes, and field-glasses, red-coated soldiers escorting pretty girls, sailors from the warships…children in lace and children with bare legs, Americans, Frenchmen, Germans, Hollanders [sic]. There were policemen everywhere [11]

At Sangatte, there were said to be 10,000 visitors. Sunday was spent anxiously watching the sky for signs, which did not come, of more settled weather. Amid gusty winds, Levavasseur consoled the patience of the crowd – the *Mail* mused there had not been so many people there since Napoleon's day – with a glimpse of the Antoinette in its tent. He removed one side of the red and white striped awning and started up the engine for a few minutes, duly astonishing those present with the tremendous noise.

The next day, Monday 12 July, fog, wind and rain persisted. At Sangatte the weather was the only subject of conversation. A trial flight was planned for four o'clock next morning. 'The eyes of the world', said the *Daily Mail*, 'were on the Pas-de-Calais.' Levavasseur remained courteous and cheerful, but also adamant:

> It is tiresome for people here and at Dover: it is also inconvenient for the Press. But for us, you understand, the people and the Press do not exist. We are concerned only to fly across the Channel. We shall wait, if necessary, weeks or even months rather than court risk of failure by starting in unfavourable conditions… Be calm, be calm, I beg of you, and when the weather is calm we too shall make a start.'[12]

★★★★★

On Tuesday 13 July, just after 7.30 a.m., Latham made his test flight. After taxiing a hundred yards, he took off gracefully and flew away towards Calais, reaching a height of some 200 feet. Having flown a wide circle, he returned after seven minutes in the air, and landed in a little valley not far from his point of departure, damaging the undercarriage slightly.

He said that no further trial flight would be needed, and gave the required twenty-four hours' notice of an attempt the next morning. All that day patient crowds thronged Dover. From five o'clock in the morning there were men, women and children on the cliffs, on the pier and on the waterfront. Many people had stayed up all night, fearing they would not waken early enough. The *Mail* posted frequent bulletins in the Lord Warden Hotel, giving the latest news from Sangatte, as it was passed down from the wireless on the roof. They put out Latham's statement that he did not need another trial, and that his next flight would be over the water.

But it was not to be the next day, Wednesday 14 July, because the weather intervened again. There were wind and fog in the Channel, and the former continued throughout the day. During the following morning the wind dropped, and at ten o'clock delightful weather gave an excellent opportunity to fly.

Unbelievably, the machine was not ready. It was suddenly discovered that the batteries were flat. According to another version, they had been stolen. By the time this trouble had

32. COMTE DE LAMBERT
SUR SON AÉROPLANE

An exasperating contender: *comte Charles de Lambert in his Wright biplane. (Harman Collection)*

been put right the wind had increased, and at 5.30 p.m. Latham told the reporters, who had been there since 4.00 a.m., that no attempt was possible.

Finally, the patience and good humour that had prevailed through so many disappointments at Sangatte began to crack. 'When this was communicated to the crowd, an angry murmur was heard on every side.' To make matters worse, the captain of the destroyer *Harpon* let it be known that he could not wait much longer, and it was thought doubtful that the government would send another vessel. To the swelling tide of resentment was added a rumour that Latham was going away for the weekend. However, a beleaguered and exhausted *Daily Mail* reporter was able to conclude his despatch thus: 'I am authorized to contradict the rumour…Mr Latham said this evening "I shall stay on day by day until my opportunity comes."'

At Dover too the mood had changed. In a despatch on Thursday night (15 July) the *Mail's* man wrote: 'It would be ridiculous to affect ignorance of the fact that as a result of what has happened today (or rather, of what has not happened) there is intense disappointment here.'

From time to time during those days of waiting for Latham, the *Daily Mail* sought to maintain interest in the enterprise by bringing news of his only competitor, de Lambert – Farman's challenge never materialized. The forty-four year-old Charles de Lambert was an elusive and, when found, exasperating contender, at least from the paper's point of view, although they never printed a word of direct criticism.

On 29 June, the *Mail* announced that de Lambert would be a competitor, and that he would use a Wright biplane which Wilbur had taught him to fly at Pau. It was reported that he had leased a large piece of land near Calais (actually at Wissant, west of Sangatte), where he had erected an aeroplane shed 'so that all his preparations are complete', and that he would make his attempt as soon as the weather was suitable.

This was a little premature. Nothing more was heard of de Lambert for a week, and then it emerged that his aeroplane was not yet at Wissant, and neither was he. However, the Wright was then expected to arrive within twenty-four hours, and as for the comte, he was 'hourly expected' at the Grand Hotel, Wissant, which was to be his headquarters. After traversing again the next day the 'half a dozen miles up and down the undulating country, with its many-hued, buttercup-embroidered fields' that led to Wissant, the *Mail's* reporter could only note that: 'Although his rooms were engaged some days ago, he had not arrived at Wissant this afternoon, and his aeroplane is also still on the way.'

By 9 July the *Mail* came as close as it ever did to outright criticism of the noble entrant, saying he was: 'still supposed to be on his way to Wissant.' On 13 July, the day of Latham's trial flight, he was there at last:

> At Wissant this afternoon I found the comte de Lambert busy unpacking the Wright aeroplane with which he hopes to attempt the Channel in about ten days. In overalls and with a screwdriver in his hand, the comte walked round the huge packing case ripping off the canvas while we talked. This is quite in the Wright manner. The comte de Lambert, as a pupil of the American flying man, has caught his master's manner and reproduces it with amusing accuracy.'

Anxious now to make de Lambert seem a believable competitor, the *Mail* reported next day (15 July) that a second Wright was expected at Wissant, and said that the rapidity of his unpacking and the engagement of three torpedo boats showed that the comte 'meant business', adding 'But he has no intention of making the attempt until he has made frequent trials.'

On Sunday 18 July de Lambert asked about the exact conditions under which notice of intention to try for the prize had to be given:

> But, he said, I should not hesitate to start without giving notice if I thought when I got into the air that I could get across. I may practise for weeks, possibly months: on the other hand, if I found on the occasion of even the first trial that the conditions were perfect, I might make the effort then. Such an adventure in a field not yet explored by aviators must, of course, not be undertaken rashly, or in response to the desire of the public for sensation. We are experimenting in the cause of science, and must work with caution. I should like to win the prize if it comes in my way; but I am more interested in crossing the Channel, and thus establishing a new record, than in gaining even the large sum offered by the *Daily Mail*…

But this Russian count (of French origin – his family emigrated during the French Revolution) was never to be ready. By the end of July he had decamped from Wissant in search of new pastures at Reims.

So all real hope still rested on Hubert Latham. At Sangatte, Saturday and Sunday came and went, but the weather was always wrong. However, on Sunday evening, 18 July, there was a feeling of optimism for the morrow in the Antoinette camp. With 'an excess of precaution' they ran the engine in a stationary test, and kept it running for a whole hour… Reassured, at midnight on Sunday 18 July, in a starlit night with very little wind and a calm sea, they had a wireless message sent from Sangatte, asking Dover to stand by at 4.00 a.m.

★★★★★

On Monday morning at 3.00a.m. there was some wind at Calais, but it soon died away. The suspense continued, however, as the wireless came to life:

> Sangatte, 4.30 a.m. – Weather here unfavourable; thick mist, slight rain, little wind.
> Dover, 4.30 a.m. – Unfavourable here; fog, followed by wind and wet.
> Sangatte, 5.05 a.m. – Stand by. Every hour wind conditions getting more favourable.
> Dover, 5.10 a.m. – Weather clearing.
> Sangatte, 5.16 a.m. – Latham wants to know is fog clearing. How far in this direction can you see? He will start if conditions not more unfavourable.
> Dover, 5.20 a.m. – Can see ten miles.
> Sangatte 5.48 a.m. – Don't leave instrument for a second. Torpedo boat arrived and exchanging signals with the shore. Mechanics preparing the machine. Weather nearly ideal excepting for mist.

Levavasseur went on board the *Harpon* saying that if he considered conditions suitable after cruising offshore for a little while he would have a signal given to start. The minutes passed, the sun rose, but no signal came. Then:

> At 6.20, with intense excitement we heard a gun boom. There were only a few people round the shed – not more than a hundred all told – but in the breast of every single one there was a flutter as all ears were strained to catch the next boom. Another and yet another! Three guns, that was the signal. At last the moment for which we had waited nine long weary days had come.
> Already Mr Latham had put on his knitted blue jersey, with cap to match. Pushed up on his forehead were a pair of motor goggles… He is a youth of marvellous self-control. While we talked in excited gasps, and felt the moment big with destiny, he was to all appearances as calm as if he were starting for a bicycle ride…[13]

At the starting place, where the grass sloped gently down towards the old Channel Tunnel workshops, there was a pause while the petrol was topped up. The small agitated figure of Jules Gastambide, standing by, betrayed all the signs of nervousness the English reporters pretended to expect of a Frenchman.

Latham looked at his watch – it was just after 6.30 a.m. – lit another cigarette and attached the waist and foot straps which were meant to keep him in his seat. Then he started the engine, briefly acknowledged the cries of 'Good luck!', and told the three mechanics who were hanging on to the undercarriage to let go. His impressions of the flight were written down a few hours later, while they were still fresh:

'Thankful to be able to start at last.' That was my thought. There also came into my mind the idea that it would have been better had there been fewer spectators – in case of a failure. My ear told me that the motor... was working splendidly. And then I was away.

There was a short, swift run down the slope towards the sea, and I launched myself into the air. My last thought was one of confidence that my motor would not leave me in the lurch. The start could not have been more auspicious. I left the ground in infinitely better style than...the previous Tuesday. Instead of wobbling on getting into the air, I went up with perfect steadiness. I flew so well, indeed, that I altered my plans. Instead of describing a circle, as I had meant to do, I went straight off over the edge of the cliff. First, however, so as to judge my height from the ground, I steered over the ruined Channel Tunnel workings. I estimated that I was then six hundred feet above the level of the water.

Everything was going beautifully: I ran up to a little masthead between the main planes a flag that I had decided should only be hoisted at the moment of leaving land.

Then I took in my hand a little camera... and was preparing to take a picture when a disconcerting sound came to my ears. My motor was showing signs of breaking down. I could hear that more than one of the eight cylinders was misfiring. Instantly, I gave up any idea of photography, and did everything I could to remedy the defect. I examined all the electrical connections that were within my reach. I tried also to alter the carburation and ignition of the engine. But it was all in vain; in a few seconds my engine had stopped entirely. It was maddening, but I was helpless. Never before had the engine played me such a trick, after so short a flight... I estimated that I was quite 1,000 feet up in the air... I took a quick glance ahead, and calculated that the torpedo boat was about a mile away. Then I glided down to the surface of the water. There was nothing else to be done...It seemed quite a long time to me before I struck the water. My speed at the moment of impact was about forty or forty-five miles an hour...

I skimmed down, so that I was able to make the contact with the sea with the aeroplane practically in a horizontal position. It settled in the water and floated like a cork. I swung my feet up on to a cross-bar to prevent them getting wet. Then I took out my cigarette case, lit a cigarette, and waited for the torpedo boat to come up...[14]

Latham's Antoinette VII under tow behind Cap Gris Nez with a mounted escort before his second attempt on the channel. The factory built for the abandoned Channel Tunnel project, and used by the Antoinette team as a base, is shown in the background. (MA 37116)

So ended what Latham gamely called his 'trial trip'. He had flown about half way across, but had not been able to see the English coast. He told Robert Gastambide that he thought a fuel lead had fractured 'I had a partial loss of fuel supply; then it became total'.[15] However, Levavasseur was quoted as saying that a small component in the distributor had broken.[16] His version was later confirmed by another member of his team, who explained that a small piece of insulation had become detached from a wire inside the distributor and had then broken one of its brass moving parts.[17] Vibration could be a cause common to both versions, and it is probable that the extraordinary procedure which had been adopted of wheeling the Antoinette along that bumpy lane at Blanc Nez with the engine running before the start had not helped. Neither, perhaps, had the very long stationary test run the night before.

Latham stepped ashore at Calais to an enthusiastic reception. There were flowers and cheers: it was almost as if he had succeeded. 'I will start again as soon as possible', he told the horde of reporters, announcing that a new aeroplane, the Antoinette VII, would be sent urgently from the factory to Sangatte.

Just as he was at last able to relax, when going into lunch at the Terminus Hotel, he was approached by a journalist he knew with sensational news. Latham turned pale as he listened while a copy of a telegram which had been received in London at ten o'clock that morning was read out:

Gentlemen of the press. Reporters concentrating on their work outside the Antoinette's tent near Sangatte in July 1909. Whether the dog is the 'fierce black' one reportedly used to guard the Antoinette from souvenir hunters is open to question. (MC 985)

Hubert Latham sits calmly on his still floating Antoinette IV while awaiting rescue after the failure of his first attempt, 19 July 1909. (P47279)

To the Editor of *The Daily Mail*

Sir. – I have the honour to inform you that I enter for the *Daily Mail* prize of £1,000 for a cross-Channel flight by aeroplane.

My intention is to compete for the prize on Thursday or Friday next on the Calais-Dover route. – Receive, Sir, my sincere salutations.

Paris, July 19   L. Blériot'[18]

8 A tide taken at the flood

A few hours earlier, in the Champs Elysées, Alice Blériot had sat waiting in their car parked outside the Aéro Club. A small, dandified figure emerged, and approached her. It was Santos-Dumont: 'It's alright', he said, 'he has sent in his entry!' That was how Alice claimed she learned of her husband's decision.[1]

During the preceding few weeks Blériot had defined his conditions for an attempt on the Channel. Firstly, he would only go if Latham failed. Secondly, he would need to have made several flights of a duration and distance comparable to those required for a Channel crossing. On 4 July at Juvisy he told the press that he thought it would be imprudent to make an attempt before he had succeeded in remaining in the air half a dozen times for periods longer than he had done that day (50min 8sec). To Alice he said that two flights of one hour would be needed. By the date Latham failed he had not achieved either of these flying objectives. Nevertheless, his achievements in the past six weeks had been astonishing, as the record shows:

2 June	Takes off with a mechanic as a passenger in the type XII at Issy.
7 June	Again takes a passenger in the XII – the aeronautical journalist André Fournier.
8 June	Two flights of 500m in the XII.
11 June	Flies a double 'S' at four metres altitude in the XII.
12 June	For the first time in history two passengers are taken in an aeroplane. Louis Blériot in the XII takes up Alberto Santos-Dumont and André Fournier at Issy-les-Moulineaux.
14 June	The XII flies for 10.5min. To demonstrate its stability, Blériot several times takes his hands off the controls.
15 June	During a flight with Fournier as a passenger in the ENV engined XII, the crankshaft breaks.
18 June	Blériot reverts to his Anzani-engined model XI, not flown since 27 May, and flies 4km at Issy.
21 June	The XI flies for 3min and 6.5min, stopped by a lack of oil. When restarting, the engine bursts into flames – the carburettor is too close to the exhaust pipe – but quick-thinking spectators at Issy pick up handfuls of sand from the surface of the parade-ground and throw them over the Anzani, putting out the fire before any damage is done.
25 June	Flight of 15min 30sec by the XI – Blériot's longest in it to date.
26 June	In the XI, Blériot excels himself by staying in the air for 36min 55sec, accomplishing twenty circuits of the field at Issy in a gusty wind. He is brought down by an excess of oil fouling the sparking plugs.

28 June	With a new crankshaft in the XII, Blériot opens the meeting at Douai by flying at an altitude of 40 to 50m.
30 June	Back at Issy, he makes several short flights on the XI, but is obliged to stop each time because of faulty adjustment of the lubrication system.
2 July	Again at Douai, he wins a prize in the XII for flying a circle of 1,500m.
3 July	He flies for 47min 17sec in the XII at Douai, covering 47.277km before the engine fails.
4 July	A flight of 50min 8sec is made in the XI at Juvisy, covering twenty-four laps at 20 to 40m altitude with a steadiness that amazed the spectators.
9 and 10 July	Several short flights of the XII at Douai.
13 July	Louis Blériot in his XI flies the 41.2 km from Etampes to Orléans in 44min 30sec (after deducting 11min 20sec for a stop at Arbouville), and wins the first Prix du Voyage.[2]

When he entered for the *Daily Mail* prize on 19 July, Blériot had made no flight lasting an hour, but he had made four of well over half an hour, all within the short span of three weeks. He felt this was enough to give him a sporting chance, but it had been obtained at an agonizing cost. His mechanic Ferdinand Collin recalled what had happened at Douai on 3 July:

> After the first fifteen minutes, he felt a great deal of heat in his ankle, which was touching the exhaust pipe. The asbestos lagging had worked loose and was soon blown away. By the time he had been in the air for thirty minutes his shoe had been burnt through and his flesh roasted: but, hands clenched, fearless, unshakeable, the man held on. In the 42nd minute [sic], when the engine gave up, and Blériot landed, it was a casualty who came out of the aeroplane… his burns took two months to heal.[3]

So it was, reflected Collin, that the *patron* showed the extent of 'his obstinacy and his terrible tenacity'. Alice was aghast at the injury. His trouser leg, sock and shoe had been destroyed, and there were third degree burns to his ankle and foot: gangrene was feared. He endured a painful treatment which lasted one hour. However, in the days that followed he continued to fly. It was only after a few weeks, when the injury was beginning to heal, that he was unable to keep on top of it. Once, on 18 July, he was forced to curtail a flight, at Douai on the XII, but that time he burnt the foot again…

Blériot's attitude to his injury is apparent from the fact that he sent in his entry to the *Daily Mail* the next morning. The wretched set-back could not be allowed to interfere with the realization that, with Latham's failure, his time had come. His conviction that there was a rising tide in his affairs cannot have been due solely to the number or duration of his recent flights, for they were in all conscience marginal in comparison to the objective to which he was now committed. What was probably decisive was the new proof that he had the capacity to mount the logistical operation which his practical sense told him was indispensable for a successful attempt on the Channel.

That proof had been furnished in abundance by the manner in which the Aéro Club's first Prix de Voyage was won on 13 July. Building on the experience of the previous

Louis Blériot in his type XI at Mondésir farm prepares to take off for the Etampes-Orléans flight on 13 July 1909. Alexandre Anzani is about to swing the propeller to start 'his' engine. (P47113)

October in setting up a base in the 'field' for flying operations at Toury, Blériot chose as his headquarters the large complex of buildings called La Ferme de Mondésir, beside a vast and fairly level field five kilometres south of Etampes. To this spot the XI, with its wings removed and folded, so to speak, against the fuselage, was towed behind the yellow Panhard by Henri the chauffeur. (The field is still used for flying and the farm with its great courtyard looks much as it did in photographs taken when Blériot was there.) In that courtyard Ferdinand Collin, working alone under the eyes of Blériot and his close friend Alfred Leblanc, with a stop-watch in his hand, assembled the type XI in twenty-seven minutes. Then the aeroplane was sheltered fully by an awning erected against a rick of straw. Collin remembered spending the night in Blériot's car, parked alongside:

> I guarded our type XI, sleeping with one eye open. God knows that the night of 12-13 July was chilly! But all went well, in the solitude and the silence of the plain, the Route Nationale Paris-Orléans in 1909 having no traffic at night, and only a few barks of far-away dogs reached me from isolated farms.[4]

The next morning, although calm, was misty, but Blériot decided to go anyway. At 4.44 a.m. he took off, climbed to thirty metres, and soon got lost in the fog, to be saved by spotting the Paris-Orléans railway line. After a brief planned stop to examine the Anzani engine which, gratifyingly, was 'scarcely warm', he was off, and soon got lost again because Artenay church spire was invisible. Picking up the railway and the road, and staying now between them, he recognized his intended landing place, which he had never seen but which had been described to him, by an iron cross standing in a field of lucerne. Tracing

97

Louis Blériot and Alfred Leblanc confer over the route to be taken from Mondésir farm, near Etampes, to Orléans, 13 July 1909. (MC 1409)

Louis and Alice Blériot with the type XI at Mondésir farm. (Royal Aeronautical Society)

a wide semi-circle to face the wind, he made a perfect landing at Chevilly, just outside Orléans. He covered 41.2km in 44min 30sec flying time.[5] It was generally recognised at the time as the highly symbolic first flight in history from 'town to town', although arguably that distinction belonged to the previous year's Toury-Artenay flight, which had been hailed simply as a 'cross-country' flight.

★★★★★

Blériot's late and dramatically timed entry was just what the *Daily Mail* needed. The paper was able to announce it on the same day and on the same page as Latham's failure, thus alleviating the great anticlimax.

The whole tempo of events altered overnight. After the interminable delays, the ponderous and at times chaotic preparations of the Antoinette team, Blériot brought a breath of fresh air to the contest. He told the *Mail*:

> My machine will leave Paris for Calais tomorrow night. It requires no shed and can be put together half an hour after its arrival. It is the smallest practical flying machine in existence – less than half the size of Latham's – and has only a 20hp motor. If the wind is northerly I may fly from Dover to Calais.[6]

This was indeed a new approach, and one to be marvelled at. Breathlessly, the *Mail* explained: 'So easily portable is his little monoplane that he need not make up his mind

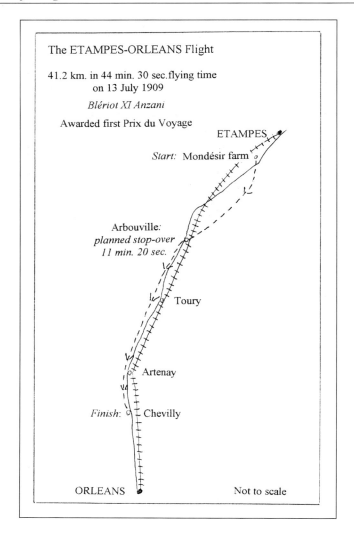

The ETAMPES-ORLEANS Flight

41.2 km. in 44 min. 30 sec.flying time
on 13 July 1909

Blériot XI Anzani

Awarded first Prix du Voyage

ETAMPES

Start: Mondésir farm

Arbouville:
planned stop-over
11 min. 20 sec.

Toury

Artenay

Finish: Chevilly

ORLEANS

Not to scale

until a few hours beforehand whether he will attempt the flight from Calais to Dover or from Dover to Calais.'

Unlike the aircraft of Latham and de Lambert, Blériot's arrived on the coast when its owner said it would:

Calais, Wednesday Night.

In the small hours of this morning there arrived at Calais town station from Paris on a railway truck all to itself a mysterious-looking object, partly concealed by striped canvas. It was the already famous monoplane of M. Blériot. All the morning it was surrounded by curious crowds, which, owing to the hasty manner in which the machine had apparently been prepared for the journey, were able to get a pretty good view of it.

Louis Blériot looking anxious before taking off from Mondésir farm on 13 July 1909. (Author's Collection)

> It is a monoplane less than half the size of Mr Latham's…Seen close, it is
> not beautiful, being dirty and weather-beaten, but it looks very business-like.
> At midday a tall, keen-eyed, eagle-nosed, heavily-moustached gentleman,
> limping slightly, descended from the train from Paris and registered at the
> Terminus Hotel. It was M. Blériot…He has been here only a few hours, but
> already he is 'making things hum'.[7]

When Blériot had taken the train that morning at the Gare du Nord he had been able
to walk only with excruciating difficulty. Alice remembered that getting along the platform
to their compartment he lifted his left leg for each step with a scarf passed behind his knee.
At Calais a pair of crutches were bought, and a local physician, Dr Doyen, attended him
twice a day, hoping to keep gangrene at bay with frequent injections. Blériot refused
opium, protesting that he did not want to experience the sensation of dying![8] He seems to
have known that the continual pain could affect his judgement, and so he wisely made up
his mind to leave vital decisions to his close and trusted friend, the indispensable Alfred
Leblanc whom he had appointed his 'manager' for the enterprise.

Although he sometimes gave interviews while resting in bed, the press and public were
not fully aware of the gravity of Blériot's condition and hence of how unlikely it was, on
any rational basis, that he would be fit to fly. What was well recognized at that time was
his courage and daring at another level. Under the headline: 'M. Blériot's confidence –
how he avoids injury in a fall', the *Mail* recounted with some awe that although Blériot
had had several falls, he had so far escaped serious injury – as he had explained:

The Blériot XI near Orléans, after the flight on 13 July 1909. The aeroplane is being dismantled for transport home. (P 47117)

> A man who keeps his head cool can never be injured through a fall. If one falls one must not try to save both the machine and oneself. I always throw myself upon one of the wings of my machine, when I have a mishap, and although this breaks the wing, it causes me to alight safely.

In just three days Louis Blériot had shown himself to be a serious and effective contender. Instead of having up to ten mechanics milling about on the coast, as Levavasseur had done, Blériot had sent just two: Julien Mamet and Ferdinand Collin. They were highly competent, and had specific experience, as veterans of Toury-Artenay and Etampes-Orléans, of setting up an improvised base. Conscientious and thorough, these were men who could be absolutely relied on to bring the right tools and spare parts from Paris, and to set up a weather-proof shelter and temporary workshop at whatever spot their *patron* would decree.

After deciding against a field near the Calais Casino, Blériot, driven by Leblanc in the latter's car, found a vast and virtually treeless plain just behind some low sand dunes by the then very small village of Les Baraques, three kilometres west of Calais town. The site could hardly have been better. Blériot and Leblanc quickly came to terms with the Grignon family, owners of a dairy farm whose small group of buildings gave directly on to the edge of the plain. There was to be no long and rocky road between shelter and flying ground for them.

A new barn stood half-built at the farm, and against one of its walls they decided to erect a lean-to shelter, sturdily constructed from the builder's ladders that were lying about, and covered by a tarpaulin. Running on its own wheels, the Blériot XI was towed gently by a horse from the railway siding at Calais to the farm.[9]

There was a lot of wind, ruling out any chance of a trial flight that day (Wednesday), so the two mechanics took their time over unpacking the tools and stores, and mounting the wings. Nevertheless, the job was completed in under two hours.

During those days at Les Baraques the mechanics were anxious in case any fault or oversight of theirs should lead to failure. They repeatedly went over the little monoplane inch by inch, checking everything. Insulating tape was put round the screw terminals of the sparking plugs, to prevent them working loose, as frequently happened. Every screw, every nut and bolt, was tightened and re-tightened, in case some small but potentially fatal defect should escape them.

There was reason to fear a fatality. The general expectation was that Blériot would come down in the sea. This was a doubly grim prospect because his smaller plane might not float as well as Latham's had, and Blériot apparently could not swim. To improve his chance of staying on the surface long enough to be rescued, a long cylindrical bag, made of rubberized fabric, was placed inside the fuselage and filled with 350 litres of air.

Alexandre Anzani arrived tempestuously from Paris. According to Collin, Anzani, after examining the engine in detail pronounced himself satisfied with its condition and state of tune, as well as with the extra precautions which had been taken. But by another account there was a great row, because Anzani discovered that the pistons, so lovingly made in his workshop, had been replaced by others. To add insult to injury, the substitutes had come from Buchet, Anzani's former employer. Anzani's rage defied all description, we are told, and was so unbearable that the offending parts were promptly removed.

What is certain is that Anzani had worked himself into a frenzy of apprehension, overcome by the responsibility he was assuming for Blériot's life which, he was persuaded, would depend upon the engine lasting for one hour. Experience had shown the lubrication system to be the Achilles heel of the three cylinder Anzani, and it was all too easy for too much oil to enter the cylinders and stop the engine by fouling the sparking plugs, or alternatively for too little oil to stop the engine by causing a piston to seize. For the engine to run long enough to get across the Channel, it would be imperative for Blériot to remember every three minutes to work the oil pump by its hand-plunger. Anzani implored him not to forget.

Apart from those moments of stress, great good humour prevailed at the dairy farm. Even the stern and usually unbending Blériot was not immune to it. Having been driven out from Calais with Alice to check on the preparation of his machine, he asked Mamet: 'Are you absolutely sure that I am going to get across?' Although the mechanics were always anxious to make Blériot feel confident, the directness of the question made Mamet hesitate. Then Blériot said 'There will be 1,000 francs for you and for Collin if I do.' Instantly Mamet replied: 'Then Monsieur Blériot, you will succeed.' They all burst out laughing.[10]

★★★★★

From these lighter moments one man now stood apart. He was small of stature, pugnacious of stance, and in normal times his wit and light-heartedness made him the best of company. But Alfred Leblanc's life throughout those days and nights had but one aim, and it absorbed him totally: to get Blériot to Dover, alive and before Latham.

All the strands of the enterprise came together in his hands. His friend and mentor, with physique, morale and judgement for the time impaired, had put them there. Continually going over all aspects of the attempt in his mind, Leblanc knew that on some counts they were in a strong position, but there were also matters of uncertainty and great concern.

He too was a veteran of Toury-Artenay and Etampes-Orléans, and knew the worth of the two mechanics. The technical preparation of the machine was in the most capable hands, particularly as Anzani was now on the scene and Blériot was well enough to keep an overview of work at the dairy. However, a political crisis in Paris created difficulties in arranging a naval escort, without which there could be no question of Blériot being allowed to start.

After several meetings in Calais, with Blériot personally taking part in the key negotiations, Commandant Piogier, in command of the destroyer *Escopette*, finally told Blériot at nine o'clock on Saturday evening (24 July) that in view of the danger to which he would be exposed by a refusal to accompany him, he was taking it upon himself to escort whichever of the two contenders started first.

The Navy's plans in respect of Blériot were set out in writing. They give a unique insight into how professional mariners viewed the venture:

Instructions on the measures to be taken by the vessels of the Second Flotilla assigned to convoy Monsieur Blériot:

During Monsieur Blériot's flight, the vessels charged with accompanying him will initially take up the following positions on the line between the Calais and Dover semaphores:

The *257* at 3 milles [sic] from the shore

The *227* at 2 kilometres from *257*

The *Escopette* at 2 kilometres from *227*

The distance between the three ships is very short so that Monsieur Blériot can be saved as soon as possible in the event of his aeroplane falling in the sea.

The lack of buoyancy of the machine means that assistance to the aviator must be immediate and that all the torpedo boats must gather around the point where he falls. If the aeroplane disappears the only remaining guide to the search will be the small flag which Monsieur Blériot should put up. His attention has been drawn to the difficulties resulting from the limited visibility of this signal: he will try to make it as apparent as possible.

The machine should be considered as sacrificed if it falls in the sea: Monsieur Blériot desires that salvage of the engine only be undertaken. He will be given satisfaction in this respect as long as there is no danger to naval property. A permanent look-out will be kept at the masthead of the *Escopette*.

Monsieur Blériot will apply himself to adjusting his speed to that of the torpedo boats by proceeding in zigzags across their course.

As soon as the aeroplane is seen in the air, the vessels will set the course indicated at a speed of 20 knots, with the exception of the last one which will go more slowly, in order to be ready to go to his assistance, until Monsieur Blériot catches up with it.

From that moment the *257* will proceed at full speed: 23 knots. The *Escopette* and the *227* will then immediately do the same.

Reductions in speed are left to the discretion of the commanders if the machine appears to be in difficulty. A flag at the masthead, prolonged blasts of the (steam) whistle, or a few rounds of cannon will signal that the aeroplane has fallen into the sea...[11]

Thus it was with much care and thoroughness – having regard to the means at their disposal – that Commandant Piogier and his fellow officers prepared themselves for their task. However, the provision that Blériot should follow a zigzag course in order to keep in touch with the flotilla seems naive in the extreme – by so greatly increasing the duration and difficulty of the flight compliance would have made failure inevitable. Perhaps the officers thought that by recording that pious hope they might protect themselves from criticism in the event of tragedy. If the frequent mentions of the aeroplane falling into the sea suggest pessimism, it should be remembered that the operation was a rescue mission – for the Navy it had no other justification.

However, for Blériot and Leblanc the Navy may have had another and more positive role: the line of ships would show the direction in which the pilot should fly. With hindsight, the most extraordinary potential flaw in the whole venture was the apparently total neglect of navigation, in both the preparations and in the flight itself. It was an omission that would come close to costing Blériot his life. While it is often possible to see right across the Channel, that is unlikely to have been the case during the weather that had prevailed since their arrival, and they were in a position to know that Latham, even from an altitude and half way across, had not seen England.

There may perhaps have been one exception to the lack of interest in navigation within the Blériot camp, but the evidence is unconvincing. Ferdinand Collin claimed that he had fitted a compass to the type XI:

> Meanwhile, I became obsessed with the risk of a deviation from a true course during the crossing, and it was when on the dunes one night that the inspiration came to me to mark out with two stakes the direction of the Dover lighthouse. Next day I bought a small compass in Calais, and having set the needle to the north, I attached a length of brass wire across the dial to show the direction of Dover: the compass was then fixed on the longeron of the fuselage.[12]

That account was written by Collin in 1929, twenty years after the event, and was repeated in substance in his book published in 1948. On the latter occasion he added: 'It would suffice therefore for Blériot to keep the needle over the north marking on the disk to be sure of heading for Dover.' However, immediately after the flight Blériot was to write: 'I carried neither watch nor compass.' No photographic evidence of the existence of a compass has been found.

Another neglected question, until a late stage and then as a result of outside intervention, was the choice of a landing place at Dover. Hubert Latham, as we have seen, had gone to England to spend half a day in touring round prospective sites in the vicinity of the town. Blériot was unwell, his team was small and otherwise occupied, and they had been installed on the French coast only for a few days, whereas the Antoinette team had been there for weeks. These factors combined to deny them an opportunity for reconnaissance, even if the inclination was there. But all that was to change, thanks to the initiative of a then obscure reporter – Charles Fontaine of the the Paris daily *Le Matin*.

Fontaine was the star of what was about to become an extraordinary episode in the early development of modern journalism. The proprietors of *Le Matin* decided to give the Channel contest major coverage, and they chose to concentrate on Blériot. Fontaine was told to travel to Calais on the same train as Blériot, and to arrange to be present at the landing, irrespective of whether the flight was from Dover to Calais or vice-versa.

Right from the start, Fontaine's limpet-like qualities made themselves apparent – as well as his good luck. Dashing along the platform at the Gare du Nord, clutching a hastily-packed suitcase, just as the Calais train began to move out, he sprang into the first compartment to offer itself. Needless to say, it was the one in which Louis and Alice Blériot had installed themselves a few minutes earlier.

Also in the compartment were two other reporters, one of them the sports correspondent of *Le Matin*, Guérin, who had been given the role converse to Fontaine's – he was to cover Blériot's departure, whether it took place from Calais or from Dover. Guerin introduced his colleague to the Blériots. 'Finding myself there', Fontaine noted somewhat disingenuously, 'I judged it opportune to stay.' He immediately engaged the couple in conversation, and was grateful for their 'charming and even affable' response to the intruder.

Fontaine remained with them throughout that day, accompanying the party to Les Baraques. Back at the Hotel Terminus at Calais he, by his own account, drew Blériot aside from the dinner table and spoke to him in conspiratorial tones. Fontaine's plan was to cross over to Dover that night and find a suitable place for Blériot to land. He pointed out that Blériot, unlike Latham, had not done this for himself. Fontaine added: 'as soon as you get within sight of the port look along the cliff-tops: I will be there waving a large tricolour. You should then aim straight for my flag, which will guide your descent.'

According to Fontaine, Blériot at once accepted this proposal, and went back to his dinner.

At 1.30 a.m. (on the Friday) Fontaine went on board the steamer *Pas-de-Calais*, for what proved to be a dreadfully rough crossing. It was obvious to him by the time he got off the boat at Dover that there could be no flight that morning, so instead of beginning his reconnaissance he went to the Lord Warden Hotel in search of some rest. At 4.00 a.m. he received a despatch from Guérin saying that no start was intended. Relieved, he went to sleep, but after a few hours arose to begin his day again.

Throughout the day, 23 July, Fontaine made an exhaustive study of the neighbouring landscape, and in the evening sat down to write a letter, which at 11.00 p.m. he placed in the hands of the purser of the *Pas-de-Calais*. It was addressed to Blériot at the Hôtel Terminus at Calais, and at the top left hand corner of the envelope Fontaine had written: 'To be given to Monsieur Blériot as soon as he awakes.' The letter read in part as follows:

> Dear Monsieur Blériot,
>   I have examined the English coast today from Shakespeare Cliff to St Margaret's Bay to find a place suitable for your landing... You must definitely give up any idea of landing on the beach... at high tide the beach

is barely twenty metres wide...

You said that during your crossing you would keep at a height of between 50 and 60 metres. Such being the case, the idea of landing on Shakespeare Cliff, which is more than 100 metres high, must also be abandoned.

I strongly recommend you therefore to come in to land to the right of Dover Castle, on the cliff called North Foreland [also referred to as Northfall] Meadow. This cliff, which is 30 metres above sea level, is shaped like a wide basin. In maintaining a height of 50 metres, you will still fly 20 metres above the cliff, which is certainly sufficient....

I have arranged with the authorities for the removal of the telegraph poles and wires which could hamper you at this spot: this will be done, I am told, either tonight or at dawn tomorrow....

I shall be there with my large tricolour flag which I will start waving as soon as you have been able to pick me out....

Ch. Fontaine[13]

After handing over his precious envelope to the purser, Fontaine walked out along the jetty where the *Pas-de-Calais* was berthed. A gale was blowing, and there were huge waves. Conditions could have hardly have been worse, but all the same when he returned to the Lord Warden he gave strict instructions to the night-watchman to rouse him at half past three in the morning.

*****

Any hope that Blériot might have the field to himself was quashed by Levavasseur. The evening before Blériot travelled to Calais, there was a flutter of excitement at Sangatte when it was announced that the new Antoinette, which had been expected in about eight days, would now arrive at 6.00 a.m. the next morning:

The machine is coming straight through tonight from the Antoinette company's works at Puteaux, near Paris, accompanied by a double staff of mechanics, and immediately on its arrival in Calais will be put on a wagon and brought to Sangatte, where it is expected to arrive at noon. The mechanics will work on the monoplane day and night and we shall have it ready in forty-eight hours from the time of arrival here. On Friday evening or Saturday morning we hope to give the machine a trial, and the second attempt to fly across the Channel will be made by Mr Latham immediately afterwards.[14]

There was a delay of twenty-four hours in getting the Antoinette VII to Sangatte, and assembly did not begin until noon on Thursday: 'Ten mechanics put their backs into it and rapid progress was made.' By evening, their work was nearly finished, but the bad weather continued to exclude any possibility of a trial flight. Yet a test was imperative because Latham apparently had no experience of the wing-warping which the Antoinette VII employed in place of ailerons.

Meanwhile, Blériot was at Les Baraques. In the presence of reporters he climbed into his seat in the XI, to see if he could operate the controls, in particular the rudder bar, without too much pain. He was relieved to find that he could cope:

> I shall start at the earliest possible moment. The Government have sent a destroyer to accompany me which can steam at fifty-five kilometres an hour. As that is also my speed, I should be in no danger even if I fell into the water. The machine would float for five minutes, which would be quite enough to enable me to be picked up. I shall start from the flat meadow behind the village and fly over the houses and out to sea. I mean to land on Dover beach below Shakespeare's Cliff. I wanted to land on the Admiralty Pier, but found it impracticable. I shall not fly more than fifty or sixty feet high, and cannot do with more than a ten-mile wind. But what wind there is must be behind me. Therefore if the wind blew persistently from the west I might still go across and fly from Dover.[15]

The *Daily Mail* correspondent concluded his report:

> "If only the wind would drop," M. Blériot said mournfully. "If only the wind will keep up," the president of the Antoinette Company had been saying to me an hour before. M. Blériot wants calm weather; Mr Latham wants time. That is the situation to-night.

★★★★★

Next day, Friday 23 July, Blériot and Latham met, and had a discussion about the possibility of both starting at the same time, according to the *Mail*. They foresaw difficulties over the naval escort if they did this. According to Robert Gastambide, it was on Saturday that Latham called on Blériot in Calais, and Blériot returned the compliment by calling on Latham at Sangatte. In any case the tension was now complete.

Throughout Saturday the wind did not relent, and gave no sign that it ever would. When night fell, however, two watchers on the coast, as they went to their beds, detected the most tentative of hints that a change was after all a possibility.

At Sangatte, Hubert Latham took a pencil before going upstairs at the Hotel de la Plage and wrote:

> Midnight – The wind appears to be lessening. If this continues, have Wimille start at 3.30 a.m. and waken me. Also send the team to the shed.

He went up to Levavasseur's room, wakened him and handed him the note. Then he went to bed.[16]

At Calais, Alfred Leblanc stayed up late. It was not until around midnight, just before he went to bed, that the wind died down.

9 The Channel Flight

Leblanc was the first to register the change in the weather:

> I was too expectant, too alert, to be able to sleep for very long. So, just after two o'clock in the morning I was up and out on the hotel balcony pacing back and forth. As the weather was ideal I decided to go and waken Blériot, who at first was reluctant: 'Do you think an attempt is possible this morning?' he asked me. 'I am absolutely certain. But it is essential to make a move now, to take advantage of the calm conditions,' I replied. My friend got dressed and prepared for breakfast. But, I have to admit, he was dejected, and not at all his usual self. I even had to force him to eat something.[1]

According to Blériot, it was worse than that:

> Getting up this morning was dreadful for me. My friend Alfred Leblanc, a devoted supporter if ever there was one, had called me at half-past two. I was not in the least inclined to get going. I could see only the black side and – to tell the truth – I would have been relieved to hear that the wind was too strong for an attempt to be possible.
>
> Indeed, I felt terrible. Leblanc urged and encouraged me. He took me in his car. I was saved. The fresh air lashing my face woke me up thoroughly. I was a bit ashamed of my moment of weakness, now that I felt in really good form.[2]

While Blériot was coming to, Leblanc's chauffeur drove them first to the berth of the *Escopette*, where Alice was put on board. It had finally been decided that the destroyer alone would escort Blériot, while the two torpedo boats were allocated to Latham. Decisively, Leblanc asked Commandant Piogier to put to sea at once and take up station offshore, and there await the signal to start. To make sure that signal would be given professionally, without ambiguity, Leblanc took a member of the crew with them in the car, which then headed for Les Baraques.

Those moments were etched on Alice Blériot's memory:

> My husband was in good spirits, although his ankle was painful. He wasn't nervous, but calm and confident. I went on board at three o'clock in the morning. My husband had gone…after having handed me his wallet however.... We had parted with no apparent emotion, calm and confident.[3]

A tall, keen-eyed, heavily-moustached gentleman, limping slightly. *Blériot radiating confidence at Calais in the days just before the Channel flight.. Alfred Leblanc is on Alice Blériot's right. (MA 28704)*

At Les Baraques, Collin, warned by a magnificent red sky at sunset, had slept 'with one eye open'. As dawn came and the limpid, glimmering sky kept its promise, he awoke, and instantly realized that this would be the day. When he was already up and getting dressed, four shots rang out in the corridor. Anzani, flourishing a revolver, had taken matters into his own hands, and decided to rouse the entire hotel when he saw that the weather was perfect.[4]

The Grignon's dairy was everyone's objective. Mamet and Collin took the Blériot XI out of the tent and wheeled it into the field. As they did so the car arrived from Calais with Blériot, Leblanc and the sailor. Petrol was put into the aeroplane while Blériot put on a brand new set of the traditional French workman's blue overalls. Then standing, on his crutches, he paused for a few moments in front of the cameraman sent by Pathé Frères, before turning briskly away and striding out towards his machine, crutches swinging.

Blériot was hoisted into his seat and the crutches were lashed to the fuselage. Collin felt they were installing a semi-invalid on board, but Blériot appeared calmly resolved, his expression energetic and determined, and he made the mechanics feel confident. Anzani took a good look at the engine. Blériot had not flown for a week, so to get his hand in and to check the set-up of the rigging he decided to make a short test flight. A mechanic grasped the propeller and rotated it half a turn clockwise, paused, pushed it half a turn anti-clockwise…then he stopped and spoke to Blériot. Another spin anti-clockwise and

Louis Blériot in his workshop in 1909. (Harman Collection)

the Anzani roared vigorously, with its habitual, uneven beat. Blériot shouted *'laissez aller!'* and those restraining the monoplane, by holding its tail, let go.

Just after 4.10 a.m. he took off, before a huge and ever growing crowd of spectators, kept more or less out of the way by the police. Nevertheless, when the plane was being pulled along to its starting point, with Blériot standing up in the cockpit, women and girls in white aprons ran after it. He flew in a circle, passing close to Calais on one side… and almost to Sangatte on the other.

> The machine takes off easily. The extra weight of the cylinder of air reduces the power only very slightly. I have a new propeller which pulls perfectly. I stay in the air for ten minutes, agreeably surprised to find there is a fresh, gentle wind blowing from the land, a tidal wind, which pushes me towards the Channel.[5]

He landed impeccably, and said he was satisfied with the machine. 'What did you think of my flight?' he asked Leblanc, 'Could I start?' 'I am quite confident', answered the man he had put in charge, 'you must get ready, now.' The petrol tank was topped up to its capacity of 13 litres. More oil was put in the crankcase. The official observer sent over by the Aero Club of the United Kingdom, Charles Rolls, stood by. Like the Frenchmen he had to be patient a few minutes longer, for an official reason, as Leblanc described:

An artist's impression of the chief contenders for the Daily Mail *prize. (Royal Aeronautical Society)*

It is 4.25 a.m. The sun appears on the horizon: that's one of the conditions in the *Daily Mail's* regulations. Therefore Blériot can go. A last look through my binoculars enables me to reassure him that there is no sign of Latham.

Suddenly Blériot asked him: 'Where *is* Dover?'

Leblanc tried to see the English coast, but he could not. He waved an arm in approximately the right direction. Blériot spoke again, as Leblanc recalled:

'I will not leave', he said to me with excessive caution, 'until the starting signal has been given to the *Escopette*.' I reassure him for the last time and, saying I will see him in Dover, take my leave. I then go over to the dunes. Reaching the high point I have chosen as a look-out place, I can see the destroyer. I wave my handkerchief, to let Blériot know that he can start. The ship's signal to start is given by the sailor from the *Escopette*, standing on the dunes.[6]

The sailor's signal was duplicated, or perhaps relayed, by two other sailors perched high on the stepped gable of a house, as the Pathé movie camera faithfully recorded. Anzani had a last look over the engine. He had donned a well-cut overcoat, a new flat cap and smart white spats for the great day. Blériot said good-bye to him, and in turn to Collin and Mamet. Their last advice was to remember to pump the oil regularly. The engine was restarted, and the Blériot XI began to move away. Above the noise, Anzani shouted once more: 'Give it oil!' The time was 4.41 a.m.

Abruptly, Blériot was by himself:

> Everything is ready. Keeping to the rules, I wait for the sun to rise. Leblanc shows me that the disc is visible by waving a flag from the dune. It's the signal. I felt anxious the moment I got into my seat. What will happen? Will I reach Dover?
>
> These thoughts flash through my mind, but I don't dwell on them. I don't think any more except about my machine, about the engine, about the propeller. Everything is in motion all vibrating. At the signal the workmen let go of the machine. There I am, off the ground.
>
> I keep going straight ahead, progressively rising metre by metre. I cross the dune from which Leblanc is sending me his good wishes. Now I am over the sea, leaving to my right the destroyer whose opaque smoke obscures the sun...
>
> I go on, I go on tranquilly, without any emotion, without any real impression. I feel as if I were on a balloon. The complete absence of wind means that the steering and wing-warping controls don't have to be moved at all. If I could block the controls, I could put both hands in my pockets.
>
> My impression is that I am not moving quickly. That comes, I believe, from the uniformity of the sea. Over land, houses, woods and roads appear and disappear as in a dream. Over water, there is only a wave, always the same wave...
>
> I am pleased with my machine. Its stability is perfect. And the engine, what a marvel! Ah! My fine Anzani, it doesn't falter!
>
> But I had my best time in the first half hour. Not wanting to be held up, I had parted company from the *Escopette*. Too bad!
>
> Come what may! For a period of ten minutes I was by myself, alone, lost in the middle of the immense sea, detecting nothing on the horizon, seeing no vessel. This calm, disturbed only by the roar of the engine, held a dangerous attraction, as I recognized only too well. Therefore I concentrated on the oil pump and on the level of fuel consumption.
>
> Those ten minutes seemed long to me, and truly I was glad to be able to pick out to the west a grey line which separated itself from the sea and grew thicker as I watched. Beyond question it was the English coast. I was almost saved.
>
> I set my course for this white mountain. But I am trapped by wind and mist. I have to struggle, with my hands, with my eyes. My machine, docile, obeys my thoughts. I aim for the cliff, but I can't see Dover any more. What the Devil! Where am I then?
>
> I can see three ships. Are they tugs, or packet-boats? It doesn't matter. They seem to be making for a port. I follow them, unworried. The sailors send up enthusiastic cheers. I would almost like to ask them the way to Dover. Alas! I don't speak English.

I go along the cliff, from north to south, but the wind, against which I struggle, has started to blow very strongly. A jagged break in the coastline opens up on my right, just before Dover Castle. A wild feeling of joy takes hold of me. I aim for it with all haste. I am over the land! I feel again a slight emotion. But on the ground a man is desperately waving a tricolour. I come down further and I recognize the reporter from *Le Matin*, the good Fontaine who, alone in the great plain, was yelling for all he was worth. *Ah! Le brave garçon!*

I want to land: the eddies are violent. As soon as I approach the ground I am lifted by a fierce swirling gust. I cannot stay up any longer. The flight had lasted 33 minutes [sic]: it was enough. At the risk of breaking everything, I cut the ignition. And now, to chance! The chassis did not take it too well, and got damaged a bit. Too bad! I have crossed the Channel.[7]

The departure and arrival times recorded in signed statements by Leblanc and Fontaine respectively were 4.41 a.m. and 5.17 a.m. and 30 seconds (allowing for the time difference between France and England), giving a journey time of 36 minutes 30 seconds. The exact distance Blériot travelled is unknown, but obviously it exceeded the width of the Channel at the narrowest, 34km, and it may well have been about 44km.

★★★★★

Meanwhile, at Les Baraques, the past half hour had had its share of anxiety, though not at first, as Collin recalled. As soon as the type XI took off:

It gained 5 metres, then 10 metres, then at 20 metres jumped the dunes, and without waiting in order to gain more height, the aeroplane headed straight in the direction of Dover.

We ran like maniacs for the dunes. The aeroplane was going well, it was gaining height, 60 metres at least. *Never before had we seen the aeroplane at such an altitude.* We were ecstatic!

It rapidly got further away, the sound of the engine fading almost imperceptibly. The weather was superb, the sea absolutely calm, in the distance the plume of smoke from the *Escopette*...and that was all.

Gradually, we lost sight of the tiny little black spot which carried our fervent hopes, and nothing remained except the luminous sheet of water and the radiant sun. We were truly overcome by the disappearance.[8]

Anzani, for once, had nothing to say. But it was all written on his face, and in his attitude. The broad shoulders stooped a shade, the usually flashing eyes showed only anxiety.

They hastened to Sangatte, and joined a great crowd that had gathered around the Marconi installation. There were French and English reporters, local people and tourists of both nationalities. Most of the English were supporters of Latham, who, reassuringly, could be thought of almost as an Englishman. All were waiting for news, but there was none. Hopes rose each time the tapping of Morse code was heard from within the hut,

Louis Blériot in the air near Calais on 25 July 1909. (MA 28707)

and fell each time, as nothing of significance emerged. The suspense for Leblanc, Anzani, Mamet and Collin was unbearable:

> In the end, and only then, a *Daily Mail* reporter, a colossus of a man, and elderly, came out slowly, very slowly from the little hut, with *un flegme tout britannique* which we found revolting. His face gave nothing away, but he had news all the same. He came forward, saying nothing.

He was greeted by a clamour of questions, to which he made no reply. When at last there was silence, the pale and impassive Englishman spoke:

> I am informed by the wireless station at Dover that an engineer of the Ecole Centrale de Paris…Monsieur Louis Blériot, born at Cambrai…piloting a flying machine of his invention…a monoplane, with an Anzani engine of 24hp, equipped with a Chauvière propeller…who at 4.52[sic] this morning left Les Baraques near Calais… has landed safely in a field at Dover Castle…[9]

He was interrupted, never to resume, by an explosion of joy. The mechanics cried in relief, and embraced one another, and amidst the excited clamour could be heard English voices calling for three cheers for Blériot.

★★★★★

But at Sangatte one man's story had yet to be told. A *Daily Mail* reporter did what had to be done:

> As I look back upon the crowded hours of this morning, I see against a background of radiant faces and enthusiastic crowds a tall, slim figure

with bent head and quivering lips and hands clenched in unavailing regret for lost opportunity. It is the figure of Hubert Latham.

Here is the story as he told it to me in a low voice, trembling with indignation and anger, later on.

M. Levavasseur, it appears, got up at two and at three. Each time he looked out of the window, shook his head at the weather, and returned to bed. About half-past four he got up again, and, partially dressed, went out on the verandah to see how the wind was then.

At this moment he heard a remark about M. Blériot having started, and simultaneously he saw a small dark object travelling rapidly over the sea several miles away.

The scene when Mr Latham awoke and learnt what had happened may be imagined.

When we were cheering M. Blériot I saw Mr Latham joining in heartily, like the good fellow he is. But it was a melancholy figure he made as he paced to and fro, while the mechanics pulled the Antoinette VII out of the tent.

But, alas! as the sun gained power so did the wind. Mr Latham, who had been standing about in a spiritless attitude, paid for a time little attention to the machine...the extreme tension of the past fortnight had told upon him severely, and this bitter blow coming at the end of it was having its natural, its inevitable effect.

Soon after, Mr Latham took his seat in the monoplane. But the wind was freshening every minute, and Mr Latham in a state bordering on physical collapse, M M. Levavasseur and Gastambide formally forbade him to start.

Mr Latham waited to hear no more. He sprang out of the car [sic], and, with the utmost difficulty suppressing his indignation and disappointment, he walked, alone, rapidly down hill, past all the people.[10]

★★★★★

The Saturday had been frustrating for Charles Fontaine. He was awakened at 3.45 a.m. with a message from Calais saying that Blériot would not start that morning. A few hours later he hired a motor boat to enable him to photograph the coast line and, he said, to pick out the highest point near the Northfall Meadow, so that he could use it to signal from when the time came. Unhappily the rough sea caused all the photographs to be spoilt, and Fontaine gave up and ordered the boat back to port. His account continues:

Although there had been no reply to my letter, I was convinced that Blériot had agreed to my proposal...I was at my post on the cliff at four o'clock in the morning...I was ready...

[later] I unroll the large tricolour which I have brought with me. 'That way', I say to myself, 'the first thing Blériot will see will be his country's flag. It will be his guide towards glory.'...I detect a vague noise, then a strange

humming....I see him getting larger as I watch. I recognize his aeroplane....Furiously seizing my flag, I wave it desperately, at the risk of falling off the cliff.

It is Blériot, [he] had seen my flag from several kilometres out at sea; he made a big turn. It's no longer an engine that rumbles: it's a trumpet which sounds victory...He is still flying. He goes over my head like an arrow, and over there, in the middle of an undulating lawn, he traces an arc, and like a bird which swoops on its prey, dives furiously at the ground. The flying man has landed. I run madly, shouting, beside myself: 'Bravo! Bravo!' Quietly, Blériot got down from his machine and came towards me. I embraced him on both cheeks…but this man, so fearless, so courageous, found nothing to say to me. His eyes were swollen and his eyelids blackened by the smoke from the ships, but there was a beaming smile upon his face. 'So, that's it!' I said.

'It's done', he answered, in the calmest tone imaginable.[11]

After briefly explaining how he had lost his way, Blériot rapidly changed the subject: 'And Latham?' he demanded. 'Latham is still at Sangatte', answered Fontaine. His paper put out a special edition the same day under the banner headline:

LE FRANCAIS BLERIOT VIENT DE TRAVERSER LA MANCHE EN AEROPLANE

Immediately underneath came this:

C'EST L'ENVOYE SPECIAL du 'MATIN' qui l'a accueilli SUR LA TERRE ANGLAISE et qui EN ELEVANT LE DRAPEAU FRANCAIS lui a fait le signal de l'atterrissement.[12]

(It was the special correspondent of *Le Matin* who greeted him on English soil and who, by raising the French flag, gave him the signal to land.)

The *Daily Mail* and every other paper had been expecting the landing to be on Dover beach. By the time they discovered their mistake, Fontaine had completed his first interview, and his colleague Marmier had got the first photographs of Blériot and his machine on English soil – with Fontaine and his flag.

The *Mail* implicitly recognized, with good grace, that it had been out-manoeuvred, but refused to allow anything to interfere with the joy of the great moment:

THE ARRIVAL
How M. Blériot came to Dover
Dover, Sunday.

Louis Blériot enters the company of the immortals. Starting from the French coast near Calais this morning, he steered his monoplane across the English Channel, and in thirty-seven minutes descended at Dover. He has accomplished what no man has accomplished, what a few months ago

Scoop! Le Matin's *reporter Charles Fontaine and his tricolour with Louis Blériot on the Northfall meadow, Dover, in the morning of Sunday 25 July 1909. (Royal Aeronautical Society)*

would have been regarded as hopeless of accomplishment, something seen at the end of a vista of dreams. His triumph is complete.

It is a triumph in which no factor that appeals to the imagination, to the emotions, to the reason, is absent. Splendid courage, superb skill, inventive genius, perseverance, enterprise, judgement, *sang-froid* – all these qualities M. Blériot displayed.

Moreover, M. Blériot made the flight in weather that was by no means ideal for his purpose…It was a crystal-clear morning, a dawn of rose and gold. But the cool, fresh breeze that blew in our faces when we went outside the hotel! And those foam-crested waves, telling of an unquiet sea! Surely no man would try to fly across with conditions so perilous as these! It is about five minutes by motor car from the Lord Warden to Shakespeare Cliff, towards which eminence M. Blériot had announced he would steer, landing, if possible, on the beach below. At twenty minutes to five I had reached the cliff.

At last the aeroplane came into view:

> In a moment we knew it was the monoplane, flying straight as a cannon ball, and flying, alas, not towards us but to the high ground behind Dover Castle, on the other side of the harbour…The next ten minutes were too exciting to be agreeable. I was in the motor car again, and Mr Igglesden was driving his machine at a pace which is by no means adequately described by the expression "defiant of the speed laws." We were in the town and through it in hardly more time than it takes to tell. We passed several policemen, who, instead of trying to arrest us, smiled amiably when we shouted "Blériot!" But the streets were clear.
>
> And then, just the other side of the castle we met an angel in a blue uniform who had seen the monoplane, and pointed out to us the right direction. He himself was running the same way.
>
> Up a hill, down it, along a stretch of level road, then another angel (this one in khaki), a providential open gate, a few bumps over a large meadow, and we came to the monoplane. It had just descended.
>
> Yes, there it was on the ground. There in front of us on a downward dip of grass lay the most wonderful thing in the world today…And there too was the Man. In the blue overalls of the French mechanic, the trousers torn, wearing a motor cap of the close-fitting kind that covers the ears and leaves the face looking like a mask, with one foot in a brown boot and the other in a slipper…he seemed as calm as if he had just got out of a hansom cab. He was smiling. There was happiness, triumph, in his keen, dark eyes.
>
> It was a moment such as one does not forget. On the way I had been composing a little speech of congratulation. It was not delivered. All I could do was to shake M. Blériot's hand.
>
> Already a crowd had begun to collect. There were half a dozen policemen, some soldiers, farmers, boys and girls from nearby houses, two or three Frenchmen.
>
> Everybody, I think, was excited to the point of incoherence. The Frenchmen were almost sobbing. M. Blériot was the calmest person there. At one end of the monoplane was a big French flag. It had been carried by two of the Frenchmen to the Northfall Meadow…These Frenchmen were the correspondent and the photographer of a Paris newspaper.'[13]

★★★★★

While this was going on, Alice Blériot was still at sea, aboard the *Escopette* steaming flat out at 25 knots. She had no idea of what had happened to her husband. He had caught up with the destroyer at 4.48 a.m., and had disappeared from the view of the watchers on board just over 10 minutes later, at 4.58 a.m. and 10 seconds. Alice was more anxious for him than she had ever been. She did not look up, she looked down:

From the bridge I kept the binoculars trained on the sea, fearing to see my husband's aeroplane with a red duster on its fuselage, if he had fallen into the water…Time passed very slowly…there was nothing to be seen. Within sight of Dover I saw something white on the grass, which I took for clothes drying. I was alone in the middle of all those men, reporters and others – keeping calm is not easy when one is young. Frantz Reichel said: "Didn't you hear? Didn't you see the smoke?" referring to the shells that were fired when the landing took place. The captain invited us to take a cup of tea in his cabin. No one could swallow a mouthful. Then we heard a disturbance, someone rushing down the stairs: "Captain, he has done it, he has done it!"…

We then stopped for the port formalities. All the men were slapping one another on the back, hugging each other, weeping…Then a signal was received from the admiral of the English fleet, bringing his congratulations. A dinghy came alongside. I was the first to go down into it to be taken ashore, and I had vertigo! I went down. I rejoined my husband with indescribable joy at five o'clock in the morning.[14]

Igglesden of the *Daily Mail* had taken Blériot in his car from the Northfall Meadow to the port. Fontaine, who had no intention of leaving Blériot's side, came in the car as well, holding his flag proudly aloft as they drove down into the centre of the town, and to the steps where Alice came ashore in the dinghy. Reunited, the Blériots were taken next to the Lord Warden Hotel, not without being stopped several times on the way to be photographed. There were cheering people everywhere.

When going into the hotel they were approached by two Customs officers. After briefly questioning him, they handed over an official certificate of the kind given to arriving ships, a Certificate of 'Pratique'. This gave the name of the 'vessel' as 'Monoplane', and stated that there were no infectious diseases on board.[15] This incident, reported all over the world, caused much merriment at the expense of English insularity and bureaucracy. In fact, the officers had acted contrary to instructions. The senior customs official at Dover, the Collector, A.S. Williams, foreseeing just such a consequence, had given orders some weeks before that:

> …the crossing of the Channel by airship was not to be treated officially by our officers…an attempt to impose Customs regulations on anyone engaged in experiments with aerial navigation would only tend to bring this department into ridicule without doing any practical good…

Collector Williams also foresaw, moreover, that:

> …a time may come when this department will have to treat their arrival seriously, and take steps to ensure that no opportunity be given for Revenue interests to suffer through indiscriminate landings of airships in this country.[16]

★★★★★

In response to a message from Blériot asking them to come over to Dover, Collin and Mamet packed up some tools and a few spare parts, and made their way to Calais. There they embarked on the *Pas-de-Calais*, one of the last paddle steamers to be used on the route. Leblanc and Anzani were also on board. It was a time, the first time, for the four to relax and to marvel together on the success in which each had played a part. But as Dover came into sight they grew impatient. As Collin put it: 'we wanted to see the *patron* in flesh and blood.'

Finally, they spotted a man, standing alone, arms raised, at the end of a jetty. He radiated excitement. A great cheer went up the moment he was recognized by those on the steamer: *Vive Blériot!* Collin was amazed by Blériot's display of feeling, and more was to come because as soon as they ran ashore he actually embraced them. So much warmth, from his reserved and habitually stern and preoccupied employer, was overwhelming.

Taken at once by Guérin of *Le Matin* in a Darracq taxi to the Northfall Meadow, Collin and Mamet instantly took stock of the damage to the monoplane, lying on a slope like an injured bird. One of the chassis' uprights was broken, as was one of its cross-members. One blade of the propellor was shattered into several pieces. There was nothing here that they could not easily deal with, but as they came closer there was consternation:

> We saw that a lot of parts had been removed by unscrupulous English admirers. Then a thing happened which could never have occurred in France. We complained to the policemen who were there and, within less than ten minutes, all the parts of the aeroplane and the engine which had been taken were handed back to us, as if by magic![17]

But no one worried about bits of the broken propeller. Fontaine had pocketed a piece, about the size of a matchbox, which he returned to Blériot's younger son, Jean, some thirty years later: it is now in the Museé de l'Air, as is a much larger fragment which bears Louis Blériot's signature as authentication.

There were moments when the mechanics were alarmed by the mass of humanity surging and pushing around the monoplane. When Julien Mamet left his shower-proof coat on the grass for a moment, it was seized and cut up into tiny pieces which were promptly handed round as 'souvenirs of Blériot's mechanic.'

Steps were taken to protect the aeroplane, first with posts and ropes; then early in the afternoon a marquee was erected, into which it was wheeled tail first. But before any of this had been done, the ground was so heavily trampled that all the grass was worn away except, of course, directly underneath the fuselage, wings and tail. Once the machine was moved, its replica in grass remained, sharply outlined by bare earth. This curious circumstance no doubt inspired the form of the stone monument soon to be constructed – a full-size plan view of the machine in granite paving stones – and it conveniently established beyond doubt the exact position.

The Dover authorities 'hit upon the ingenious idea of charging sixpence admission (to the marquee) the money being divided among local charities.' Apparently there had been an idea that money raised would go to Blériot, towards his expenses, but he had declined in favour of Dover's poor. Throughout the afternoon an endless file of people who had come from far and wide passed through the tent. When at last all the money was counted, it was found

The Blériot XI, showing its flotation cylinder, shortly after landing at the end of the Channel flight. (Harman Collection)

that twelve thousand people had paid to see the monoplane for a few moments.[18]

Meanwhile, the American owner of a London department store sent this letter round by hand to the editor of the *Daily Mail:*

> Sir, – While motoring in the neighbourhood of Folkestone today I learned that the wonderful little aeroplane in which the plucky Frenchman M. Blériot crossed the Channel could be seen.
>
> We immediately turned our car towards Dover, and motoring as far as we could completed the journey with a half-mile walk in the rain up the chalk path to the cliff near Dover Castle.
>
> There in a tent to which each paid admission we saw this epoch-making little machine. So greatly were we interested and so enthusiastic were all who looked at the bird-like monoplane, that it at once seemed desirable that as many as possible of the London public should also be permitted to see it. I therefore suggest that we place this aeroplane for three days in one of the floors of our store to which all will be admitted, without charge, of course.
>
> If this seems feasible to you we will pay the expenses of bringing the aeroplane to London, and in addition propose donating a sum of, say, £200 to any London hospital you may name.
>
> H. Gordon Selfridge[19]

Now Blériot wanted to get home as soon as possible, and his intention that afternoon was simply to get his machine packed up on board a steamer and return with it to Calais.

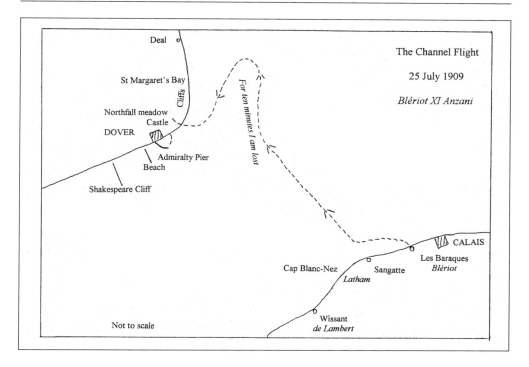

Deal

St Margaret's Bay

Cliffs

Northfall meadow
Castle
DOVER

Admiralty Pier
Beach

Shakespeare Cliff

For ten minutes I am lost

The Channel Flight

25 July 1909

Blériot XI Anzani

CALAIS
Les Baraques
Blériot

Cap Blanc-Nez   Sangatte
Latham

Wissant
de Lambert

Not to scale

But it was a Sunday, and the Dover authorities wanted to give him their long-planned official reception, and that could not be done on an English Sunday. Also, there was the matter of the *Daily Mail's* prize, which Harmsworth wished personally to present to him. And now there was Selfridge.

Sitting in the coffee room of the Lord Warden, a most reluctant Louis Blériot was at last persuaded by his then large entourage to change his plans. But on one point he was immovable: he would return to Calais that night, he owed much to Calais and he had given his word…He would come back to Dover in the morning, and the monoplane, well, London could have it for three days.

Hart O. Berg, the Wright brothers' agent in France, was in Dover for his own purposes. He of course knew Blériot – it was he who had invited Blériot to watch Wilbur flying at Auvours the previous August. When Blériot arrived at the hotel he had no change of clothes with him, so the American lent him one of his own suits, and an overcoat. Blériot washed and changed out of his overalls in Berg's room. Returning downstairs, Blériot found himself the centre of a continuous press conference in the coffee room and took some breakfast.

A flood of telegrams kept coming in. Among the first were congratulations from the French and British aero clubs, from the French parliamentary group for 'aerial locomotion', and from Hubert Latham: 'Cordial congratulations. Hope to follow you soon.' By a happy coincidence, because it was unrelated to that day's achievement, another telegram, an official one from Paris, informed Blériot that he had the previous day been made a Chevalier of the Legion of Honour. (He may already have been told this by Alice, as soon as she landed at Dover.)

Blériot began sending telegrams. The first, according to Fontaine, was to his father: 'I have made the crossing. Louis.' Before lunch he said, to general surprise: 'Tell Latham that if he comes over today I will share the *Daily Mail* prize with him.'[20]

After lunch he and Alice were driven to the Northfall Meadow, Blériot looking surprisingly rested, and smart in Hart O. Berg's elegant overcoat with its dark velvet collar. At this point he was able to dispense with crutches. With Leblanc he looked over the monoplane and smiled at everyone. Dogs barked and ran about; small boys chased one another, and the horses which had drawn the wagon bearing the marquee grazed contentedly. The *Daily Mail* reported the scene:

> M. Blériot was immediately recognized, and there was a cheer that equalled that of the destroyer's men. 'Brave old fellow' cried one enthusiast. 'Bully for you,' 'Well done,' shouted others, and then 'Speech, Speech,' the crowd all cried at once.
>
> M. Blériot, hat in hand, waited till he got to the middle of the crowd beside the monoplane. '*Vive l'Entente Cordiale*', he said, waving his hat in the air. The rudder of the machine was already covered with pencilled signatures of Doverites. '*Blériot est un brave homme*,' was one well-meaning effort.[21]

Then the Blériots went to the port and boarded the *Escopette* for the return crossing to Calais. Their longest day was not yet over, but by that time Alice knew, beyond doubt, that: '*C'était le commencement de la gloire*'.

Collin and Mamet stayed at Dover. That evening they removed the wings of the Blériot XI and placed them in the 'folded' position, for transport by train to London that same night. Exhausted, the two young men decided not to travel with it, but to get a meal and some sleep at Dover first. Next morning they took the 5.00 a.m. train to London.

At Victoria station soon after seven o'clock they bought a copy of the *Daily Mail* and were astounded to see their charge depicted, wings folded, already on display at Selfridges! Arriving hurriedly at the store, they mounted the wings and made a few repairs. Either that day or soon after Robert Grandseigne from Blériot's workshop also travelled to London, and perhaps brought a new Chauvière propeller.

Collin recalled the people who came to see 'the marvel':

> Imagine a queue six or eight deep, meandering through the immense shop, and outside stretching almost right round the building…continuing for four or five hundred metres down Oxford Street, under a steady drizzle…'[22]

That Monday 18,000 people came to see the aeroplane. On Tuesday there were 26,000, on Wednesday 36,000, and finally on Thursday, an extra day that could not be refused, there were 40,000.[23] Each day the store stayed open until midnight: on the Wednesday evening there was a private viewing for members of both Houses of Parliament. From 2 to 7 August the aeroplane was exhibited at the White City, during the Imperial International Exhibition.

10 Le Grand Blériot

Having reputedly burst one of her boilers in the desperate attempt to keep Blériot in view that morning, the *Escopette* crossed back to Calais at a more sedate pace. Blériot bought champagne for the crew, and spent the time giving an interview to the aviation correspondent Harry Harper, who would speak of this day for the rest of his long life. One of the things Harper remembered most vividly in later years was Blériot's delighted amusement over the encounter with the customs officers.[1] According to his daughter Simone, Blériot had the Certificate of 'Pratique' framed and hung over his bedside table.[2]

At Calais, two thousand people massed on the quay to acclaim 'their' hero. He limped off the ship, his leg hurting, to a delirious welcome of applause, music and flowers. The municipality gave an official reception, followed by a dinner at the Hôtel Terminus. Anzani and Leblanc were there to be feted too. A great many French journalists were present. As the evening wore on, tiredness caught up with Blériot and his leg got worse. He managed to get away from the party at ten o'clock and got to bed in a cabin on a waiting steamer. Alice continued giving interviews for some time more, but came on board before the boat left at 1.00 a.m. The sea was very rough, and the crossing slow. They docked at Dover at 5.00 a.m., having slept little, but were then able to rest on board for two hours.[3] These were their last moments of respite before being carried off on a wave of public adulation.

Although a few special editions had been published on Sunday, it was from the Monday newspapers that most people learned that the Channel had been crossed by an aeroplane. The event was reported in sensational detail. The *Daily Mail's* coverage extended over a page and a half, while an early tabloid, the *Daily Graphic*, devoted four pages to the story. If the latter caught the prevailing mood, with a full front page photograph of the aviator headed simply: 'BRAVO Blériot!', it was the headline of the former which remains, to an extraordinary degree, engraved in the English memory:

BLERIOT
FIRST MAN TO FLY THE CHANNEL

What is remarkable, in the present day, is not that this is all most English people know of Blériot, but that so very many know that much.

The reason the event penetrated the English consciousness as it did, and why it caused a greater stir in England than in France, was instantly highlighted by the leader writers:

GREAT BRITAIN IS NO LONGER AN ISLAND

was the discovery made by the *Daily Express*, while the *Morning Post* predicted that the news would come as a great shock to most English people, because the progress in flying made in only one year would lead to a major change in military strategy, and threatened the traditional means of defence on which the country had relied in the past. Some papers expressed regret that the feat had not been accomplished by an Englishman.

As for H.G. Wells, – the author of *The War in the Air* and much else – he was not just sorry about it, he was eloquently furious:

> This thing from first to last was made abroad... Gliding began abroad while our young men of muscle and courage were braving the dangers of the cricket ball...The foreigner is ahead of us in education...His schools are places for vigorous education instead of genteel athleticism, and his home has books in it, and thought and conversation. Our homes and schools are relatively dull and uninspiring, and to that we owe this new generation of nicely behaved, unenterprising sons, who play golf and dominate the tailoring of the world, while Brazilians, Frenchmen, Americans, and Germans fly.[4]

The Times offered Blériot:

> ...hearty congratulations upon a success fairly won by long and scientific study of the conditions to be satisfied, by careful adaptation of means to ends, by originality of views, by faith in his ideas, and, finally, by courage and promptitude in seizing upon an opportunity which others have missed. He has won by the combination of deliberation in planning with celerity in execution, which is the secret of success alike in war and in business...

A leader in *The Times Engineering Supplement* the next day, 28 July, was more clinical and detached:

> The successful flight by M. Blériot across the English Channel in his monoplane marks a distinct advance in engineering science. It is true that the passage across 22 miles of open sea lends to the achievement a certain amount of importance which would not be associated with a flight over an equal distance of land, for such distances have been traversed by monoplanes within the last two years without exciting a corresponding amount of attention. We have no doubt that other forms of aeroplanes are equally capable of a voyage such as M. Blériot has made, though to him belongs the credit for a notable achievement in practical aeronautics.'

As was to be expected, a more exalted view of the event was taken by *Le Matin*:

> One has perhaps the right this morning to feel a little French pride. After all it was France who, with Zédé, invented the submarine. It was France which created the motor car, it was the Frenchman Vielle who discovered smokeless powder, it was the Frenchman Lesseps who opened the isthmus

of Suez and began the Panama canal, it was the Frenchman Pasteur who gave science new life. We wrote in *Le Matin* on 14 January 1907:

Since there is today a new invention to be made, since the air in which the Frenchmen Montgolfier and Charles raised the first balloons should tomorrow belong to man just as the ground does, it is natural, it is necessary that this invention takes place on the soil of France, because it is a soil which brings good fortune to the human spirit. Blériot leaving Calais, quietly, for a little stroll in the air, and less than an hour later, alone and for his own amusement, invading the unattainable England and all the armour in the world could not have prevented it. *Vive la France!* Our special correspondent did well to salute Blériot in triumph in the three French colours. It is French genius which, this morning, has brought back another victory.

Le Petit Parisien adopted a more thoughtful tone:

When the moment comes when aeroplanes are fully practical, all the conditions of battle on land and at sea will be changed. War will take on an aspect such that one may ask oneself whether it will still be possible. Unless there is fighting in the sky, can one imagine armies and fleets ready to have a rain of destruction fall on them? The annihilation of towns will be a risk so terrible that governments will be obliged to draw back from the idea of war.

In Germany, there was a succinct riposte to those English papers like *The Times* which, while applauding the event in sporting terms, were reluctant to see in it any larger implications. The *Lokal Anzeiger*:

England is no longer an island. Those among the English newspapers who try to play down the importance of this event are not convinced. Blériot has flown as he wanted to. Within a year from today we will probably see a race taking place in the air.

As for Wilbur Wright, he admitted to being moderately impressed. When informed in the middle of the night by a reporter, he said that the news was worth being wakened up for. He added that a flight proposed by Orville, over hill, dale and woodland between Fort Myer and Alexandria would surpass Blériot's, 'because the air pressure over such broken ground was vastly different from that over the water, which was even' He said that he knew Mr Latham's engine was unequal to the passage across the Channel.[5]

★★★★★

At Dover, the Blériots' brief rest ended, and another remarkable day began, as Alice recorded:

Le commencement de la gloire: *Louis Blériot acknowledges applause as he is driven from Victoria Station with Lord Northcliffe on their way to the Savoy Hotel the day after the Channel flight. (The Flight Collection at Quadrant Picture Library)*

We made our appearance presentable and were given a civic reception by the Mayor of Dover at 8.00 a.m. My husband was obliged to sign autographs on shirt cuffs, collars, handkerchiefs, etc. Then we took the train to London…received in London by Lord Northcliffe at Victoria Station – arrival at the Savoy where a lunch for forty had been planned, becoming one for 400 – we had a magnificent apartment with flowers everywhere – I had never seen so many – grand luncheon – speeches – photographs – interviews all afternoon without pause – in the evening dinner (with Rolls Royce [sic] among others). I had to appear at all these festivities in the clothes I had travelled in, because we had brought no evening dress. That very evening the film of our arrival was shown at the Empire in London. Recognized by the crowd, we were greeted by the tune 'Marlborough'…The next day: the press, then a grand luncheon at the French Embassy…the afternoon visit Selfridges where the aeroplane is on display…The evening: grand dinner at the Ritz (Aero Club).

The Times on Tuesday morning described the Blériots' tumultuous welcome in the detailed and measured terms habitually employed on great occasions of state:

> From Dover the successful aviator, accompanied by Madame Blériot, travelled to London in a saloon carriage attached to the ordinary train due at Victoria at eleven minutes past one. The train stopped at Herne Hill, where a large crowd had assembled on the platform and loudly cheered M. and Mme. Blériot. But the crowd there was small compared with that at Victoria. People filled the space allotted to them in the station and overflowed into the carriage yard and so on to Victoria Street itself… M. Blériot, with his wife by his side looking very happy indeed, limped forward, and the two were introduced to Lord Northcliffe…More presentations followed, and then Mr Blériot, with Lord Northcliffe, entered a motor car and was driven away to the Savoy Hotel amid the enthusiastic cheering of the crowds. Mme. Blériot followed in a second car.

At the Savoy, the Secretary of State for War, Mr Haldane, greeted Blériot in French, telling him that his great success was due to his great courage. The British Minister's words were ecstatically received in France, where they made headlines next day, along with the statement: 'London gives Blériot a triumphal reception.' This led the *Times* in its turn to report from Paris:

> The cordial enthusiasm with which the 'invader,' as M. Blériot is called, was welcomed in England. is recorded with a gratification scarcely inferior to that with which the news of the triumph of a French aeronaut was first received here.

Before presenting the *Daily Mail* prize to Blériot (two £500 notes in a silver casket), Northcliffe expressed his congratulations at some length in both languages, remarking, after a long list of French inventions, and amid cheers and laughter, that: '…many ideas which we calmly assumed to be our own have, like M Blériot, come out of France'[6]

Blériot was no orator, and he understood little if any English, but he had a shrewd, instinctive sense of what the occasion called for. When his turn came to reply, he at once outdid the English in understatement, and they loved it. Speaking in French, Blériot said he was very much touched by the welcome that had been extended to him which he thought was out of proportion to what he had accomplished. (Shouts of 'No, no!') Hitherto France and England had been united by the right hand across the sea; now they were united also by the left hand across the air. (Cheers.) He raised his glass and drank to 'England and her King.' (Loud cheers.)[7]

Louis Blériot, wearing the ribbon of his newly conferred membership of the Legion of Honour in his buttonhole, photographed during the ceremony at which the Daily Mail *prize was presented to him. (Harman Collection)*

★★★★★

Messages of congratulation had begun to arrive at the Lord Warden Hotel on Sunday morning, and soon increased to a flood which followed Blériot wherever he went. Telegrams, cards and letters, at least 1,250 of them, came from all over the world, from friends and from strangers. There was no need to know Blériot's address: 'M. Blériot, Dover' would do, while a letter from Siberia to 'M. Blériot, France', was delivered punctiliously to his house at Neuilly. From the famous, the obscure, the altruistic, the self-interested, and the anonymous, the good wishes poured in:

> M. Blériot Dover Je vous felicite vive la France. Un anglais.
> Blériot Aviator Dover England Enthusiastic congratulations Aéro Club France for Glorious Crossing. Besançon.
> Please convey my congratulations to M. Blériot and my sincere wishes that aeroplanes may soon travel through space with the same ease as the electric waves which convey this message. Marconi Caronia Atlantic Ocean.
> Reply paid Blériot Savoy Hotel Strand Heartiest congratulations will you honour me by accepting my offer for smart suit to measure free. Shall I call with patterns. Ellis 201 Strand.

Bravo your name is chiselled on the cliffs of Dover and on the Walls of Fame
for all time. Accept congratulations from brother inventor Ernest Osborne
(Birmingham).

Brother Osborne followed this ingratiating missive with another in which he offered
unspecified royalties for the rights to manufacture and sell Blériot's aeroplane 'in England
and the Colonies'.

Among the messages were 120 letters and many telegrams in response to the following
agency report, which appeared in the *Star* and other papers:

It is reported at Dover that Blériot is offering £50 to anyone who will accompany
him back to France later in the same machine, says the Central News.

The wording suggests that this was not believed by the papers which printed it, and of
course the story was preposterous, but the response shows the avidity with which
anything to do with Blériot was read, because those few lines were buried in a dense
column of small print. Typical of the rather touching letters it provoked was this:

197 High Street Kensington
To M. Blériot, London
Dear Sir,
I have been informed that you require an Englishman who will cross the
Channel with you in your Monoplane. I shall therefore be pleased to accept
your offer. I am 26 years of age, weight 7 stone 2 lbs, height 55 inches and
of absolute Iron Nerve.
Awaiting your reply, I am Sir,
Yours obediently
H. W. Atkinson

★★★★★

Beneath the surface of the universal adulation, a curious little controversy was brewing.
Among the reports in Monday's papers were several stories presented in the first person,
purporting to be written by Blériot, some of them over a facsimile of his signature. (The
one published by *Le Matin* was given in Chapter 9.) There is no doubt that these accounts
of the flight were written up by journalists following the many interviews he gave on
Sunday – Blériot certainly had neither time nor inclination to write anything himself. The
various accounts differ on several points, and of these the most intriguing concerns what
actually happened when Blériot arrived over the English coast.

The article 'signed' by Blériot which appeared in the *Daily Mail* on Monday morning
contained this passage:

...steadily I fly westwards, hoping to cross the harbour and reach the
Shakespeare Cliff. Again the wind blows, I see an opening in the cliff.

> Although I am confident that I can continue for an hour and a half, that I might indeed return to Calais, I cannot resist the opportunity to make a landing upon this green spot. Once more I turn my aeroplane, and, describing a half circle, I enter the opening and find myself again over dry land. Avoiding the red buildings on my right, I attempt a landing; but the wind catches me and whirls me round two or three times. At once I stop my motor, and instantly my machine falls straight upon the land from a height of 20 metres. In two or three seconds I am safe upon your shore. Soldiers in khaki run up, and a policeman. Two of my compatriots are on the spot.. They kiss my cheeks. The conclusion of my flight overwhelms me. I have nothing to say.

The difference between that description and the one given in *Le Matin* was essentially that in the *Mail* he omits mention of Fontaine's flag-waving and states that several other people were present at the landing. According to the historian Michel Lhospice, this discrepancy upset the editor of *Le Matin* so much that he insisted on Fontaine persuading Blériot to sign a note repeating that Fontaine had been the first person to welcome him on land.

The *Daily Mail* no doubt perceived that it would be counter-productive to draw attention to the discrepancy. They knew, and had published as shown earlier, that Fontaine and his photographer were already with Blériot by the time their men arrived at the meadow. They did not know for certain whether Fontaine, as he asserted, had guided Blériot with his large French flag, or whether he had been the first person to speak to him on English soil, but it was a good story, so why not leave it undisturbed? Fontaine even managed to embellish it by claiming in his quickly written book that he had been the only eye-witness of the landing. And undisturbed it was for fifty years, at least in public. Then, in 1959, Alice Blériot gave a newspaper interview in which she was reported as saying that her husband had been alone when he landed. So, finally, after half a century, the record was set straight, or was it? Far from settling the question, Alice had unwittingly given it a new lease of life, because a few days later she received a letter from a Mr Leonard Mersh writing from Bournemouth:

> You are in error regarding his landing alone, I was the only one who actually witnessed the touchdown. I can see him now as he limped towards me with slightly bloodshot eyes and embraced me. We stood alone for some minutes then a journalist friend of his came running up with a big French tricolour flag which he planted in the plane. This gentleman could speak English and he told me he had been sleeping on the Dover Cliffs all night awaiting the arrival of Louis Blériot. I was a lad of fifteen years and had joined the Territorial Army as a bugle boy, this was my first night in camp on the Dover Cliffs, I did not sleep. At dawn about 3.30 a.m. I got up and went over the cliffs for a stroll on the way back about 5.00 a.m. this thing came in from the sea, I was scared until then I had not seen an aeroplane, I thought it was a flying bicycle, it crash landed almost at my feet, a piece of the propeller struck my leg, I still have the piece also a large photograph of your husband

and his friend talking by the crashed plane. The Police did not get to the scene for another forty-five minutes, I could not stop longer as I had to blow reveille at a nearby camp at 6.00 a.m. I would add that this incident inspired me to become a pilot in World War 1.

Yours very sincerely,
Leonard Mersh[8]

That soldiers were early on the scene is proved by photographs, and they are the persons mentioned first in the *Daily Mail* article attributed to Blériot, but Mr Mersh states that he was alone, not with other soldiers. Mr Mersh's description of Fontaine planting his flag proprietorially in the plane has a decidedly authentic ring, but his assertion that the police did not get to the scene for another forty-five minutes is certainly mistaken. (Blériot landed just after 5.17 a.m., and if Mr Mersh had waited for forty-five minutes he could not have blown his bugle in his camp at 6.00 a.m.). Mr Mersh's claim to have been the sole witness of the landing has not been corroborated. However, his letter does add to the already strong doubt about whether Fontaine was 'the sole witness', although it sheds no light on Fontaine's primary claim that he guided Blériot to his landing.

A categoric but not entirely convincing rebuttal of all of Fontaine's claims came in 1979, when the one person who could have been in a position to settle the matter – Louis Blériot himself – was reported by the historian Charles Dollfus as always having told him'…this man was not there and I never saw his flag.'[9] That conveys more exasperation than exactitude. It is entirely possible that Blériot never saw the flag, but Fontaine was on the meadow (no vast area of land) when he landed, he certainly witnessed the landing, and he was beyond doubt the first reporter to speak to Louis Blériot in England. Whatever else he had done or not done, Charles Fontaine had obtained a scoop thanks to his imagination and determination.

★★★★★

On Tuesday, 27 July, while Blériot was being lionised in London, a crowd gathered again at Sangatte. Hubert Latham had resolved to try again. The morning was calm and a trial flight was decided upon. It was a great and total success, Latham displaying immediate mastery of the new system of lateral control by wing-warping in several graceful turns. On landing to refuel before making his attempt he bent the propeller, but the damage was slight and by 5.00 p.m. the Antoinette was again at the starting point. After further checks, during which parts of the machine were covered to protect them from rain that fell steadily, he got away at 6.00 p.m.

Latham set off at a speed which amazed the enthusiastic onlookers, disappearing from their view after only five minutes. At Dover, informed by wireless, prearranged signals of ships' sirens and a special flag alerted an eager public. A crowd estimated at 40,000 rushed to the upper promenades and other vantage points.

Nothing could be seen for some minutes, but soon with the aid of powerful glasses it was possible to make out a dark speck in the sky which rapidly

The Mayor of Dover greets the Blériots before an enthusiastic crowd in front of the Lord Warden Hotel the day after the Channel flight, 26 July 1909 (Harman Collection)

grew larger and larger until the aeroplane was seen approaching quickly from the south-east at a considerable speed.

Fall of the Aeroplane

The machine came on steadily, its appearance being like an enormous seagull, but in a moment it was seen to make a partial circle and then dip, and it was evident that Mr Latham was in difficulties. At the time, the aeroplane was at a height which was none too high to clear the cliffs with success. After the manoeuvre by which the aviator brought the machine round, it again dipped and went ahead, and then, like a bird which has been shot, took a series of slight lurches and dropped into the sea. When the aeroplane began to drop the enthusiasm of the spectators was changed to consternation, and then as they realised what was happening there were cries of 'He's falling into the sea.' As the aeroplane struck the water, apparently just off the Admiralty Pier, shouts were raised and there was a wild rush along the piers.[10]

In the floating Antoinette, its wings dipping alternately below the surface in the strong swell, Latham stood up to show that he was all right. An armada of steam, sailing and rowing boats sped to his assistance: 'there was a great race out to the wrecked aviator', and he was quickly surrounded by would-be rescuers, French and English, naval and civilian. Although it could now be seen that his face was covered with blood, he did not care to be picked up by the first boat to arrive (a steam pinnace from the battleship *H.M.S. Russell*) but calmly selected a French destroyer to be rescued by. On board he was bandaged before being landed at Dover, where he explained:

> I had had a splendid flight across from Sangatte up till the time this accident happened, and at that time I seemed to be within about half a mile of Dover and I could hear the sirens of the shipping quite plainly. The accident was due to my motor breaking down in a very similar manner to that in which it did on my last attempt. The motor failed very suddenly, and my machine at once began to fall. Seeing that the monoplane must go into the sea I lay down in order to lighten the force of the blow as much as possible. The monoplane struck the sea fairly easily, but with greater force than on the last occasion, the descent being a very rapid one. It was this that caused the injuries to my face. I was wearing goggles to protect my eyes against the great wind force that there is when one is motoring through the air at this tremendous speed. My goggles were broken.[11]

A fuel pipe had fractured.[12] Latham's failure was touchingly gallant, and so very nearly a brilliant success. For the crash had occurred only sixteen minutes after take-off, and he had reached a point between one and two miles mile short of Shakespeare Cliff. Another minute or so, and he too would have crossed the Channel, second to be sure, but almost twice as fast as Blériot! What a way it would have been to even the score. As it was, people on both sides of the Channel recognized that it was Latham who had 'shown the way'. Thus the Paris correspondent of *The Times* wrote:

> It is no disparagement of M. Blériot's feat to say that M. Latham's first attempt, which showed that the crossing was possible, robbed Sunday's dash across the channel of some of the magic glamour that it might otherwise have possessed.

Latham had also shown that the crossing was difficult and perilous. Today, on the coast of France each man has his monument: Blériot's is an obelisk by the road-side behind the dunes at Les Baraques, now renamed Blériot-Plage. Latham's is five kilometres further on, at a windy spot where the road rises beyond Sangatte, just behind Cap Blanc Nez. It is a life-size bronze of a young man. The inscription translates:

> To the aviator H. Latham, 1883-1912, in memory of his audacious flights above the Channel, his admirers and friends have erected this monument under the patronage of the Aéro Club of France.

Latham was killed near Lake Chad on 7 June 1912, by a charging buffalo.

★★★★★

The successful cross-Channel Blériot on display at the White City, London, August 1909. (MA 295)

By the time Louis and Alice Blériot got to the Ritz Hotel for the Aero Club's dinner in their honour that evening, the news of Latham's second attempt and its result was known in London, and was the subject of sympathetic references in the inevitable and flowery speeches. According to Robert Gastambide, when Blériot went on board at Dover later in the evening to return to Calais, a silent passenger with a bandage on his temple kept to his cabin: it was Latham, who during the three long hours of the crossing heard the joyous laughter of the passengers on deck, celebrating Louis Blériot's victorious return to France.[13]

The Blériots slept at Calais, and at last, on the Wednesday morning, they had a few hours to themselves – a chance to realize that it was only a week since they had first come to Calais. In this brief interlude snatched from the midst of his triumph, as its crescendo approached, Blériot must have wondered what the future held for him. It was a moment when time stood still, when the flood of decisions rushing towards him to be made was for an instant held back. Around noon they took the train for Paris, as Alice remembered:

> We were acclaimed at every stop – there were even special, extra stops – a compartment had been reserved for my husband and myself, and another one for all the presents and flowers which had already been sent to us from here, there and everywhere…boxes of toys for the children, pyjamas for my husband…[14]

The Gare du Nord outdid Victoria. Fontaine, admittedly not a disinterested observer, speculated on whether the crowd in and around the station numbered 100,000 or 200,000.

From on board the train, where he still clung to Blériot and waved his tricolour at every opportunity, our intrepid reporter described the scene:

> A whistle blast was heard from afar, the atmosphere became heavy with billowing smoke, and slowly, with undeniable majesty, the Calais express pulled into the station. On the platform, the scrimmage was indescribable. People were jostling, and trampling one another. The train stopped, a door opened, and suddenly, drowning the puffing and whistling of the locomotive, an immense clamour arose. It was formidable, deafening, and getting ever louder, because the crowd outside realized that he had arrived, and without being able to see him as those on the platform did, shouted *'Vive Blériot!'*[15]

The delight caused in Paris by London's reception of Blériot made it certain that his welcome in Paris would be extraordinary. Forty or fifty of Blériot's employees were at the station to present an *objet d'art*, a bronze statue called *Le Cri de la Victoire*, which they had clubbed together to buy. Two members of the cabinet were there. One, the newly appointed Minister of Justice, Barthou, had before been Minister of Public Works and in that capacity had brought about the recent admissions to the Legion of Honour of Blériot and other aviators – including the Wright brothers. Barthou now congratulated Blériot formally on behalf of the nation on his 'splendid achievement which had increased the renown of France all over the world.' He added that Paris was waiting at the door to express its joy in welcoming a compatriot of whom all Frenchmen were proud. Blériot, too moved to reply, was then taken with Anzani and Alice to an open carriage: Fontaine and his flag occupied the seat beside the coachman. Then, escorted by a detachment of the mounted Republican Guard, and followed by a procession of carriages and motor cars they made their way through cheering throngs to the Aéro Club in the Champs Elysées.

In one of the carriages Alfred Leblanc kept an eye on the five Blériot children. In the tumult at the Gare du Nord their governess had been unable to get them through the crowd to meet their parents, and it was only at the Aéro Club that the family was reunited.

Of all the receptions and banquets given in Paris in honour of Blériot, with their endless speeches and awards of gold medals, none was marked by such breath-taking candour as the lunch given by the directors of *Le Matin* on 30 July. The Editor, Henry de Jouvenel, began his speech by going straight to the point which evidently preoccupied him:

> It's not for us to welcome you. The French government did that the day before yesterday. What we offer to-day, in all sincerity, is our profound gratitude to you for having wanted to remember that it was a Frenchman, a reporter from *Le Matin* who, tricolour in hand, first welcomed you on English soil...[16]

The Blériot monument at Dover, during a celebration in 1929 of the twentieth anniveersary of the Channel flight. (Royal Aeronautical Society)

11 Business booms

It has often been claimed, although never specifically by Blériot himself, that at the time of the Channel flight he was on the brink of financial disaster, and that only his success saved him from bankruptcy.[1] For some, he was already a ruined man when he took off from Les Baraques.[2] 'When he started that flight, M. Blériot had spent his last penny', said Sir Sefton Branker, then British Director of Civil Aviation, in 1929, at a celebration of the twentieth anniversary of the flight.[3]

Although Blériot had been using Anzani's engine since 27 May, by July it had not been paid for: some have interpreted that as a sign of inability to pay. The reason, it has been said, why Blériot entered for so many competitions that summer was that he needed all the prize-money he could collect. Without money provided by Leblanc, said some, Blériot could not have met the expenses involved in staying at Calais and preparing for the flight.

A charming and much repeated anecdote supports the view that Blériot was in dire straits. It was Alice, the story goes, who dramatically, if inadvertently, saved the situation. She had been visiting the home of neighbours where, with great presence of mind, she saved the life of a small child who was about to fall from a balcony. The parents came to the Blériots' house to express their gratitude, and the father got into a conversation with Blériot (resting at home with his burnt foot after Douai) which ended with him handing over a cheque for 25,000 francs as an 'investment' in aviation! With this sum, the story concludes, Blériot was able to pay Anzani and then go ahead with his entry for the *Daily Mail* prize.

No corroboration of Alice's adventure or of its sequel has been found, either in her memoirs or anywhere else. Moreover, if Blériot did receive the sum stated he certainly did not then use it to pay Anzani. At Les Baraques the latter, in one of his transports of rage and frustration over the weather, had threatened to take away 'his' engine if it was not paid for in full immediately.

Later, Anzani stated that the engine had been 'on trial before purchase' when used for the Etampes-Orléans and Calais-Dover flights.[4] Apparently the two entered into an agreement for the future supply of engines in some quantity, and perhaps one of the conditions was that extended credit would be available for the first engine, the price of which was probably in the region of 5,000 francs. Alternatively, Blériot may simply have delayed payment as long as prudently possible.

Parts of an interview given by Blériot in 1909 could be taken to imply that he was in financial trouble, but it is ambiguous. After describing his success at Toury-Artenay with the Blériot VIII, and the failures of the types IX and X which brought 1908 to a close, he added this:

On 31 December we took stock of the situation: the results achieved were problematic, but the expenses were certain: they were 780,000 francs. It was a disaster!

At that moment when I also took stock of my inward hopes and doubts, at that awful moment, I felt the true meaning of my wife's looks of reproach, and all the pitiful little fair heads danced before my eyes!

I must go on, because I can no longer do otherwise. I must go on because, like the gambler, I must recoup my losses. I must go on because it's certain, my calculations are right… and I should fly… I must go on…

I built the number XI, the last one probably: I made it with all the fervour of a shipwrecked man lashing together the planks of a raft. This machine was everything for me… and it was everything I was going to ask of it.

There was a great blow to be struck. Having done Etampes-Orleans was good, but not enough. It was necessary to attempt what no one else had yet been able to do - to cross the Channel. It's dangerous, certainly, but what of it! It's the best French way of falling into the water![5]

This tells us a lot about his general attitude, but the only specific piece of financial information is that his aviation had cost him 780,000 francs up to the end of 1908. Even that is uncertain, however. Discussing the costs up to July 1909 Michel Lhospice has noted that: 'according to indications given by Blériot or by others, the figures vary between 500,000 francs and 700,000 francs.' Fontaine mentions a figure of 800,000 francs.

An account book for aviation found in the family archives suggests, from the sporadic way in which it was kept, that Blériot could not in fact have known precisely what his aviation was costing, and that perhaps he preferred not to know. Many pages are blank, and the entries – all in Blériot's own hand – are intermittent, but at no time are any receipts recorded – only outgoings. One period when the expenses were put down systematically was during the months of July and August 1907.

Blériot wrote down payments such as: 'Bois divers' 193 francs on 2 July, and the same day three francs to 'Freins Bowden' for a cable. Paper, used for covering wings, cost 214.20 francs on 31 July. But most of the entries are the fortnightly payments of the wages of his workmen, of whom there were then about six. The skilled mechanic, Julien Mamet, earned 250 francs a month, while the pay of the apprentice 'P'tit Louis' Paragot was approximately forty francs a month, or twenty francs a fortnight. When he did make entries in the book, Blériot was meticulous. Thus when 'P'tit Louis' was paid on 1 July he was given only 16.50 francs, Blériot noting: 'He owed me 3.50 francs.' Despite all this attention to detail – at that particular time – Blériot did not even then go so far as to add up the columns of neat figures. He knew he was spending a lot of money, but he did not care to know how much.

There are two possible explanations: either he was irresponsible, which from all that is known about him is unbelievable, or he was not as short of money as has been supposed. Another discovery in the family archives indicates that the latter is the true explanation. This is a balance sheet of his personal net worth at the end of the year 1909. It shows that he owned assets, chiefly stocks and shares and commercial property, worth more than 1.5 million francs, then equivalent to about £60,000.

Alfred Leblanc learns to fly in a Blériot XI at Issy in August 1909. (P 47526)

This was a very substantial fortune, conservatively valued, which cannot be explained by the success of his aviation business from August 1909 when he began to make and sell aeroplanes in considerable numbers. In no way could profits in the last months of 1909 have been translated into personal wealth of this magnitude. It was a fortune that already existed, and it had existed on Sunday morning, 25 July 1909. The man who flew to Dover was not a potential bankrupt, he was a well-to-do engineer, which is not to say that he had not made great financial sacrifices for his research in aviation.

In France there is an old bourgeois principle: '*Chaque affaire est indépendante des autres,*' meaning that each enterprise [in common ownership] is independent of the others. Blériot was undoubtedly following that principle – to him it would have been a matter of instinct to do so. When he spoke of 'disaster' and the need to continue desperately to try to recoup his losses, he did not mean that he was ruined, but only that he had spent already on aviation almost all that he considered justified or could reasonably afford.

In her memoirs Alice noted:

> If he had not succeeded [in the Channel flight] then no doubt he would
> have had to give up aviation, because from a financial point of view he
> would have been unable to continue his experiments, which were very
> expensive, since he sought no finance from banks, preferring to meet the

costs entirely by himself…He worked out that his Channel flight had cost 780,000 francs…

Now it was time to get something to enter on the receipts side of the cash book.

★★★★★

Five days after his return from London, Blériot was at Issy-les-Moulineaux at five o'clock in the morning to give the first lesson to his first customer, who was none other than the redoubtable Alfred Leblanc. Just two years later 500 Blériots had been sold;[6] they went to countries all over the globe. Probably there were more Blériots in the world than all other makes put together. At the end of 1911 the French army had 249 aeroplanes: 175 of them were Blériots. The British, Russian, Austrian and Italian armies had Blériots too.[7]

Dramatic success over the English Channel gave Blériot an extraordinary opportunity to become a manufacturer of aeroplanes, and he seized it with energy and conviction. Orders for replicas of his number XI arrived by telegram and letter from many parts of the world. People in South America who had never seen an aeroplane ordered one from him. The first hundred machines are reputed to have been ordered within three months, although some say it was within two days of the landing at Northfall Meadow. (No record of these orders has been found.) The Blériot XI had a useful price advantage over its competitors: in August 1909 it sold for 10,000 francs (equivalent to the cost of a middle-of-the-range car) whereas an Antoinette cost 25,000 francs and a Wright 30,000 francs.

★★★★★

It is time to describe the product that would be the basis of Blériot's new career, the original Blériot XI, and to give some account of how it was made. The detailed design, a logical development from the type VIII, is generally considered to be mainly the work of Raymond Saulnier. Wood was the predominant material used in the construction. That is a fact which today may convey an impression of ease and simplicity, but this was far from the case. Great skill was called for at every stage, from the decision on what type of wood to use for a particular part, the selection of the actual piece (according to its original position in the tree, among other criteria) to the cutting, shaping, planing and finishing. An authority on the use of wood in aeroplanes, J.G. Robins, has pointed out that:

> Aircraft construction requires more from the natural qualities of timber than any other structural industry in which wood plays the major part. The highest quality material is demanded and its selection and preparation must be stringently inspected, therefore incurring a greater degree of wastage and expense.[8]

The Anzani engine and the Chauvière propeller on the original Blériot XI. (P 46891)

Failure to attain the standards this implies was not unknown. In 1911 the editor of *The Aeroplane*, C.G. Grey, wrote: 'I have seen wing-ribs with the bark still on them, showing they were cut from the wrong part of the wood…'

The fuselage of the Blériot XI is rectangular in section, with four longerons of American (Sitka) spruce. The vertical and horizontal struts, braced with piano wire, are attached to the longerons by U-bolts of a pattern patented by Blériot. These ingenious devices enable the struts to be fixed directly to the longerons in a flat joint, without traditional mortises which would weaken the longerons.

The original weight of the fuselage was 20.5kg and it could support at its centre a weight of 300kg without permanent distortion. At the rear the fuselage comes to a point, as seen from above, and here are fixed a pair of hinges which hold the rudder – there is no fin, the vertical plane is all rudder. The forward part of the fuselage is covered with fabric, the rear is uncovered.

At the front, the fuselage is attached to a 'chassis' of some complexity which will be described presently, and here also are the engine mountings. The fuselage contains the pilot's seat, the engine and the flying controls.

The wings, in contrast to the simple design of the fuselage, are of astonishing complexity, but with the saving grace that the leading and trailing edges are parallel, so that virtually all the ribs could be made the same length – not like the Antoinette, whose tapered wings required every rib to be different. There are two main spars (76mm x 19mm), and three shaping stringers, in addition to the leading and trailing edges. All these parts are of solid spruce. The ribs are hollow, built up from ash components glued together, wonderfully light yet strong.

The wings are concave beneath, and they are fully covered above and below with rubberised cloth of the 'Continental' marque. The angle of attack is about 7°. At rest, the wings are supported from above by cables attached to a steel pylon (the *cabane*) fixed to the fuselage in front of the pilot. In flight, support is provided by bracing wires underneath the wings. The tautness of all the wing bracing wires is adjustable by tensioners of a special Blériot pattern placed in each wire. The outer ends of the wings were flexible so that they could be warped. There are reinforcement struts of dowel, attached flexibly between the main spars, between the fixing points for the warping cables.

The tail-plane, apart from the rudder already mentioned, comprises a fixed horizontal stabilising plane with a movable elevator beyond it on each side. The elevators are linked rigidly by a transverse metal torque tube which passes through a housing in the stabiliser.

The 'chassis', a visually striking feature of the aeroplane, is a strong, almost square frame with ash uprights and tubular steel cross members. The two undercarriage wheels are sprung by elastic rope and swivel like castors. Although each wheel can move up and down independently of the other, the wheels are linked in their castor action – if one swivels so does the other. (Elastic rope was also used in some later versions to automatically bring the wheels back into line, but this probably did not work quite as well as intended.) The spoked wheels are derived from motorcycle practice, certainly adapted to take side loads. There is also a small pivoting rear wheel (in some versions with a telescopic spring). Thus all three wheels castor.

The flying controls comprise a central lever, or control column, leading down to a Blériot *cloche* (bell) placed at floor level, and a rudder bar operated by the feet. The *cloche*, a bell-shaped dome of aluminium mounted on a universal joint, had attached to it around its circumference at diametrically opposed points the control wires leading to the elevators at the tail and the warping wires leading through pulleys to the wings. The two kinds of control could be operated separately or together.

There were three kinds of movement:

1. Ascent and descent were achieved by using the elevator. To make the machine rise the control column, at whose foot was the *cloche*, was pulled back in a straight line. (The wheel at the top of the column did not turn – its purpose was to improve the pilot's grip, and it was perhaps also a safety feature in the event of a fall.)
2. Lateral movement – banking or levelling out after banking – was achieved by moving the control column sideways to warp the wings. What warping did was to increase the angle of incidence of one wing and reduce the incidence of the opposite one. To bank by lowering the left wing, for example, the column was pushed to the left. This reduced the incidence of that wing, causing it to fall, and had the opposite effect on the right wing.
3. Turns were made by a combination of warping the wings and pushing the rudder bar.

Business booms: *Blériot XIs under construction in the factory at Levallois after the Channel flight. (BL 195)*

The Blériot XI had reached its Calais-Dover form after a good many modifications. The change from an REP engine to the Anzani has already been described. Other important changes concerned the propeller, a fixed vertical fin, fuselage covering, the rudder and the dimensions of the wings.

When it first appeared, at the Salon in December 1908, the type XI had a four-bladed metal REP propeller. When the Anzani was installed it was replaced by a superbly designed and crafted two-bladed propeller made by Lucien Chauvière. This was carved from laminated walnut and polished to the standard of high quality furniture. The diameter was 2.10 metres and the weight only 4.5kg. The lamination procedure, requiring thinner pieces of wood, facilitated their selection, gave increased strength, and of course helped the carver by giving him a rough shape to start with, since the laminations were staggered.

At first a tear-drop shaped vertical fin was attached to the top of the pylon, but by May this had been removed and a higher rudder installed. At the same time, the front part of the fuselage was covered in fabric. Originally the wing area was 12sq.m, but this was increased to 13 then 14sq.m – while the wing span grew from 7.20m to 7.80m, and finally to 8.40m.[9]

★★★★★

Blériot's response to the clamour for copies of his aeroplane was not entirely improvised. Already in the spring of 1909 he had brought out an aeronautical catalogue under the name and style of 'Recherches Aéronautiques L.Blériot Ingenieur des Arts et Manufactures.' He had 1,500 copies printed, at a cost, including 'numerous corrections and changes', of one franc a copy. This forty-seven page booklet shows beyond doubt that he wished to make and sell aeroplanes. However, that first catalogue, not surprisingly, was vague about what he had to offer, with much space given over to discussion of the comparative merits of different kinds of wood and paper used in aircraft construction. Cautiously, a page or two were devoted to headlamps, in case they were what the reader was looking for after all.

A few months after the Channel flight a new edition appeared. The difference is startling. Now there are specific machines on offer, at fixed prices. A 'Calais-Dover' model, virtually identical to the original cross-channel machine, and with a similar Anzani engine, sold at the increased price of 12,000 francs. The number XII, with an ENV engine, was also put on sale. (but only three were ever made, and none was sold new.)

Not all the old ideas were abandoned. Blériot would still welcome orders to build aeroplanes to customers' own designs, just as Gabriel Voisin had done four long years before. This is how Blériot explained the two alternative ways of buying an aeroplane:

> We can always make aeroplanes of any kind, either according to our customers' plans or our own. The great experience we have acquired over many years in aeronautical construction, as well as our building methods, leaves us better placed than anyone to make new models of aeroplane, but it goes without saying that we cannot guarantee that such prototypes will work. The price of such machines is always negotiated individually with the customer, either on the basis of an estimate or according to the time taken.
>
> We can deliver several types of monoplane straight away, with a guarantee that they will fly. We give this guarantee only for machines built entirely to our specification. Any alteration requested by the customer annuls this guarantee.
>
> We particularly recommend the monoplane type, which we consider has less wind-resistance than the biplane, and is consequently more efficient. Another appreciable advantage, nowadays when one tends already to fly beyond the boundaries of aerodromes, is the great ease with which the wings can be fitted or removed: it doesn't take more than twenty to twenty-five minutes. Easy transport by road is allowed by a special system for holding the dismounted wings alongside the streamlined body.
>
> The only drawback of the monoplane is the great difficulty of construction, and consequently its higher price. It goes without saying that our machines can leave the ground under their own power, and the pilot can take off without leaving his *nacelle*.

Although Blériot was preparing to become a manufacturer before he flew the Channel, there is no firm evidence that he had actually sold any aeroplanes before then,

Louis Blériot in his uniform as a Lieutenant in the Artillery reserve. (MA 29865)

with the exception of one Goupy biplane built to the customer's design. It has been asserted by several writers[10] that he had sold, or at least received orders for, fifteen machines of his own design up to that time, but this has not been corroborated and the identity of the customers, if they existed, is unknown. It seems inconceivable that the aeronautical press of the day would have failed to report such spectacular sales, if they had taken place.

In January 1909 Blériot had received an enquiry from an engineer in practice in Berlin, asking on behalf of an anonymous client whether an aeroplane 'of your system' could be supplied. Rumpler wanted to know the catalogue price, and also the price 'for me', saying bluntly that he hoped the latter would be at least 15% and preferably 20% less than the former. He also asked to be appointed Blériot's exclusive agent in Germany. Blériot refused him the agency, and ignored the request for a catalogue price, but he did reply that the price would be 19,000 francs 'to him'.[11] No order was placed, but Rumpler went on to become an important aircraft manufacturer in his own right.

There can be little doubt that Alfred Leblanc was indeed the first customer for a Blériot aeroplane. The experienced and well-known balloonist was said by several of his contemporaries to have been very keen to learn to fly for some time. However, as we have seen, even as one of Blériot's closest friends he had to wait until after the Channel flight for his instruction to begin, and this took place on a replica of Blériot's own XI. It was the first 'production model' of a Blériot. The next one was delivered, also in August 1909, to Léon Delagrange, who had learned to fly on a biplane built for him by the Voisins in 1907, and had since become, for the times, an experienced pilot.

The demand that Blériot at first set out to meet was for single-seater aeroplanes for sporting use. But by September he was speaking in public about his wider vision for aviation. He was invited again to London – the festivities there in July, although impressive enough to be sure, had been hastily improvised, and there were many who wanted him to be entertained on a grander scale than had been possible at only twenty-four hours notice.

At a lunch in his honour at the House of Commons and attended by a distinguished company that included David Lloyd George, Blériot said, after speaking of his affection for England:

> I admit to you that I had also other strong feelings, that day, leaving French soil on my frail aerial boat I found myself soon, as in a dream, above that magnificent English fleet in which you justly take such pride. I dominated your ships; I saw beneath me all those powerful vessels, and I said to myself: what does the future hold? What do those courageous sailors think of this little bird which is passing over, a friendly bird that announces a revolution?…It is for you, as it is for us Frenchmen, to develop this superb realm of aviation for the great benefit of our two nations, and for the great good of humanity. Can you not catch a glimpse already, Gentlemen, not just of *raids* like the crossing of the Channel, but don't you see breaking through on the horizon, and very soon, real companies for aerial transport? And doesn't this prospect justify what I said to begin with about a revolution?

On the terrace of the House of Commons, a theatrically attired Samuel Franklin Cody sits on Blériot's left..
(MA 29085)

> Gentlemen, let me say that if aviation exists, it is thanks to England. You
> have made Blériot your grateful friend; by not allowing the ground to be
> dug for a tunnel so that one could come here in comfort, you have made
> those who, like us, have affection for you, find another way…[12]

Blériot had alluded, diplomatically but clearly, to the military potential of aircraft and, with unerring accuracy, had specified 'real companies for aerial transport'. However, the immediate future, back in Paris, lay with aviation as a sport. Men and some women, who could afford to, as well as several who could not, wanted to fly. For the first time there was a dramatically successful aeroplane of reassuringly small size and apparent simplicity of construction and operation to be bought, and moreover it came from the only aeroplane manufacturer in the world with a previously established and first class reputation as an industrialist and businessman. This, combined with Blériot's modesty, and his protracted and courageous struggle to master the air, meant that he was believed when he claimed that: 'Each component, each part… has only been adopted and definitively selected after experimental study and comparative testing carried out over long months of work.'[13]

Rarely can a new career have been more auspiciously launched. Blériot had so many advantages, both innate and acquired. Not the least of the latter were his skilled and trusted staff. Changing from an experimenter to a series producer meant that their

149

talents had to be redeployed, a process which gave many of them wonderful opportunities. Julian Mamet became a successful pilot, Ferdinand Collin was put in charge of pilot training, while Bertrand, Grandseigne, and later Paragot, had key management roles in the factory. Inexplicably, however, the design side was neglected: Raymond Saulnier was let go, and he joined Morane to found a famous marque. Weaknesses in design capability would be keenly felt later on, but for the time being business boomed.

12 Revelation at Reims

It was the *Belle Epoque*. There was no fairer place on earth to be in the last week of August 1909 than the commanding, lofty grandstand restaurant at the Reims aviation meeting. Well-laden tables covered stepped terraces. With a panoramic view of the plain of Béthenty, where 2,500 acres had been marked out for the purposes of the 'Grande semaine d'aviation de la Champagne', a diner could enjoy a fine and leisurely meal, accompanied by the music of a gypsy orchestra, and return Monsieur Blériot's wave as he flew past at eye level.

If there was one thing every man, woman and child wanted that summer, it was to see an aeroplane fly. While Blériot's Channel flight had inflamed the public's imagination, only a few hundred people had been able to see any part of it. But when Latham tried again three days later, 40,000 people watched in awe from Dover and its cliffs as the Channel claimed him. People would travel long distances, accept much inconvenience, and tolerate hours of simply waiting for something to happen, just on the off-chance of seeing an aeroplane fly.

When flying was said to be a certainty, and when there was a prospect of seeing not just one aeroplane, but two, or maybe even three, in the air at the same time, when Blériot would be seen, and Latham, and perhaps those two actually racing one another, there were the ingredients of what was probably the largest peaceful public event ever held until then in the western world. More than half a million people were there, including 250,000 on the final day. Reims was not the first aviation meeting, but it was the first to be international, and in grandeur it was unique.

In 1908 some clear-sighted magnates of the Champagne region had foreseen the enthusiasm there would be if they could organise races and other competitions to bring together a large number of different aeroplanes. Led by the head of the Pommery champagne house, the comte de Polignac, firms like Mumm, Heidsieck, Cliquot and Krug put up between them financing on a grand scale for an eight-day festival of flying, and guaranteed at least 150,000 francs in prize money. Nothing was to be done by halves.

A city of wood and canvas was erected on the vast plain of Béthenty, with its centre some five kilometres north of Reims at a small racecourse. A special railway station, Frenois-Aviation, was built on the line going north from Reims. In addition to the grandstands and innumerable restaurants, there were gardens, a hairdresser, a shoe-shine parlour, newspaper and tobacco kiosks, a florist, and the largest telephone and telegraph installation that had ever been set up for a public event, with special direct lines to Paris, London and Berlin.

Just as had happened when the motor racing track at Brooklands was opened two years earlier, the organisation of the air racing at Reims was based on the arrangements developed in horse racing over the previous two centuries. There were members'

The Blériot type XII with 40hp Anzani engine (P 48068)

enclosures, a paddock, a huge results board, and each entrant prominently carried a number. Stewards, and their inevitable enquiries, were also in evidence.

One problem which exercised the stewards was how to be sure that aeroplanes did not come into contact with the ground at any time during a competition. The rules were adamant – touch the grass and disqualification was automatic. In vain did pilots try to convince the stewards that, far from being helped by contact with the ground, an aeroplane's progress would be impeded because of the loss of momentum. They would be no more helped by touching the ground here and there than would a jockey who fell off his horse and remounted! But the stewards were understandably preoccupied by the idea that flying races should be won by flying, not by hopping. At first they thought each aeroplane should be fitted with an apparatus to record any contacts with the ground, but the technology for this was wanting. Instead, they hit upon a simple idea which worked perfectly: at intervals nine strips of sand were laid across the 250m wide circuit, and kept raked smooth. Any wheel, skid or wing-tip which touched the sand would leave its tell-tale mark. The stewards stationed at each strip had only to glance at their piece of sand each time an aeroplane went by, and if it was marked, telephone to the stewards' room. Twenty kilometres of underground telephone lines had been laid over the plain.

The great circuit – ten kilometres long – was rectangular, marked at each corner by tall, white-painted wooden pylons of simple but distinctive design. Unfortunately, these pylons were not easily seen by the pilots in some lighting conditions, and they consequently had to be attentive to other, more distant, landmarks as well.

There was of course no public address system, so in order to keep spectators informed on a variety of matters not covered by the results board, a naval officer among the officials

Revelation at Reims...nickel steel polished to a mirror-like brilliance: *a 50hp Gnome rotary engine on a test rig in 1909. (Royal Aeronautical Society)*

had set up beside the stewards' room and timekeepers' office what looked like the full-sized mast of a square-rigged ship. From the five spars of this structure, known as the *semaphore*, various flags and symbols were hung in frequently changing patterns.

The only problem was that hardly anyone knew what these meant. But wait – there is a small boy at that table over there who is explaining to his parents that such and such flags mean that the wind speed is so much...and so forth. Gazing over the restaurant, it becomes clear that every family group containing a boy aged between seven and ten is reasonably well-informed, and that everyone else is going up to them with questions. It is, notes the good Captain Ferber, 'an encouraging sign for the future of humanity'.[1]

But even dull-witted grown-ups soon learned that the white sphere which keeps being raised aloft means that a new world record has been set. This was the week when men flew further, for a longer time, higher, and faster, than ever before.

It was the fourth day, 25 August, that marked the beginning of the end of the Wright brothers' supremacy in aviation. It was not to Blériot that the honour fell, but to another Louis. For on that day a twenty-six year old aeromodeller called Louis Paulhan, who had first sat in an aeroplane just two months earlier, flew further and for longer than anyone had done.

The day started badly, with a violent wind preventing all flying. Then at four o'clock in the afternoon, when the wind had eased slightly but was still strong, gusting at nine metres per second, Paulhan brought out his Voisin. The major contest of the meeting, with a first prize of 50,000 francs, was the Grand Prix de la Champagne, a distance event. The rules required the contestants to have completed a minimum of 50km by five o'clock in the afternoon – then they were entitled to continue. Paulhan's bold move provoked his rivals to get into the air as well, but none could stay there. The best of them, Latham, had to come down after only 31km. Other ineffectual attempts were made by Blériot, Tissandier, and the one American pilot at Reims, Glenn Curtiss.

Meanwhile, Paulhan continued lap after lap with a regularity that dismayed those who had fallen by the wayside. Through binoculars he could be seen calmly operating the forward elevator of the Voisin, apparently unperturbed by the bumpy conditions and the difficulty of keeping a true course round the pylons. When, just before five o'clock, the semaphore showed that he had completed 50km, five laps, in 1 hour 51 seconds, there was a stir of excitement in the crowd. Light rain began to fall, dark clouds rolled up and blotted out the view of the distant cathedral, but Paulhan kept on. Approaching a pylon he was blown no less than 300 metres off course, passing the pylon on the inside instead of the outside. Making a wide turn he came back and passed it again, correctly. He flew on.

As soon as the semaphore showed that he had completed ten laps, a great murmur went up. Then each time he passed the finishing line in front of the grandstands people clapped and waved handkerchiefs, car horns were blown. Would he or would he not beat Wilbur Wright's world record? Had he enough fuel? Those in the know, standing outside the hangars, where all work had stopped, reckoned that he had, but only just.

When he was on his twelfth lap a white sphere was hauled up the mast. Paulhan had flown for more than 2 hours 18 minutes 33 seconds, and the duration record set by Wilbur at Auvours on 31 December 1908 was broken. Paulhan flew on.

Suddenly, half way round the fourteenth lap, at the most remote part of the circuit, he came down slowly and landed gently. There was no fuel left. Stewards jumped into cars and dashed to the spot. To stop everyone else doing the same thing, two squadrons of cavalry, 1,200 infantrymen and 400 gendarmes were standing by.

Another white sphere went up. Paulhan had also broken Wilbur's distance record of 123.2 km, by covering 133.7 km. Although not hiding the fact that he was by then very tired, Paulhan told the stewards that if some petrol could be brought quickly, he would take off again and fly back to the grandstands, about 3.5km away, so as not to disappoint the main part of the crowd.

When he glided down in front of the central *tribune* the comte de Polignac gave him a glass of...champagne, while the gypsy orchestra, in diabolic frenzy, played *La Marseillaise*. Everyone joined in the singing, flowers were thrown, and Louis Paulhan was carried slowly, shoulder high, back to his hangar, to tumultuous cheers.[2]

★★★★★

How, spectators asked one another, could Paulhan's brilliant performance be accounted for? Was it that the Voisin was a superior kind of aeroplane? Hardly, his was one of eight Voisins entered at Reims and the others did little to speak of, indeed they were quite out-classed by at least four other marques. No, the reason for Paulhan's success was a new kind

7187 B   M. PAULHAN ON BIPLANE.   ROTARY PHOTO, E.C.

Louis Paulhan, Voisin, who first revealed in public the potential of the Gnome rotary engine. (Author's Collection)

of engine of astonishingly radical design, the Gnome. Although it had been exhibited in 1908, not until the year of Reims could any aviator be persuaded to take the strange engine seriously, and even then the hesitation was such that inducements had to be offered, even to the needy. Louis Paulhan had obtained his Voisin as a prize in a model aeroplane competition, but it had no engine and he had no money to buy one. So it came about that he was ready to accept a Gnome from the Séguin brothers, Laurent and Louis, who had made it, on the basis that he would hand over to them half of the prize money he earned until the engine was paid for.[3] It soon was, because Paulhan went on to earn, it was said, one million francs in prize and appearance money in 1910.

The Gnome *Omega*, the model used by Paulhan, employed the four-stroke cycle, had sparking plugs and was air-cooled, but in most other respects it was radically different from all other aero-engines which had been used successfully until then. Most conspicuously this engine was its own flywheel – virtually everything except the carburettor rotated round the crankshaft. (This was not the first rotary engine, but it was the first to succeed in a full-sized aircraft.) An inlet valve was located in the crown of each of the seven pistons. These were spring-loaded poppet valves which were opened and closed by the difference in pressure between the cylinders and the crankcase, into which the fuel and air mixture was drawn through a hollow crankshaft, which was capped by the carburettor. The exhaust valves were in the cylinder heads and operated by pushrods, much in the manner of an Anzani.

Weight was designed out of the Gnome, and the design was executed with exceptional refinement – the Séguin brothers were members of an engineering dynasty celebrated for the originality and quality of its productions. The main material used was nickel steel, every part being machined and polished to a mirror-like brilliance evocative of a fine watch. The seven cylinders were machined from solid billets, and their walls were nowhere more than 1.5 millimetres thick. The 50hp Gnome of 1909 was almost twice as expensive as most alternatives, but its power-to-weight ratio was superior to most, and its cooling – such a problem in those days – was excellent. When expertly maintained – the adjustment of the inlet valves inside the pistons was particularly exacting – reliability was good. [4]

★★★★★

At this stage in aviation flight endurance was generally considered more important than speed or altitude. Now, thanks to Paulhan, and his Voisin-Gnome, both world endurance records were safely in French hands. Moreover, Paulhan seemed a certain winner of the Grand Prix, with only forty-eight hours remaining before the result would be declared according to the performances achieved up to that time. But next day Hubert Latham went out, and in wind and rain flew 154.5km in 2 hours 18 minutes. He was bravely applauded, but without the delirium that had greeted Paulhan. Few were in any doubt that the Grand Prix was won, and a boisterous party went on late that night in the grandstand restaurant.

Meanwhile, in Paulhan's hangar mechanics worked on through the night, fitting larger fuel and oil tanks but, as it turned out on the morrow, to no avail: the Voisin had been made unstable by these too hasty modifications. There seemed no chance now that Latham could be beaten, but that was to overlook the magic of Reims, where as the reporter Paul Rousseau put it: 'we go from surprise to surprise, from astonishment to astonishment.'

The repercussions of Paulhan's flight were not over. After seeing what the Gnome had done, Henry Farman bought one on the spot and immediately substituted it for the Belgian Vivinius engine he had been using earlier in the week. He then went out, the day after Latham, on 27 August, and flew 180km in 3 hours 4 minutes and 56 seconds. So it was the victor of *la boucle* who returned from a period of comparative obscurity to win the Grand Prix de la Champagne and to set new world records for distance and duration. Farman survived a stewards' enquiry, which overruled objections that he should not have used an engine different from the one he had qualified with. As for Blériot, he had managed to cover only 40km, and was placed ninth, out of the prize money.

Oddly, Farman's victory was an anticlimax, arousing little enthusiasm. Rousseau explained why:

> Henry Farman is an old sportsman, not born yesterday: he prepared his attempt the way a race should be prepared for. It is sufficient to be ready at the right moment, not before. Farman understood all that...He won, he was the victor. But his success was no masterpiece. It must be admitted that the public were not with him. In reality he merely complied with the rules: flying a flat course level with the ground and three to four metres

992   J. H.

ARCHDEACON

Henri FARMAN
Vainqueur du prix   KAPFERER

A 1908 photograph of Henry Farman, centre, winner of the Grand Prix de la Champagne at Reims in 1909. Gabriel Voisin is on the extreme night. (Harman Collection)

Blériot XII, 60hp ENV, with Claude Grahame-White at the controls, 1909. (MC 2177)

up, he never exceeded that low altitude, he did not give the impression of
flight, he showed none of the prowess of Latham and Paulhan. And if
Farman was the winner on paper, his performance yesterday did not show
us the machine that flies. This is not the one, or so it seemed, that will soar
over the countryside.[5]

★★★★★

Farman's uninspiring, although effective, way of flying brought home to the public
something which European airmen had known for twelve months – since Wilbur Wright
had flown at Les Hunaudières. This was that there were different ways of flying. The
British engineer F.W. Lanchester had offered a perceptive insight in December 1908 when
he compared the Voisin and Wright machines. Lanchester pointed out that in the case of
the Voisin, the designer's intention was: 'that the machine should be automatically and
inherently stable, and unquestionably he has succeeded.' But in the case of the Wright
machine, Lanchester said:

> It is claimed by Mr Wright himself that the (longitudinal) stability depends
> entirely on the skill and address of the aeronaut (sic); in fact, if we are to
> credit the account of Mr Wright's declaration on the subject, he does not
> believe in the possibility of safety, under ordinary weather conditions, being
> achieved by the inherent properties of the machine. He says that sooner or

The Belle Epoque: spectators at the first international aviation meeting, at Reims. (P 48274)

later the fatal puff must come that will end the flight...The position of the machine, with the leading planes fixed, is comparable to an arrow travelling feather first, and this condition is one of instability. In brief, not only does Mr Wright design definitely for hand-controlled equilibrium, but he has no belief in the possibility of making a machine safe by its own inherent stability. The success of the Wright method shows that there is at least more than one way to fly.[6]

★★★★★

Even without the technical insight, Lanchester's last point became abundantly plain to even the most casual spectator at Reims. The undulating flight of the Wright machines, rising and falling like a raft bobbing on one wave after another but in slow motion, could be contrasted with the slow, ethereal, unforgettable, side-to-side oscillations of the Voisins. Then there were the superb sweeping glides of the Antoinettes, the most bird-like of all, especially with Latham at the controls. Beside these the Blériots were unspectacular, keeping in the main a straight and level course.

Blériot's approach to Reims lacked the single-mindedness of the Channel flight. He did not, as might have been expected, simply bring along a replica of the aeroplane that had served him so well and concentrate on racing it. Instead, he seemed to want to hedge the risks, by entering no less than three machines, all different. There was a type XI, but also two type XIIs, one with a 60hp ENV engine, and one with a 40hp Anzani. The type XI took little part in the proceedings, perhaps because it had been built in haste and was not yet correctly set up. (Two other type XIs were entered, by Leblanc and Delagrange.)

Blériot's resumed interest in the type XII was perhaps due to its ability to carry a passenger, and he may have expected improved reliability from an Anzani engine, although in the end it was the ENV version which was used principally at Reims. Whatever the reasons, the type XII exercised a near-fatal attraction for its creator, but its days were numbered.

★★★★★

The hopes of Blériot at Reims rested on the Gordon Bennett cup. This event, although it carried less than half the prize money of the Grand Prix, aroused wider interest because it was an international competition between national aero clubs. It was a speed contest, the winner to be the competitor completing 20km, two laps, in the fastest time. There could be up to three pilots in each nation's team. The American aero club had selected just one pilot, Glenn Curtiss, on the basis of a good performance at Long Island a month earlier. He had come to aviation with an impressive record in motorcycling, as a race and record-breaking rider, and as a manufacturer. He is generally credited with, among other things, the invention of the twist-grip throttle control. He was the only competitor at Reims to have constructed both his engine and his airframe. The British club's nominee was George Cockburn who had learned to fly on a Farman just a few weeks before. He had no chance and represented his country by default. 'I feel as a Britisher,' said David Lloyd George who was there, 'rather ashamed that we are so completely out of it.'[7]

For the French aero club the problem was that they had to select a team from an entry of some twenty pilots and thirty-six aeroplanes. This was done by choosing the three fastest finishers in qualifying trials held earlier in the week over 10km. The resulting team consisted of Lefebvre (Wright), Latham (Antoinette), and Blériot. The inclusion of Blériot was based on a specific qualifying flight over two laps by his Anzani-engined type XII (race no.23), but as he was the fastest Frenchman over one lap on his other, ENV-powered type XII (no.22), he was given permission to use whichever of these machines he wished in the contest.

On 24 August the French President, Armand Fallières, visited the meeting amid dense protocol. He spoke to Blériot at his hangar and congratulated him on the Channel flight. There was brilliant flying that day but, unfortunately for the President, the best of it took place after he had left for Paris. Blériot, practising on his XII with the ENV engine caused a stir by taking 38 seconds off his best lap time of the previous day, handsomely beating Curtiss' fastest time to date by some 31 seconds.

The next day, Wednesday 25 August, while Paulhan was making history, Blériot and Curtiss tried but failed to improve on their best practice lap times of 8 minutes 4 seconds and 8 minutes 35 seconds respectively. On Thursday Blériot flew past the packed grandstand restaurant at lunch-time with a passenger, Alfred Leblanc: 'the hero of the crossing of the Channel carries in the air the man who organised the famous flight.' They were warmly applauded, as well they might be. Shortly after 6.30 that afternoon Blériot was returning from a short initiation flight he had given to Paul Rath, designer of the ENV engine. When preparing to land in front of the grandstand he saw a squadron of dragoons about to ride across his path. With a desperate manoeuvre he avoided them, but in doing so collided with the paddock rails. There was aloud crack as a ten-metre length of the wooden fence was shattered by the right wing, and the type XII came to rest tipped on its nose. Hearts stopped in the grandstand, but Blériot and Rath at once stepped out quite unhurt. Blériot's men worked all night to repair the badly damaged machine, successfully, because it was then able to do a lap in the good time of 8 minutes 4 seconds. The following day Curtiss put in a lap of 8 minutes 9 seconds.

At last, on Saturday 28 August, came the final contest for the Gordon Bennett cup. At 11.45 a.m. Curtiss made his attempt – 20 km against the clock. His first lap was covered in 7 minutes 57 seconds and the second in 7 minutes 53 seconds. While he was in the air Blériot, on his ENV type XII did a practice lap in 7 minutes 58 seconds.

Suddenly it was apparent that an extremely close contest was taking place. Moreover it was a duel, because no one else could approach the times of the American and the leading Frenchman. The rules allowed only one attempt, so Curtiss had no chance to improve his time. The result would depend entirely on the time Blériot could achieve. In the restaurant in the grandstand every place was taken. Cars, cycles and pedestrians choked the roads for miles around. Overloaded special trains arrived every four minutes at the temporary station.

At 2.00 p.m. Blériot made another attempt at the lap record, but managed only 8 minutes 14 seconds. The wind was then rising and he would not yet commit himself to his cup attempt, knowing that the rules gave him until 5.00 p.m. for that one chance. After some mechanical adjustments had been made at his hangar, he tried again at 2.30 p.m. to do one fast lap, but came down after only one kilometre. Ominously, the ENV was misbehaving, and the mechanics struggled anxiously with it throughout that torrid afternoon. It began to look as if Curtiss would win by default, but at the very last moment Blériot got away, as the hands of the clock taunted Curtiss.

The drama was not over, it was just beginning, for Blériot did his first lap in 7 minutes 53 seconds, exactly the same time as Curtiss' best lap. Alas for Blériot and for France, the second lap took 8 minutes 3 seconds and it was all over – Curtiss had won by a margin of 6 seconds, with an aggregate time of 15 minutes 50 seconds. (As for the best of the Wright machines, its time was 20 minutes 47 seconds.)

The sad irony for Blériot was that only an hour later he took out the same aeroplane again and did a lap in 7 minutes 47 seconds – 77 kph – thus securing the prize of 7,000 francs for the fastest single lap of the meeting, and reaching the highest speed ever officially recorded for an aeroplane up to that time.

There is an anecdote, related by Blériot's mechanic Collin, that Blériot, in an excess of friendliness, sealed his own fate in the Gordon Bennett cup by advising Curtiss to fit a smaller fuel tank and carry only a minimum of fuel in order to save precious weight.

A versatile speed merchant in his prime: Glenn Hammond Curtiss at Reims in August 1909, when he won the Gordon Bennett cup. He is generally credited with the invention of the twist grip throttle for motorcycles in around 1903. In 1907 he was acclaimed as 'the fastest human' after setting a new world speed record for motorcycles of 220kph in Florida. (MC 105)

Reims: Blériot's long-time manager in England, Norbert Chéreau, facing camera, with, on his left, Lord Northcliffe, owner of the Daily Mail; Sir Henry Norman, a prominent scientific adviser to the Government; and David Lloyd George, the Chancellor of the Exchequer and a future Prime Minister. The British establishment was beginning to take notice of aviation. (P 48113)

Blériot may well have said that, but it is rather difficult to believe that Curtiss would not have thought of the idea himself. His background in motorcycle speed events at the highest level would surely have made such points second nature to him.

But the meeting was not yet over, one day remained. Blériot described how, on Sunday 29 August, the historic occasion ended for him:

> Fortunately I was flying quite low, when suddenly my engine stalled. Flames shot from it, immediately setting the aeroplane on fire. I don't know why or how. But I made an abrupt forced landing at 80kph. I was covered in flames but managed to protect my face. However, in the fall I hurt my forehead, bruised my shoulder, and above all was badly shaken. I consider myself very fortunate to have come off so lightly, and to have been able to get out of the machine, which was utterly destroyed.[8]

The type XII ENV, which the previous day had been all but unbeatable, was reduced to ashes before the bemused eyes of Louis Blériot, who had got to his feet unaided after rolling on the ground to put out the flames from his overalls.

★★★★★

Léon Delagrange with his Blériot XI, the first to be fitted with a Gnome engine. Contrary to what became the usual practice, the propeller is mounted behind the engine. 1909. (MA 29571)

Of all the wonders which came out of Reims, the most marvellous beyond doubt was the Gnome engine. A revelation, it burst upon the scene of struggling aviation, transforming the performance of every machine it powered. Blériot did not at once get one for his model XI. His omission to do so may have been partly due to caution induced by the daring of the design, or perhaps because his hands were for a time tied by a commitment to Anzani to take up a considerable number of his engines. But above all, he would have been concerned by the structural implications for his entire airframe of installing an engine of double the power.

Unfortunately, no such prudence restrained Léon Delagrange, a customer who would not wait, and so became the first to put a Gnome in a Blériot. It is easy to imagine that to this sculptor the aesthetic appeal of the Gnome was irresistible – it was an object to be admired as a work of art. If that were not enough, there was the expectation that it would turn the type XI into a 100kph aeroplane. But the attraction proved fatal. Soon after, on 4 January 1910, at Croix-d'Hins near Bordeaux, Delagrange was killed in this machine, in circumstances heavy with consequences which will be described later. Not until November 1910 did Blériot begin to supply type XIs with Gnomes as original equipment. Jacques Balsan was the first customer for what was to be a long line of factory-built Blériot Gnomes.

★★★★★

'Our factories were under-employed, now they have been invaded by a river of gold!', wrote Ferber after Reims. But the river would keep on flowing, Blériot knew, only for those whose products were successful, and were seen to be so. This could not be achieved, in the autumn of 1909, by more distance flights across land or sea because insufficient technical progress had been made to enable any journey more difficult than the Channel crossing to be undertaken with confidence. A time for solitary exploits would return to aviation, but now, with the brilliance of Reims as its guiding star, the time of the meetings had come.

There was no alternative to the competition and intense publicity they offered, and for Blériot hard-pressed as he was by the demands of a rapidly expanding business, there was that year no alternative to piloting himself, and taking time away from the factory to travel to venues all over Europe.

Thus September found him at Brescia, and October in Budapest and Bucharest making the first aeroplane flights ever in Hungary and Romania, always using a type XI with an Anzani engine. Promoters paid him large sums, but they were to be hard-earned. In December at Istanbul, before a large, unruly and extremely impatient crowd he took the risk of flying in a violent and erratic wind, fighting for control and being blown about like a leaf before Collin's horrified eyes. Losing height, the Blériot came down hard on the roof of a house in the Greek quarter. Somehow, Blériot got himself out, despite internal injuries, broken ribs and various superficial injuries. By the time Collin reached the garden into which the machine had tumbled, the injured man had been carried off in a sedan chair to the French hospital, where in three weeks he made an apparently good recovery.[9] However, he was warned that he would probably suffer adverse consequences in later life.

The wreckage of Blériot's aeroplane lies in the garden of a house in Istanbul on 12 December 1909. This was his last and most serious accident, and its long-term consequences probably shortened his life. (MA 29080)

Thereafter, Blériot made only infrequent flights in public, and he did not take part as a pilot in any major meetings or displays. However, he continued for many years to fly for his own enjoyment, and was particularly fond of skimming low over La Beauce at harvest time, just two or three metres above the corn stubble, often at the end of the day.

13 Onward and upward

The interval between the first Reims meeting and the beginning of the First World War was five years, almost to the day. No subsequent five-year period was to see such progress in the performance of aeroplanes and the spread of aviation throughout the world. The world records are eloquent. The highest speed attained at Reims was 77kph – by Blériot: by the time war broke out the record stood at 203.60kph – set in 1913 by Prévost on a Deperdussin – more than two and a half times faster. Aeroplanes had begun to go faster than cars. Henry Farman's distance record at Reims of 180km had been increased almost six-fold, to 1,021km, by Séguin – also on a Farman. However, it was in altitude that progress seemed to border on the miraculous, for where Latham had amazed people in 1909 by attaining 155 metres at Reims, the height reached by Legagneux on a Nieuport at St Raphael in 1913 was nearly forty times more – 6,120 metres.[1]

During that time the making of aeroplanes evolved from a craft activity into a complete industry. Annual production in France increased more than seven-fold – from 57 aircraft in 1909 to 411 in 1913. In other countries too, aircraft were built in growing numbers, notably in Russia, Germany, Italy, the United Kingdom and the USA. French manufacturers set up factories within most of those markets, but indigenous design and production also became established.

These years saw immense development in flying schools, the first use of parachutes from aircraft, the comprehensive development of aerobatics – largely by one man – the creation of the seaplane, and many other examples of innovative thinking about the design and uses of aircraft. They also saw the demise of the Wright type of aeroplane, and a series of at first unexplained catastrophes with monoplanes of the Blériot type which might have made the marque as obsolete as the Wright Flyer, but did not. These too were years of bitter and protracted litigation in many countries over alleged infringements of patents on virtually every kind of apparatus used in powered flight.

But despite all the progress and its tumultuous accompaniments, aviation throughout those five years continued to conceal the greater part of what it had in store. The main ultimate uses of the aeroplane remained obscure, and in some ways progress was more apparent than real. As the economics historian Emmanuel Chadeau has pointed out perceptively: 'Ultimately, meetings had the perverse effect of encouraging prowess to the detriment of the development of practical applications of the aeroplane.' He also noted that: 'Attempts to create a civil market failed more or less completely in 1911-13. The creation of a military market began in 1910, and was confirmed between 1911 and 1914'[2]

However, that early military market had an exceedingly narrow view of the roles, if any, aircraft might perform, and isolated examples of employment of aeroplanes in colonial conflicts did little to enlarge this. It was not until experience was gained of hostilities in which both sides possessed aeroplanes that their full military potential came to be generally recognized, and to evolve, but this did not happen until after August 1914.

Sport and 'tourism' did not suffice to generate a stable and sizeable civil market, and in those last years before the First World War the aeroplane never gave more than rare fleeting glimpses of its true destiny, which would be to carry great numbers of people over great distances, at a speed, on a scale, and at a price which would change the world.

★★★★★

In all the triumphs and disasters of aviation in those years, in all its tentative strivings to find its place, no man did more for it than Louis Blériot. His energy and example had influence in every country where aviation sprang into being. Only one design of aeroplane survived in readily recognizable form from 1909 to 1914: it was the Blériot XI. Almost immediately after his Channel flight Blériot became the world's leading aircraft manufacturer, a position he maintained throughout the period. Not the least of the reasons for this pre-eminence was his early recognition of the value of providing organized training for pilots. The rosters of the Blériot schools are a truly international *Who's Who* of aviation, a vast assembly whose influence as customers, or simply as proud and loyal alumni, lasted well into the 1920s and beyond. But Blériot did more than just recognize the potential harvest that might be reaped from pilot training, he quickly committed substantial human and financial resources to it, and did so at a time when his small initial manufacturing capacity was fully stretched to meet the first great surge of demand for copies of the machine which had flown the Channel. The whole-hearted development of training facilities – in different parts of France to enable work to continue in winter as well as summer – was accompanied by some subtlety in his approach to potential clients. His catalogue of 1911 contains three pages of advice about learning to fly, written with the tongue-in-cheek presumption that the pupil will be teaching himself.

A clever balance is maintained between making flight sound easy enough for an ordinary mortal to actually achieve, and on the other hand emphasizing difficulties and the need for prudence and attention to detail. Thus we read that the first thing the aviator should do, having positioned his aeroplane: 'if possible' facing into the wind, and shouted to his assistants to let go of the tail (chocks were not yet in use) is to:

> Advance the control column slightly so that the tail of the machine rises until the fuselage is exactly horizontal. The angle of attack of the wings is thus almost completely eliminated and they offer no resistance to forward motion, acceleration is then very rapid. When the pupil has completed several straight runs in this manner, and when he feels thoroughly in control, he may attempt to rise a little. For this he must have at least one kilometre clear in a straight line before him. When he feels that the fuselage is definitely horizontal, he should bring the control wheel gently towards him, in order to incline the elevator, and the machine will leave the ground. He must then immediately put the *cloche* back into the vertical position, that is to say in neutral. If the engine stops suddenly at a certain height, the aviator must not lose his *sang-froid* and above all not pull on the control column, because then the machine, loosing its speed, will fall back heavily onto the ground, tail first....

After all this, at just the right psychological moment, the reader turns the page and is told:

> To put into practice all the advice we have just given about learning, we have established in France two Schools of Piloting: one at Pau, the other at Etampes. Our school at Pau operates during the winter, when the weather does not allow flying in the neighbourhood of Paris. We have chosen Pau because of its quite exceptional situation, and because of its ideal winter temperatures. When the fine weather returns we bring our school back to Etampes, sixty kilometres from Paris, in the great plain of La Beauce, well-suited to enable young aviators to make fine flights, while running as few risks as possible. We have just opened at Hendon, near London, a third school for our customers in England...

A few would-be aviators, however, seem to have taken the catalogue's advice more literally than was intended – in any event they resolved not to go to school, but to teach themselves to fly. One such was a Yorkshireman, Percy Richardson. In August 1909 he had:

> ...motored over to the aviation meeting held at Reims....learning as much as was possible for a spectator who had to bluff his way into that strictly guarded paddock...each day getting keener until I worked myself up to order a flying machine....My choice settled on a Blériot monoplane of the Cross-Channel type.

The first time he taxied the aeroplane Richardson inadvertently took off:

> At first I felt rather alarmed, but then, gathering my wits together, decided the best thing to do was to stay up for a short distance and then come gracefully down, so I put all the theories I had collected into practice with a view to staying at the height I had reached (which I presumed was only just clear of the ground) so I could make an easy and safe landing. For some reason or other, which I expect I shall learn in the future, theory and practice did not seem to agree, and the machine continued to rise until my experience seemed to indicate the possibility of "looping the loop" backwards; so I thought it time to do something drastic. I did this by altering the angle of the elevating planes so as to bring the machine down, and sure enough it came surprisingly quickly. I landed with rather a hard bump on the near-side front wheel which immediately collapsed. However, I had flown...[3]

In April 1910 Richardson, or anyone else who wanted to start flying in England, had no choice but to teach himself, for there were then no flying schools in the country. Despite much optimistic publicity, by August of that year the situation had in reality scarcely improved, as another aspirant, one Maurice Ducrocq, was to discover:

> I began operations by a close survey of all schools and so-called schools of aviation in England. I mention no names, but there is no harm in saying that

last August there were no schools actually in being within easy reach of London. One there was which had neither engine nor pilot; another had an aeroplane but no engine; another had an engine but no pilot; another, even others, had insufficient engines, or planes which declined (very properly) to take to the air.[4]

More fortunate were those who lived in France or who were in a position to go there, like Claude Grahame-White. Blériot leased large tracts of land, first at Etampes and then at Pau, on which hangars and other buildings were erected. The investment was considerable, especially in the context of only seasonal use of each facility. More important than money, Blériot also assigned some of his best men to the management of schools, at considerable sacrifice to the manufacturing and commercial sides of the business. Alfred Leblanc, no less, spent substantial periods of time at Pau, and the pioneering school at Etampes was placed in the hands of Ferdinand Collin, the mechanic. He seems a strange choice, someone who apparently never became a keen or experienced pilot himself. Although he worked like a demon, sometimes twenty hours a day, and made a success of his new role, one cannot but wonder whether he might not have made a still greater contribution back at the factory in Paris. The fact that he was sent to Etampes may denote that the long, sad, and obscure process of his estrangement from the *patron* had already begun. But then Blériot had a just handful of trusted and competent men from whom to choose.

Collin recalled how in the spring of 1910 he had searched the plain of La Beauce in Blériot's old Panhard searching for a suitable site for an aerodrome and school. At last he chose an area of some sixty hectares, lying beside the Route Nationale from Paris to Orléans, some six kilometres beyond Etampes near the farm called Mondésir, where Blériot had 'stabled' his monoplane the previous July before the famous flight to Orléans. A little later, Blériot announced to Collin that they would go together to the place he had found, to make a start. The younger man remembered Blériot leaving him there that evening, saying:

> There you are, you are in charge of the school, of the hangars that are going to be built, of the aeroplanes, of the supplies, of the staff, and of the pupils I will send you. *Au revoir*, Collin, sort things out for yourself and work hard.[5]

So the twenty-six year old mechanic was left alone with, as he put it: '...my radiant enthusiasm and a beautiful field of grass.' He soon had hangars put up, engaging for the task young unskilled men of the neighbourhood, whom he found more agile and open-minded than experienced construction workers, but he had to train them. Soon the first aeroplanes arrived, and it was at once evident why a first-class mechanic was needed at Étampes, for they were in a sorry state, being second or third-hand machines which Blériot had taken in part exchange for new ones. A British pupil, Lieutenant Reginald Cammell, arrived at the end of June, and found the flying ground 'in its earliest state of establishment.' The surface was extremely rough:

> ...which would render preliminary essays very expensive, as breakages were certain. There are absolutely no facilities for repair here beyond the little

portable tool chests which the mechanics carry about with them, and no spare parts, so that if any serious breakdown occurs the machine has to go off to Paris.

Within two weeks, Cammell was able to report much progress in developing the aerodrome. The grass had been cut and a circular track rolled:

> ...so that it is now quite respectably smooth for ground trials. There is also an instructor, and tools and spare parts are gradually arriving. There are also three pupils, whose first lessons I have watched. It seems fairly simple, all having flown at the third or fourth try.[6]

In the midst of his many other tasks Collin had not had much time to work out how to turn himself into 'the instructor', but the idea came to him of dividing the training into four stages. The first was to learn how to operate the engine with the machine stationary, sitting in the slipstream and in a spray of castor oil. The second was to taxi in a straight line on the ground using one control only – the rudder. The third stage – and it was a large one not lending itself to sub-division – was to take off, fly at an altitude of between one and six metres, and land again, all more or less in a straight line. The fourth stage was to meet the requirements for the *brevet* (licence) of the Aéro Club, which would evolve as aviation developed. In 1909 – the year was well advanced when the rules were established – the applicant was required to fly three circles of one kilometre each, all on different days. From the beginning of 1910 the length of the circuits was increased to five kilometres, and landings had to be made within 150 metres of a designated point. In January 1914 an additional test was introduced – flying two figures of eight at a height of 100 metres – and landings had to be made just 50 metres from the chosen point.

The time taken to acquire the *brevet*, according to Collin, varied between eight days for the most apt pupils favoured by good weather to six weeks for the most refractory suffering the added handicap of bad weather. The actual time spent in aeroplanes by pupils totalled only two to five hours, in lessons lasting ten to fifteen minutes at a time. It was important, Collin found, for pupils to have intervals between lessons in which to think over and discuss their experiences and problems. Surprisingly, it was not the third or the fourth stage of Collin's programme that caused pupils the greatest difficulty, but the second. When taxiing the Blériot XI was as disinclined to follow a straight path as many a modern supermarket trolley, and for the same reason. The castor action of the wheels gave immense advantages when landing in any sort of side wind, avoiding many breakages that would otherwise have occurred, and that was of course its purpose. Although the castor action of the main wheels took place against a light spring force and was mechanically constrained within a certain segment of movement, to taxi was always difficult even for experienced pilots. For the beginner it could be a nightmare. An American pupil at Pau, E.L. Ovington, wrote that:

> It is necessary for those who wish to learn to operate any aeroplane to do considerable 'grass-cutting' at first, in order that they may be thoroughly acquainted with the control of their machine and also become accustomed to rushing through space at a high velocity. It may seem easy to steer a machine

on the ground, from one point to another, but until you have tried it in a monoplane, you do not realize how difficult it is. Even to an experienced operator, it is more difficult to steer a straight course on the aerodrome, when the machine is rolled along the ground than when flying. This is due to the fact that the rudder is designed for operation at a mile a minute, and not for slower speed on the ground: hence the surface is not very great.[7]

Cammell found the mown track very narrow, and bounded by standing corn on both sides: 'the result is that one has to be very nippy in jumping off [the aeroplane] to save it from running into the corn'. The pupils were fined two francs fifty centimes if they did that.[8] Collin found that a good third of his pupils were panic-stricken on their first attempt, losing all control. Thus his final order to each one before starting was always to stop the engine the moment anything began to go wrong. This at least reduced the risk of collision with something solid on the ground. Another likely hazard was involuntary take-off, as Richardson had found. This was such a frequent and serious problem that finding a solution became imperative. It was probably Leblanc who had the happy idea of replacing the normal wings with much shorter ones, making flight impossible, but permitting hops of a few feet and giving the pupil the same 'feel' as a standard aeroplane while running about on the ground. Baptised 'Penguins', these modified machines, which in their perfected form had reinforced wheels and undercarriages, quickly became a feature at all Blériot schools, replacing the standard type for the first two stages of training. When there was a temporary shortage of Penguins they would be supplemented with ordinary machines whose engines were on their last legs, rendering them incapable of flight.

However, involuntary take-off did not totally cease. When teaching people of a particularly apprehensive disposition Collin sometimes thought it a good idea to make a 'mistake' when allocating aeroplanes. Thus a student lacking the confidence to progress beyond taxiing, could suddenly find himself taking to the air in a machine which he firmly believed would be for ever earthbound. These unfortunates, if that is what they were, invariably – it was claimed – returned safely, absolutely delighted to have succeeded in spite of themselves. The difficulty of keeping a straight course on the ground was so well-known that it became exaggerated. There was also an expectation of extreme discomfort, which often did not materialize. For example, Richardson:

> ...found it delightfully smooth and comfortable, more so, if anything, than a perfectly sprung car. There appeared a tendency to sway about a little, which at first made one feel somewhat insecure.[9]

The Penguins undoubtedly contributed to safety, and so did the continued use, right up until the war, of the otherwise obsolete 25hp Anzani engines in virtually all school Blériot XIs. It was Collin's proud claim that one entered the Blériot school 'alive and intact', and left it the same way. Yet the risks were alarming enough, as may be deduced from Ovington's advice:

> ...the principal thing about which I wish to warn embryo aviators is not to make sudden movements of their control. In order to rise, for instance, it is

not necessary to pull the control towards you six or eight inches, as usually one or two inches is all that is necessary. I have seen so many students get into a machine, give the control lever a pull towards them, and then practically stand the machine on end in mid-air.[10]

From 1910 to 1914 the Blériot schools trained not far short of 1,000 pilots for the *brevet* of the French Aéro Club – about one half of all the licences issued. There were Americans, Austrians, Belgians, British, Chileans, Dutch, Greek, Italians, Mexicans, Peruvians, Rumanians, Russians, Spaniards, Swedes, Swiss and Turks. It was, said Collin, 'a tower of Babel'.

Most flying was done in the few hours after dawn, and again before sunset, which meant very long days for the staff, and many idle hours for the pupils, whose patience was frequently strained by interruptions for days on end because of bad weather and shortages of aircraft. Frequent crashes and short intervals between engine overhauls resulted in a lot of machines being out of commission at any one time.

But a school was a place where someone was always busy. In the three months from mid-November 1910 until mid-February 1911, there were sixty-seven pupils in Blériot's school at Pau, of whom thirty-six obtained their *brevets*. Forty-two aeroplanes were in use, twenty-eight of them belonging to pupils and fourteen to the school. Seventeen large hangars were occupied. 15,000 litres of petrol and 3,800 litres of castor oil were used. The staff numbered fifty-nine. On one day, 21 February 1911, fifteen aeroplanes were counted in the air at once.[11]

Purchasers of Blériot aeroplanes paid no fees for pilot training, but were charged for the repair of any damage they did to school machines. Other pupils paid fees of 2,000 francs, until 1912, when the figure came down to 800 francs, in addition to repair charges – which were sometimes ruinous for those on slender budgets, forcing some to give up aviation.

★★★★★

The 900 or so aeroplanes which Louis Blériot sold between 1909 and 1914 were model XIs and direct derivatives of that famous monoplane. During that period at least fifteen other designs were produced in his drawing offices and actually built as prototypes – but not sold – while countless further designs were merely proposed, and a great many astonishing ideas were patented – ranging from vertical take-off to launching aircraft from wires. Fervent and fertile as was the activity of Blériot and his technical team, the one thing that seemed beyond them was to design a successful replacement of the type XI. The brilliant test pilot Edmond Perreyon would perish in one ill-conceived attempt in November 1913. The mould seemed too strong to be broken.

The first important change in the production versions of the type XI after Reims was the fitting of the 50hp Gnome rotary engine, accompanied by alterations to the fuselage and an increase in wing span from 8.40m to 8.90m. As cinematographic evidence confirms, the consequences for the aircraft's appearance in flight were dramatic: it was almost as if a donkey had become a racehorse.

But the Anzani engine still possessed some advantages, because it was about half the price of a Gnome and its lower power made it more suitable for beginners. Thus a new version of the XI with a 25hp Anzani was also introduced during the course of 1910, and called the XI bis. Its wing span at 9.00m was greater than any of the previous ones, but the length was only 6.60m.

Two-seater versions of the XI appeared as early as 1910 and continued to be made until 1915. In some, the two occupants sat one behind the other, in others they sat side-by-side, an arrangement favoured for pilot instruction. The former were designated XI-2, the latter XI-2 bis. There was also a three-seater in 1912, the XI-3, in which the two passengers sat in tandem behind the pilot. This was the largest and most powerful of the type XIs. The wing span was 11.35m and the length 8.50m. The engine was a 120hp Le Rhône.[12]

The many derivatives of the cross-Channel XI owed much to the availability of more powerful engines. But another influence was the requirements of the French military authorities, in a period when the civil market remained small and the industry became dependent on military orders. Although some sort of bomb-dropping may have been contemplated vaguely, for practical purposes the only military use then envisaged for aeroplanes was observation of enemy positions and movements, and for this two-seaters were thought best.

After the sweeping vision of the future 'superb realm of aviation' with which Blériot had captivated his audience at the House of Commons in September 1909, the reality from 1910 was a major anticlimax. Where were those 'real companies for aerial transport' which had been expected to break through on the horizon very soon? They were nowhere to be seen, and neither were the kind of aeroplanes that would have made them possible, except for a tantalizing glimpse offered by one solitary, eccentric precursor of the airliner which was created by Louis Blériot in 1911. This was the *Blériot Limousine* (type XXIV), hailed as the first aeroplane in which the comfort of passengers had been seriously considered. Made for the petroleum magnate Henri Deutsch de la Meurthe, it had a fully enclosed *berline* cabin built by the coachbuilder Rothchild to accommodate four passengers, who were to sit on pneumatic cushions while they gazed out through mica windows. The sumptuously appointed vehicle carried an outside seat at the front, and on this the pilot took his place, in the manner of a coachman, and received his instructions through a speaking tube, 'as in a taxi'.

Aeronautically also, the *Limousine* was a throwback, at least to the extent of having a forward elevator and a pusher propeller. It was a high wing monoplane with a 100hp Gnome engine placed just behind and above the cabin, which one commentator thought: 'savours a little too much of the Sword of Damocles to be to our liking'. This bizarre combination of ancient and modern concepts of transport was tested over a period of at least six months, which was long for those days, suggesting that all was not well with its behaviour or performance. Nevertheless, in June 1912 Edmond Perryon made a thirty-five minute flight in it at Etampes carrying 300kg of ballast at an altitude of 65 metres. It was reported that the engine used then was a Gnome of 140hp.[13] No record has been found of Deutsch de la Meurthe taking delivery of the *Limousine* or actually using it.

★★★★★

New and visionary technical ideas were what kept Blériot going: they were his constant preoccupation and consuming interest. Mechanical invention was his passion in middle age, as in youth. The man who used to sit up half the night to perfect the fine detail of an acetylene burner now stayed up late to devise ways to get an aeroplane into the air 'without

The Blériot XXIV Limousine of 1911-12. The four passengers in their luxuriously appointed cabin were to communicate with the pilot outside through a speaking tube, 'as in a taxi'. (MA 33185)

a preliminary horizontal run', or to construct a radiator like a venetian blind, with each of its layered planes contributing some lift.

The inconvenience caused to early aviators by the need for a 'preliminary horizontal run' can hardly be exaggerated. It was often difficult to find a suitable site near a city, and the state of the natural surface of the ground, in different weathers, caused further trouble. The intense, if premature, interest in helicopter flight in the early 1900s may in some part be attributable to anticipation of this constraint on the operation of aeroplanes with fixed wings. Be that as it may, the problem was identified, and addressed in characteristically original ways, by Wilbur and Orville Wright. They provided a rail along which their 1903 Flyer could run and take off – entirely under its own power – from the soft and uneven sand of Kitty Hawk. When they transferred their operations the following year to the Huffman Prairie near Dayton they found the surface so badly poached by cattle that a rail was again needed. But changes in the direction of the wind continually obliged them laboriously to lift and re-lay the joined lengths of rail. They then had the idea of reducing the work by using a much shorter rail. This was made possible by employing at the moment of launching the energy of a weight falling in a derrick, to supplement the thrust produced by the Flyer's engine. These two different methods of take off were frequently confused with one another, sometimes wilfully, so that the first was overlooked and the damaging claim was made – chiefly in France – that the Wright aeroplane was incapable of taking off under its own power. That myth was not finally laid to rest until 1910 when some customers of the Wrights, not the brothers themselves, fitted wheeled undercarriages and the biplanes took off perfectly, with no assistance.

The Wrights' system of take off had no emulators. Blériot, as has been described, had arrived after many breakages and accidents at a highly effective form of undercarriage, which represented a sound practical solution to the problem of making the preliminary horizontal run. But before getting to that stage he had, as early as 1907, devised two alternative methods of vertical take off, both of which he patented in France and in England.

The first scheme involved an aeroplane to which was attached at the rear a strong cable, two or three times as long as the fuselage. At the other end of the cable a circular metal ring was fitted, and this was threaded over a steel tube placed vertically in the ground, with three or four metres protruding, like a flagpole. Held captive in this way, the machine was supposed to rise until the ring worked its way up to the top of the pole, where it would come off, allowing the machine to fly away.

It is odd that a trained engineer – or indeed anyone else – should ever have expected this to work, and perhaps Blériot did not, but simply wanted to pre-empt anyone else who might think of a more realistic variant of the basic idea. An apparatus did not have to be built, or shown to be able to achieve its objective, in order for a patent to be registered. Patents were to be important pawns in a convoluted series of bitter commercial conflicts which plagued the first two decades of heavier-than-air aviation.

Blériot's second idea for vertical take off was hardly more convincing. Here it was the aeroplane itself which was redesigned, and no outside installation on the ground was needed. The principle, or hope, was that an airstream directed back from a propeller against wings set at an incidence of some 45 degrees would produce vertical lift. Further, the effectiveness of the process would be enhanced if the trailing edges of the wings were as close as possible to the ground, so that strong pressure would build up beneath the wings, forcing them upwards. The transition from vertical to horizontal flight would be achieved by adjusting the wings to a lesser and more usual angle of incidence.

It was proposed to apply these concepts by employing a hinged fuselage, with the joint just behind the monoplane wings, and the axis of the hinge running horizontally across between the two top longerons. For take off the hinge would be winched open by the pilot, thus lowering the trailing edges to the ground, and when he left the ground he would winch it closed, thus straightening out the fuselage.[14]

There is no evidence that either of these schemes was the subject of actual experiment, but there is evidence of at least an intention to construct an apparatus which may have had some connection with the one just described. A list of experimental aeroplanes apparently planned to be built in the Blériot factory during the year 1911 includes an *appareil à hélice verticale s'enlevant de pied ferme* (machine having a propeller on a vertical axis, raising itself from a stationary position).[15]

That list includes 'propellers of variable pitch' and 'flexible wings'. Some of the planned aircraft were certainly built and flown, among them the four-seater type XIII (a forerunner of the *Limousine* described earlier), and a set of wings whose camber could be altered in flight was certainly constructed earlier, because Cammell saw them on 1 July 1910. Grounded by high winds at Etampes, he decided to go to Paris, hoping to visit the Blériot factory, although: 'they may not allow me in, as I believe there is a secret new type on the stocks.' In fact, he was welcomed at the factory ('it really is a marvellous place') and there he saw 'several very interesting new types, and some old abandoned ideas in the direction of wings of variable camber.'

Cammell noted on another occasion:

> Whatever the secret of the aero-curve may be, it must be admitted that M. Blériot has gone a long way to solve it. With the same fuselage and motor he

Géo Chavez, first across the Alps. On 23 September 1910 Chavez flew his Blériot XI Gnome from Brig in Switzerland to Domodossola in Italy. He was fatally injured in the crash-landing which followed, due to failure of the monoplane's wing bracing. (MC 5114)

can turn out a racer, a slow weight-lifter, or a general utility vehicle [by using different wing sections].

There was a principle here which Blériot had taken a step further, by designing a wing whose camber could be altered by the pilot during flight. The wing Cammell saw was: 'put aside and dusty, so I rather imagined it was an abandoned idea'. Conscientious as always, he made a sketch all the same, and wrote a thoroughly professional description of its operating mechanism.[16]

★★★★★

Blériot's inventive energy could not for ever be concentrated on fantastic schemes. Anticipating the future by fifty years was a luxury which fate did not for long give him leisure to pursue. A fearful problem, a matter of life or death, was to present itself, and to form the first of many threats to his position as the world's leading aircraft manufacturer, even to his ability to stay in business.

There was at first no sudden crisis, rather an unease which developed gradually until the moment when hindsight suddenly put things in a new and frightening perspective, and the Minister of War shocked the aeronautical world in February 1912 by ordering the indefinite grounding of all monoplanes in the French army.

Beginning with the fatal accident to Léon Delagrange in January 1910, followed in September of that year by the fatal injury of Géo Chavez in his moment of triumph after successfully making the first aeroplane flight across the Alps, a number of fatal crashes occurred when Blériot monoplanes fell out of the sky. Expert 'eye-witness' accounts differed (not surprisingly, because what was actually happening was a phenomenon very difficult to observe), souvenir hunters made off with vital evidence, and pilots did not live to say what had happened to them, so that for a long time no particular connection was made between one accident and another. Then came a rapid succession of four crashes, three of them involving military pilots, Lantheaume, Ducorneau and Sevelle, and a civilian, Blanchard. That there might be a connection between these was a hypothesis so compelling that Blériot was bound to investigate it. What he found is best told in the words of his report to the French Government:

> The death of Lt Sevelle was not, as have been so many preceding calamities, useless to the cause of aviation. It has brought to light a new conception of the forces to which aeroplanes are subjected in flight. It has come to explain the series of mysterious accidents that have overtaken Chavez, Blanchard, Lantheaume and Ducorneau. Up to the present no one has admitted that the wings of monoplanes can carry top loading. After Chavez's death, witnesses affirmed to having seen the wings fold down beneath the machine. No one heeded their words, regarding them as the outcome of an optical illusion: meanwhile the wings (of monoplanes) were strengthened once more. Then came Blanchard's death, followed by a second reinforcement of the wing spars. Following upon that came the death of Lantheaume, which caused a military commission to decide that the wing spars should be strengthened yet a third time, and it was with these newly reinforced wings that Lt Sevelle met his death.
>
> Alas, it was not the weakness of the wings that caused these accidents. These four deaths occurred under similar circumstances; the machines had remained for a long time in the air amid most violent air turbulence. Chavez had crossed the Alps. Blanchard had journeyed from Orléans to Paris. Lantheaume had just finished a flight of 50 kilometres, and Sevelle a flight of 2 hours 10 minutes duration. Their machines had resisted perfectly the buffeting of the wind, when suddenly, as they (the pilots) proceeded to descend by *vols planés* [glides], the wings which carry very little positive loading at this time, broke and doubled up. I do not speak of Lt Ducorneau's accident, for that constitutes the first occasion on which the upper guys were broken, and is probably due to an analogous cause. In Lt Sevelle's machine the four upper guys were completely broken.
>
> All these accidents having resulted in the same conditions led to the idea that the wings must be forced from above, and had to resist pressure acting vertically in a downward direction.
>
> Then it was that I realized how the momentum of an aeroplane flying in a straight line, and made suddenly to descend by a *vol piqué*, would reverse the loading on the wings, and now this phenomenon cannot be doubted by any who care to analyse the problem.
>
> A machine moving horizontally will, when the motive power is diminished, descend by a parabolic path, which will be longer in proportion

to the initial speed. If, by a strong movement of the elevator, the pilot transforms the trajectory into a straight line slanting at a steeper angle towards the earth than the parabola, the machine is immediately subjected to a force from above. In order that it (the machine) should make this descent to earth, which takes place more rapidly than that resulting from the gravitational influence of its own weight, a downward force must act upon the wings.... It is then the change (of direction) that causes the danger to the pilot and not the *vol piqué* [dive] itself, which if performed slowly and progressively presents no objections.

There is no longer room for doubt that the deaths of Chavez, Blanchard and Lantheaume were caused, not as has been believed up to the present, by the breaking of the wings, that have withstood their trials and tests of positive loading successfully, but by the failure of the upper guys, which have no strength to resist these forces coming from above. It is therefore necessary to test monoplanes with a top loading on the wings, so as to obtain a system of upper bracing that will be of corresponding strength to the lower bracing now in use.[17]

The government accepted Blériot's report, and the suspension of the use of military monoplanes continued until they had been modified by strengthening the upper stays (landing wires) in a manner which he worked out. Blériot's confidence that he had found the true explanation of monoplane failures was not shared by all of his contemporaries, but there was diffidence about publicly disagreeing with him, and such alternative explanations as were put forward gained little support. In the light of much later scientific understanding, T.D. Crouch suggested in 1982 that the probable explanation for the collapse of early Blériot wings was a complex phenomenon (explained by Crouch) which engineers call 'beam column failure'. Significantly, Crouch observes: 'But in spite of his inability to analyse the condition properly, Blériot had reached an empirical, common-sense solution to the problem by mid-1912'[18]

Right or wrong, Blériot's report made an immensely favourable impression at the time, as *Flight* noted:

One of the most important documents dealing with the technical side of aviation that has yet been prepared...That it should have been written by the pioneer designer of monoplanes and should form such a frank and lucid exposé of a hitherto unsuspected weakness in such machines, is the finest possible vindication of the Établissements Blériot as a scientific concern.[19]

The historian R. Dallas Brett wrote:

M. Blériot was the largest manufacturer of monoplanes in the world at that time and the principal contractor to the French Government. His frank exposure of the inherent weakness of his own products was an act calling for considerable

Edmond Perreyon, Blériot's outstanding test pilot, at Etampes in May 1912 with a type XI specially made for the Artillery with a folding fuselage to facilitate ground transport. (MC 8727)

moral courage. He faced ruin at that moment, and accepted the risk calmly and courageously for the sake of his brother pilots who were flying his machines.[20]

Although Blériot's handling of the crisis was effective, and carried through in a way that enhanced his reputation just when it might have been lost, the episode probably did affect the future course of aviation. The monoplane went into a long period of unpopularity by comparison with the biplane from which it did not emerge until the design and construction of wings had completely changed and external bracing wire was no longer needed.

★★★★★

Shortly after presenting his report to the government, Blériot went off to Russia on a promotional tour, which was quickly followed by his first visit to North America – a journey which had nothing to do with aviation but which reflected the position he now held in society. He and Alice were asked to be members of an official mission composed of government ministers, deputies, and other prominent French citizens whose purpose was to present Rodin's bust of Champlain to the town of Ticonderoga. They sailed for New York on the maiden voyage of the *France*, a few days after the sinking of the *Titanic*, and returned a month later, after a gruelling round of official banquets, interspersed with continual travel throughout much of eastern Canada and the USA. (They made a similar trip in 1921.)

14 Foreign affairs, with aerobatics

While Blériot the engineer was preoccupied in 1912 with solving the menacing problem of monoplane failures, Blériot the industrialist was setting up his first manufacturing operation in a foreign country.

Like the other French manufacturers, he had supplied a great variety of foreign customers with aeroplanes made in France virtually from the beginning – in his case from the autumn of 1909. Exporting was a normal and essential part of business, but by 1912 it was being replaced in the major markets by the establishment of local manufacturing capacity.

Whether or not it was worthwhile to set up a factory abroad depended above all on the availability of substantial military orders from the country concerned. This reality was well-demonstrated by Blériot's dealings with England and Italy. Both countries were in the second wave of those in which local aviation industries developed, and both were importers of civil aircraft. For Blériot, as a result of his personal impact on the national consciousness, England was much the more important of the two civil markets, yet it was in Italy that he first set up a foreign factory. He did this when he had an order, or sufficient prospect of an order, for more than half the aeroplanes called for by the Italian Government's first major military aviation equipment programme. Nothing comparable was to come from the British authorities for another eighteen months, and when it did he at once began to manufacture in England – with, as it turned out, momentous consequences for his future fortunes.

In July 1912 Blériot personally provided nearly all the capital for a new company, Societa Italiana Transaerea, invariably known as 'SIT', which promptly erected a factory in Corso Peschiera, Turin. This was purpose-built to the highest standards for the batch-production of Blériot XIs: there were joiners' and propeller-makers' departments, mechanical workshops, and the spacious halls needed for assembly. The management of SIT was entirely Italian, and all the senior executives made small investments in the company.

The Italian Ministry of War's initial procurement programme in mid-1912 specified the construction within Italy of seventy aeroplanes by the following spring. The business was distributed among five firms, with SIT, the newcomer, receiving orders for forty-two machines. The total was increased after a time to 150, of which SIT's final share was eighty aircraft. Most were 50 and 80hp Blériot XI-Gnomes, but a few were M. Farmans built under license. Forty of the SIT machines were delivered to squadrons by April 1913, and the rest by the end of that year.

This was a remarkable industrial performance. Blériot had at one stroke become the principal constructor in Italy and had made himself indispensable to the government: without SIT they would either have had to rely on imports, which was strategically undesirable, or do without. But SIT's success was not universally welcome in Italy, and resentment at this intrusion of foreign capital and know-how may well have been behind the company's dramatic disqualification from the Italian Military Aeroplane Trials of 1913.

This decision, potentially disastrous for future sales, was taken by the committee of scrutineers on 1 April before any flights had been made by the two Blériots entered by SIT, and apparently on the flimsiest of pretexts. These machines had no doubt been carefully prepared, and were, we are told: 'built and finished in faultless fashion'. However, official inspection revealed that some tie-rods had not been connected, whereupon the committee eliminated both aircraft.

> This decision did not fail to arouse very bad feelings and induced Ing. Triaca [technical director of SIT] and Blériot to launch an advertising campaign for their products and to plan an enterprise which could not fail to attract the attention of the whole country...[1]

Inwardly furious, but calmly, methodically, taking care over every detail, Blériot prepared a devastating riposte. A flight, he announced, would be made from Turin to Rome and back – in one day. An aeroplane which showed itself capable of such a performance would, he thought, 'be worthy of consideration by the authorities...'

Such an enterprise by its failure could turn revenge into ridicule. It must not fail. A pilot of exceptional skill and dependability was called for, and he must know the route perfectly because he would not have time to spare for getting lost and coming down to enquire the way which was still then – and until much later – a feature of much cross-country flying. Blériot's choice was Edmond Perreyon, who had then emerged as the chief among his test-pilots in France. While Perreyon was studying the route between Turin and Rome, the best brains and hands in the Turin factory were getting ready a two-seater SIT Blériot with an 80hp Gnome engine. The preparations were intense but unhurried: there was a determination to take the time that was needed, but at last came the day which would either restore or destroy Blériot's prospects in Italy:

> On 28 May at 4.56 a.m. Perreyon, with the mechanic Dupuis aboard, took off from Mirafiori aerodrome and headed for Pisa, where he landed at 7.57 a.m. At 8.45 a.m. he started off again in the direction of Leghorn, continuing his flight along the coast. The excitement was intense everywhere and the flight was accompanied by a succession of telegraphic and wireless messages which gave the place and time he was due to pass. In Rome he landed at 11.26a.m. amid the enthusiasm of the crowd who had flocked to Centocelle to see his arrival. The rapid, safe flight from Turin to Rome of the Blériot-SIT was an uncommon undertaking in itself, but after refuelling Perreyon started off again north. It was 13.07. Three hours later he arrived at Pisa, stopped for some minutes to refuel and at 16.41 was again in the air.
>
> In Turin the exploit was followed with an anxiety that became apprehension when, with darkness coming on, people began to think of the serious difficulties which Perreyon would encounter in picking out Mirafiori.
>
> But suddenly, about 20.50, the Blériot-SIT passed over the aerodrome,

The insouciant and irrepressible Pégoud: *Célestin-Adolphe Pégoud, creator of aerobatics, in his Blériot XI in 1913. Note the reinforced wing bracing. (Author's Collection)*

the lights and signal fires were immediately put in operation and at 20.57 Perreyon and his flight companion Dupuis happily touched ground and were carried in triumph.[2]

Its honour vindicated, its stature enhanced, SIT resumed its place as the major supplier of the Italian government.

★★★★★

In August and September 1913 there took place the most impressive demonstrations of prowess in the air that had been seen since Wilbur Wright amazed the world at Les Hunaudières five years before. As on that occasion, this was done, as one commentator observed: 'in a manner which dumbfounded the sceptics and silenced every accusation of chicanery.'

An extraordinary programme of three flying experiments conducted by the Blériot firm led within five weeks to a major change in attitudes towards safety in the air, and to the discovery of aerobatics. Whether the initiative for these sudden and dramatic developments came from Louis Blériot or from his daring pilot, the insouciant and irrepressible Pégoud, is uncertain, but what is clear is that together they led aviation into a new phase, amassing fame and some fortune in the process.

Célestin-Adolphe Pégoud was born a farmer's son at Montferrat, Isère in the Dauphiné in 1889. At the age of fourteen he declined to become a butcher, and left for Paris.

Nothing is known of him for the next four years. Then in August 1907 he appeared in Algeria as a soldier in the 5th Regiment of Chasseurs d'Afrique, having signed on as a volunteer for five years. He continued a modest military career with service in Morocco, enlivened by a spell at the cavalry school at Saumur, and transferred to the 3rd Regiment of Colonial Artillery stationed at Toulon where he became a corporal in 1909. An officer in his new regiment, Captain Louis Carlin, took up flying in 1911 and gave Pégoud his first flight as a passenger in the autumn of that year.

From that moment aviation took possession of Pégoud. Carlin transferred to the 'Aéronautique militaire', formed in March 1912, and perhaps sensing something of Pégoud's precocious talent, arranged for him to come along as an assistant mechanic. But Pégoud was impatient to become a pilot in his own right, and the quickest way to achieve this was to leave the army and train as a civil pilot, which he did, being awarded *brevet* No.1243 of the Aéro Club of France on 7 March 1913. How this costly transformation was paid for is unclear, but it is known that he trained at Bron near Lyon and qualified on a Henry Farman.[3]

Six days later he started work for Louis Blériot, one of three young pilots recruited on 13 March 1913, a day of destiny for the marque, for that was the day Edmond Perreyon joined as well. Pégoud's beginnings with Blériot are obscure, although he may have worked as a mechanic for a time, as well as familiarizing himself with the handling of the Blériot-Gnome, then approaching the zenith of its development. This more advanced training took place under the personal direction of Ferdinand Collin, who found his new charge a handful:

> His passion for the air made him a *redoutable indiscipliné*, very hard to manage, who fumed and threatened me when I restricted his flights. In Pégoud there was everything, the best and the worst, and the miracle is that the worst did not prevail. He was twenty-four years old, with a constitution of iron and the physique of an athlete, fiercely determined, defiant of everything, even death, to attain his goal: as for courage, I have never seen more than he had...[4]

By mid-summer Pégoud had somehow managed to control himself sufficiently for his temper not to overwhelm his ability, and he was chosen by Blériot to carry out unusual tests requiring the ultimate in precise flying. The French Navy was in search of a method by which aeroplanes could be operated from battleships which, of course, lacked the deck space for even the short runs then needed. Blériot's proposal, evocative of the fantasies described earlier, called for a wire stretched between two booms protruding from the side of the vessel, and an aeroplane fitted with an overhead forked device with which the pilot could attach it to, or detach it from, the wire. To take off, the plane would 'taxi' suspended beneath the wire until enough speed to fly had been acquired, whereupon the pilot would disconnect from the wire, and 'take off', then presumably swerving promptly to avoid collision with the boom which cannot at that moment have been very far distant. 'Landing' entailed flying parallel to and just beneath the wire until it could be grabbed by the fork, and then the suspended aeroplane would be brought to a halt by friction between fork and wire.

Such was the reputation of Louis Blériot that the Navy Minister and two admirals were prepared to travel out to Buc to witness these procedures being rehearsed on dry land, and such was the skill of Pégoud and the quality of Blériot engineering that the tests, on a wire strung between two pylons only 80m apart, were pronounced an unqualified success. But it must rapidly have been borne in upon those alert, if untutored, naval minds that they were in the presence of flying skills so exceptional that the tests gave no useful indication of what average pilots might achieve, and of this almost unbelievable system little more was heard.

However, Blériot now knew beyond doubt that in this twenty-four year old ex-corporal, licensed for only four months, he possessed a pilot with qualities not before brought to aviation. From that time onward, Pégoud had a position of prestige in the firm, and seems to have had freedom to chose which experiments to undertake.

Circumstances determined that the next subject to engage his attention would be the parachute, that deceptively simple apparatus whose spasmodic and largely incoherent progress throughout the nineteenth century had cost many lives. A more systematic, and ultimately successful phase in its development began in 1910. This was stimulated by a number of fatal accidents to pilots and by the radical idea that a parachute might provide a way of escaping from a doomed aeroplane, instead of being merely a circus-like attraction used by entertainers for leaping from balloons. The new purpose necessitated a folding parachute, in place of the rigid-frame models used until then.

The first successful parachute jump from an aeroplane was made on 1 March 1912 by Captain Albert Berry from some 1,500 feet, near St Louis, Missouri. His method required a perilous climbing out from inside the fuselage to a seated position on the undercarriage axle before jumping. On 16 March a less conclusive, but promising, experiment was conducted by G. Bonnet, a restaurateur in Grenoble, from the balloon park at St Cloud. In this, a mock-up of an aeroplane fuselage, with a dummy pilot and a folded parachute inside, was hung beneath a balloon and released. The fuselage then duly crashed to the ground, but first the parachute had opened, and plucked the dummy out of the cockpit. Slowly it followed the fuselage down, and landed completely undamaged. The vital difference between the two systems was this: Berry's required a pilot to fly the aeroplane while the parachutist was preparing to jump, but Bonnet's presumed that the parachutist would be the pilot himself, and he would not even need to jump because the parachute would take him out of the aircraft.[5]

For a full test of his parachute, Bonnet turned to his fellow Dauphinois, Pégoud, who was prepared to use an old school Blériot XI which, we are told ominously, was 'sacrificed in advance'. Hearing rumours of what was about to happen at the little aerodrome of Chateaufort near Versailles, the Gendarmerie tried to get it stopped, but failed. In a first attempt on 16 August the parachute refused to come out of the box, 'resembling a coffin', in which it was folded inside the rear of the fuselage, and Pégoud made one of the rough, bouncing, bad-tempered landings for which this *redoutable indiscipliné* was notorious. Three days later he tried again, with results best described in his own words:

> Brilliant; I take off smartly and climb to 100 metres. I fly along the valley,
> turn in a wide circle and head back towards Chateaufort, facing directly into

the wind. I go into a dive and release the parachute, which opens within two seconds. Then I am dragged the length of the fuselage, hitting my shoulder very hard on the fin. The machine slips away quietly. My parachute holds up amazingly well, even though several cords are broken. For several seconds I swing like a pendulum. Then I go down very gently, while my old *coucou* plays the clown all alone. This rascal, liberated from my presence, feels himself lighter, dives, climbs up again vertically, side-slips, recovers himself, dives again, recovers once more, and in a final dive crashes on Monsieur Quesnel's land beside the aerodrome.[6]

As for Pégoud, he landed in the branches of a tree from which he easily climbed down, with no damage apart from an enormous tear in his overalls.

Relief, and satisfaction over the success of Bonnet's parachute, were quickly eclipsed as Pégoud and Blériot awoke to the significance of what the old type XI had done, when left to its own devices. If it could perform those extraordinary gymnastics alone, *a pilot should be able to achieve the same results.* Which of the two first thought of this is uncertain, but it may very well have been Blériot who proposed the next practical step,[7] although later he was keen to give Pégoud the credit. The evolutions performed by the empty aeroplane were confusing to look at, and made additionally difficult to describe by the absence of terminology for the different manoeuvres: it was necessary therefore, if public attention was to be caught, to think of one easy-to-see but dramatic thing which it could be announced that Pégoud would do. The answer was simple: fly upside-down. When this was put to Pégoud he is reported to have replied: 'Monsieur Blériot, I am broke, I have no wife, and I am thinking of committing suicide, so I agree.'[8]

Sensational press coverage duly resulted when this intention was announced, on 21 August 1913. Even in informed aeronautical circles excitement was apparent. From the beginning of flying there had been the greatest reluctance to make any movements in the air beyond what was essential for going up or down, or turning round. As Dallas Brett has explained:

> Pilots were very nervous of attaining any unusual attitude in the air, and it was generally considered that if an aeroplane was turned vertically on its side, or inverted, it would inevitably become uncontrollable and crash.
> Until the summer of 1913 the majority of pilots performed very flat turns and brought their machines down cautiously at a shallow angle with their engines running. The more accomplished descended by means of glides, known as *vols planés* and some of the experts introduced gliding turns (spiral *vols planés*) or even gentle dives, which were regarded with awe and alluded to as *vols piqués*.[9]

To emphasize what he was going to do, Pégoud in great glee had a fuselage inverted on trestles and 'sat' strapped into it, to practice being upside down, so he said, but also offering good photo opportunities. That was on 27 August. On 1 September at Juvisy the feverishly awaited exploit took place – and was repeated the next day at Buc. What actually happened was so extraordinary, went so far beyond what was at best expected, and was so confusingly and inaccurately reported, even in the serious aeronautical press, that Blériot was obliged to have an official statement put out by his man in England. Norbert Chéreau, General Manager of L. Blériot Aeronautics' 'Head Office for the British Empire' at Belfast Chambers, 156 Regent Street, London, took care to explain what Pégoud had done, but also why:

> It has not been done simply with the idea of making a stunt or astonishing the world, but with the set purpose of demonstrating that, should through any cause whatever, this monoplane be turned upside down at a good height, the pilot need not lose his head, or have the awful sensation that probably all is over, but that on the contrary he has simply to use his controls to come back to the normal position of flight without fear or the thought that the monoplane will not obey immediately...
>
> It was at the insistence of Pégoud that Blériot consented to let him try this extraordinary feat. Monsieur Blériot hesitated for a long time, not because he did not think that the monoplane would answer readily enough, and stand the test, but because he had the very natural apprehension that the pilot might lose his nerve when he was upside-down, but M. Pégoud felt so sure of himself, and insisted so much, that in the end M. Blériot gave way, and had the machine prepared for him...(it) was an ordinary Blériot monoplane of the XI single-seater type built in 1912, the position and height of the upper *cabane* being slightly modified, and the bracing of the fixed tail plane reinforced...
>
> What actually took place was this. When at a height of 3,000 feet Pégoud deliberately stopped the engine and put the nose of the monoplane down starting a descent as nearly as possible to 'the vertical', and when at about 1,600 feet pulled (sic) his *cloche* [control column] and gradually brought the machine on its back without twisting it or making a corkscrew. The machine started then what we might call a very flat *vol plané* on its back, and continued in that position for about 500 yards coming down gradually meanwhile. At that moment the pilot pulled his *cloche* and the machine assumed again by degrees a vertical position, which it kept for a few seconds only, and gently came back to the ordinary position of flight, after which M. Pégoud indulged in all sorts of twists and stunts before alighting...
>
> The experiments have proved that the Blériot monoplane must be very seriously and strongly constructed to go through such hard tests...
> It may be also that a little later M. Pégoud might attempt the 'looping the loop'...but this will be purely a stunt, and will not have the same value as the feat reported above...[10]

It was Pégoud's belief that a pilot who kept his head and used his controls intelligently should be able to recover the normal flying posture in any wind, or from any bad position in which he might find himself. Weight was if anything added to his claims by a frank admission of the failure of one manoeuvre. Despite at least four public attempts he could not get into the upside-down position by rolling over sideways – what was later termed a

187

half roll. He could only do it from a dive, but he could *recover* from inversion by a half roll. Since inadvertently rolling over sideways was a thing greatly feared by other pilots, Pégoud was able to turn his failure to good account by claiming that it proved his Blériot was, as he put it, 'uncapsizeable'.

Declarations of serious purpose – and undoubtedly there was an element of that – did not inhibit this 'modern d'Artagnan', as someone called him, and on 21 September at Juvisy he did indeed carry out the one manoeuvre which, unusually, had a name before it happened. Stranger still, it was an English name, soon abbreviated by the French to *looping*. Yes, on that day Pégoud looped the loop.

The seal was set on his dazzling reputation. Once again aviation had a hero, for not since Blériot had flown the Channel had any pilot attracted such adulation, and the extrovert Pégoud was as eligible as anyone could be for the vast acclaim that immediately followed. Proclaimed the *Roi de l'Air*, his popularity in Paris:

> ...surpassed any example of hero-worship hitherto seen, even in France. Crowds surrounded the new aerodrome at Buc, near Versailles [acquired and lavishly set up by Blériot that year], all day long in the hope that Pégoud would fly, while on one occasion his presence was discovered in the audience at a theatre and the performance was held up for fifteen minutes whilst the people cheered themselves hoarse.[11]

Pégoud promptly began a European round of demonstrations, and in the weeks that followed he became a hero successively in England, Belgium, Austria, Italy, Rumania, Norway, Holland and Russia. In England there had been some scepticism, but:

> the authorities at Brooklands, however, managed to persuade him to come over and give a demonstration. On 25, 26 and 27 September, Pégoud flew his Blériot monoplane above the Weybridge track in a manner which dumbfounded the sceptics and silenced every accusation of chicanery. To say that the British pilots were staggered would be inadequate to express the complete stupefaction which was felt by all who witnessed his beautiful exhibition of perfect control.[12]

There could have been no better way for Blériot to show the world that he had successfully put behind him the appalling problem of structural failures in his aeroplanes. (Although the climax of that affair in France had come in 1912, a similar military ban on monoplanes in England had lasted well into 1913.) Pégoud's achievements also helped to compensate for the loss in the same year of several world speed and altitude records held by Blériots. Last but not least, Pégoud's activities were remunerative. His three days at Brooklands produced a net profit of £1,440 (36,000 francs), a substantial sum at the time, which Chéreau transferred the following week to Blériot's bank account in Paris.[13]

★★★★★

Pégoud in a Blériot XI looking type 80hp Gnome, with reinforced wing bracing, 1913. (MA 3426)

Pégoud's breathtaking performances gave a new impulse to Blériot's affairs in England. The gratifying financial results of those three days, which must have exceeded expectations, no doubt stimulated Blériot to consider the further development of his English business, while the resounding publicity success created conditions in which that could be done.

As soon as he got back to Paris, Blériot wrote to the man who was then undoubtedly the most aeronautically competent engineer to be found in the public service in Britain, Lt-Col. Mervyn O'Gorman, Superintendent of the Royal Aircraft Factory at Farnborough. Blériot asked what O'Gorman thought of the idea of a Blériot factory being opened in England, and he wanted to know whether, if he did decide to set up a factory, the British government would give him a promise to buy thirty aeroplanes a year.

O'Gorman's first reaction is perplexing. Evidently much excited over being so consulted, he went to Paris to see Blériot, but strangely he made no appointment, and did not even let Blériot know that he was coming. When he got there Blériot was away, and no meeting took place. Once back in England, O'Gorman sent a personal letter from his London home. He wrote to Blériot:

> It will be a very great move if you can make a start over here…but I must inform you that I have no authority in this matter of purchasing aeroplanes…The assurance of the purchase of thirty aeroplanes per year would be a difficult promise to get as not even our own constructors over here have such an undertaking.

O'Gorman then delivered his considered judgement:

> It is I suppose a question of whether the future of aviation is sufficiently assured in the world to be able to speculate to the extent of starting a Blériot Factory here. I trust that aviation is really a *certainty* and its development to an enormous extent quite inevitable.[14]

Blériot had quite extensive, and long, experience of doing business in England. Although unknown to the general public before 1909, his name had been esteemed among the small motoring public for his lamps since the late 1890s. Their manufacture in London dated from 1902, when he started a factory in Gatesby Street, and opened his shop in Longacre.[15]

In 1910 Blériot had set up his flying school at Hendon, where he erected eight hangars, stocked five of them with type XIs and appointed Pierre Prier as chief pilot instructor.[16] From 1 October the public were admitted as spectators, and the week-end flying exhibitions given by pilots associated with the several company schools using Hendon – among them Grahame-White and Farman – continued until the war to be a feature of London life. The profits of the English lamp business provided the capital needed to set up Blériot's considerable establishment at Hendon.

Even before the approach to Mervyn O'Gorman, Norbert Chéreau had been negotiating with the Director General of Military Aviation, Brigadier-General Henderson, about possible orders for Blériots to be 'made in England'. Whether a specific order had been obtained, or whether they simply judged the prospects to be sufficiently propitious, is unclear, but late in 1913 the decision to go ahead with an English factory was taken.

Once again, according to Blériot's later declaration, the profits of the lamp business produced the wherewithal, and a small factory - no more than a shed or two - was erected beside the aerodrome at Brooklands, inside the motor-racing track. Soon this became a hive of profitable activity, meeting substantial orders for the Royal Flying Corps. At first manufacturing there consisted mainly of the assembly of parts made in France, but in due course the British-made content rapidly increased.[17] By August 1914 a total of 104 Blériot XIs had been produced in England for military use. RFC squadrons Nos 3, 5, 6, 9 and 16 had been the chief recipients, but a few had gone to the Navy, equipped with floats.[18]

★★★★★

While successful in so many ways as an aircraft manufacturer, since his debut after the Channel flight until the war, a persistent shadow had lain over Blériot, a nagging anxiety that could never be made entirely to go away. At the Salon held at the end of 1909 he was accused of infringing the Wright brothers' patents for wing-warping. Thus began an appalling saga of acrimonious litigation which would drag on, with spectacular twists and turns, for more than a decade.

The Wright brothers, preoccupied from the earliest days of their success as experimenters by fear that their work would be copied by others and that they themselves would be unable to reap an adequate financial reward, had tried to protect their crucial system of lateral control. They registered patents in every country where emulation was probable and the legal system afforded worthwhile safeguards. In France those patents were held by the company formed specifically to exploit them: 'Compagnie Générale de Navigation Aérienne' (CGNA), in which Wilbur and Orville were shareholders along with several important French industrialists.

Blériot was not the only one accused by CGNA of contravening the wing-warping patents. Antoinette, Farman Frères, Robert Esnault-Pelterie and other French firms were similarly and simultaneously sued.[19] If Blériot derived any comfort from being in such company, the feeling did not endure, because the affair divided the community of French pioneer aviation, and placed ancient friendships under unbearable strain.

Although it has been fairly described as an engineering heresy, wing-warping was what had made aviation possible. Early attempts to use ailerons failed, and only Gabriel Voisin had succeeded in designing an aeroplane with no lateral control, but his concept was not capable of great development and was abandoned comparatively early. Blériot's own experiments rapidly became much more successful once he had seen Wilbur Wright fly at Auvours and then re-adopted warping himself, towards the end of 1908.

Yet wing-warping was to be only a temporary solution, because of its fundamental drawbacks, as C.C. Turner described (in 1927):

> It seems only yesterday that the warping, or flexing, of the rear extremities of aeroplane wings was regarded as the most excellent method of regulating lateral stability. It was Nature's method, exemplified in the birds; and it was the method adopted by the Wright Brothers...[but] the constant operation of flexing the tips of the wings sooner or later had seriously detrimental effects; the wings got "tired", and the control by this method weak; worse still, permanent distortion, more or less serious, appeared, affecting the machine's behaviour in flight by no means healthily. The tips, for example, took on a slight permanent twist. Constructors...sought to overcome this usually by loosely mounting the ribs round the spars so that there was a certain amount of "play", and not much actual bending of material...[wing-warping] was not the ideal method, and on all hands one heard the demand for something less delicate and more easily repairable.[20]

One good consequence of the proceedings launched by the CGNA was the stimulation it gave to the search for satisfactory control systems based on ailerons. Some makers 'adopted the aileron, or the flap, not usually because of any acknowledged superiority of this contrivance, but to obtain the same result without copying the Wright Brothers.'[21]

Blériot was not one of these. He stuck exclusively to warping for more than five years after the action began, no doubt considering that he had done nothing that was not covered by patents of his own which went back to 1907. But he was to be disappointed, for in May 1911 the Tribunal of the Seine found in favour of the CGNA against him and most of the other defendants, without at that stage assessing damages.

An appeal was lodged, and at about the same time Blériot and Esnault-Pelterie brought actions for alleged patent infringements against five other French manufacturers, and asked the court to confirm the validity of their respective batches of patents relating to lateral control systems, registered in the period 1906-1907. Their argument was that the CGNA patents related only to the description of manoeuvres in flight, while their own patents covered the layout of the actual apparatus used for manoeuvring. Blériot relied chiefly on 1907 patents relating to control systems, which refer to the application of a disc to the control of the elevator and 'the warping components', and also to the *Cloche Blériot*, fixed to the base of an 'inclinable shaft', and from which radiated the cables leading to the flexible wing tips and the swivelling elevator. Esnault-Pelterie's 1906 patents mention a *manche-à-balai* (broomstick) movable in the four 'horizons', linked to discs to which were attached cables dedicated to each type of manoeuvre (steering, climbing or diving).

With fine understatement, the historian Chadeau has commented:

> At this point, the affair became important. Already it had been taking place in an unhealthy atmosphere, with the plaintiffs sending in their writ-servers at every salon and meeting in front of the public. From then on, enormous sums of money were at stake, because 10% of all aviation sales since the beginning might be awarded to the 'disposessed inventors' as compensation. Faced with this possibility, a committee of experts was formed, but the war caused it to be adjourned. Esnault-Pelterie did an about turn, separating himself from Blériot, whom he then attacked… for infringement of his *manche-à-balai* patents.[22]

In an astonishing judgement in March 1914, the court on that issue decided in favour of Esnault-Pelterie, and attributed to him 'the original invention…' No small part of Blériot's reputation as an inventor rested on the renowned *Cloche Blériot*, and the failure to have its primacy upheld was a hammer blow. The arrival of the war prevented any chance of an early solution, but it also aggravated the problem, because contingent liabilities for possible damages in respect of infringements would accumulate in direct proportion to massively increased production.

15 The war

When the war began in August 1914 Blériot's aircraft factory abruptly closed down. This startling result so early in the conflict was achieved not by any brilliant stroke of enemy action, but by the inexorable march of military bureaucracy. Blériot and all his fit men were simply called up by the army. The general order to mobilize issued on 1 August exempted only those Frenchmen who were unable to fight because of age or infirmity. Factories of all kinds throughout France, with the exception of those already staffed largely by women, stopped work at once.

The manner in which the army dealt with the recall of their reserve Lt Blériot suggested that they did not really mean it, and would soon change their minds. He was ordered to Le Havre, with instructions to place himself under the command of the officer in charge of a squadron of the Royal Flying Corps recently stationed there. This British colonel evidently feared that the presence of his famous guest would be less of an honour than an embarrassment, and took what he curiously deemed appropriate steps as soon as the idol of many an English schoolboy came into view.

It was in an armoured car impressively equipped with a machine-gun that Blériot arrived in Le Havre with Alice and their five children. Seizing the pretext of highly fanciful 'sightings' of German patrols in the area – the nearest Germans were in fact several hundred kilometres away – the worried colonel said they must leave at once and gave them two of his troops for their defence. Without even getting out of the car they set off again, this time in the direction of Le Mans.

'The first of the wounded were brought to Le Mans at the same time as us,' Alice remembered, 'the hotels were overwhelmed, with people sleeping on billiard tables and in the bathrooms.' Blériot obtained another car, in which he sent Alice and the children off to the relative safety of Bagnères-de-Bigorre. They could drive by day only, because by night many roads were blocked by chains strung across them. Keeping to minor roads to avoid encounters with the enemy, they traversed France from north to south, and eventually reached Colonel Védère's home early in September. Alice immediately resumed her service with the French Red Cross, which she had joined shortly before leaving Paris:

> About the twenty-third of September we received [at Bagnères-de-Bigorre] the first convoy of wounded. These poor men had not been able even to change their socks, and to get rid of their vermin we had to wash them with the hose-pipe we had for cars.[1]

A week later Blériot and the other aircraft manufacturers who had been swept up in the mobilization were released by the army and allowed to go back to their factories. But what were they to do, what was expected of them? At first no one could say. Remarkably little effective thought had been given to what aeroplanes could and should actually do in war.

Yet military use of aviation had been envisaged from the beginning. After all, it was to various Ministries of War that the Wrights directed their first marketing efforts. Earlier still, extraordinary proposals had been made in France, as Louis Blériot wrote afterwards:

> Before even having been able to make the first hop ever achieved by man in a heavier-than-air machine, Clément Ader had worked out a comprehensive scheme of aircraft constructions for war use. He had outlined plans for a 'military airframe factory', and had foreseen the need for specialization of aeroplane types: 'three categories: torpedo planes, scouts and aircraft of the line'. He had worked out aerial strategy and tactics, and envisaged several types of aircraft (ten in all), each intended to perform a specific function. All this, his clairvoyant mind conceived with total clarity from the final decade of last century… It is terrible to think that man, hardly provided with still uncertain wings, wanted to turn them into weapons…[2]

Despite the interest of the French military authorities in aviation since 1910, underlined by the doubling, at least, each year of the number of pilots obtaining the ever more difficult military *brevet*, scant attention had been given to practical operations. Isolated experiments had taken place, in connection with large army manoeuvres held in Picardy in 1912, and in competition for a prize awarded by the Michelin brothers for accurate bomb-dropping, but such lessons as may have been learned were not followed up. There was an expectation that aircraft would be useful for obtaining a view of the enemy not available from the ground, but what this implied in practice had not been thought through. That, like so much else, remained to be worked out.

Military aviators were a minute minority in the armies. There was little that they were able to do in peacetime, or even early in the war, to counter extreme scepticism about their usefulness. In this respect the German high command was no more advanced in its thinking than its counterparts in France or England. A German General Staff report of 1 October 1914 noted: 'As experience has shown, a true combat in the air, as described by journalists and writers of fiction, should be regarded as a myth: the duty of an aviator is to see, not to fight.'[3]

★★★★★

When the war began, the general expectation in France was that it would be over in six weeks. Therefore it would be fought with the resources then to hand. The question of producing more aeroplanes, let alone any different ones, simply did not arise and the aircraft factories, as we have seen, were closed. Similarly, there would be no point in training any more pilots, so all the flying schools were shut down, and their military pupils were ordered back to their regiments.[4]

In the battle of the Marne an observer in an aeroplane had reported a change of direction by a huge body of advancing German troops under von Kluck, enabling, it was said, the plan which saved Paris to be worked out by General Gallieni. After the battle of the Marne the common estimate of the war's duration was increased – to six months. At the same time, the conduct of air operations day after day in wet and windy autumn weather resulted in an alarming consumption of aeroplanes, due more to wear and tear and to accidents than to enemy action at that stage. For all these reasons, the French army decided to order a great many aircraft, sufficient to increase the number of squadrons from twenty-seven to sixty-five.

Less welcome to the industry was a drastic decision made in October 1914 not to order any more aeroplanes of types which had been deemed unsatisfactory during the first two months of the war. Only Caudrons, Maurice Farmans, Morane-Saulniers and Voisins were retained. All the other constructors had to devote themselves to making those types. Blériot was to make Caudrons.

The new policy had some justification in terms of design, as well as in obvious industrial logic. Amid all the uncertainty about what aeroplanes should be used for, one quality had emerged as an imperative necessity: the ability of a pilot or observer to see what was happening on the ground below. Designs in which the wings significantly obscured that view below were no longer acceptable – or so it was claimed. With that policy the operational career of the most popular aeroplane of its epoch, the Blériot XI, came to an end, for in so completely blotting out downward vision it had few rivals. No more Blériots were to be ordered by the French army, and most of those still in service or yet to be delivered (ninety-three type XI-2s had been ordered in May) would be assigned to school use, a role in which diminishing numbers continued throughout the war.

Blériots survived longer – another nine months – with the British forces in France, who 'could not afford to strike off an aeroplane on the mere account of its unfavourable comparison with other and more successful types.'[5] Among the aircraft taken to France at the outbreak of war by the Royal Flying Corps were seven Blériots, all with No.3 Squadron. In one of these, a two-seater, Captain P.B. Joubert de la Ferté carried out the first aerial reconnaissance of the war on 19 August. He was followed on this historic occasion by Lieutenant G.W. Mapplebeck on a Farnborough-built B.E. (signifying 'Blériot Experimental'). Both officers, it is recorded, 'lost their way but succeeded in returning.'

The British in France found their Blériots less suitable under active service conditions than they had expected:

> After remaining several nights in the open, they showed signs of 'flabbiness' which were not found in the other aeroplanes then in use, and consequently their performance in the air fell off noticeably…The Blériot therefore although very satisfactory when new, came to be looked on as a bad machine for war service.[6]

Strangely, British sources are silent about the conspicuous feature which condemned the Blériot in the French army. In all, 104 Blériots were issued to the RFC: twenty-three went overseas in 1914 and nine in 1915. The last Blériot to be struck off the strength of the Royal Flying Corps in France was in use up to 6 June 1915.

The policy adopted by the French Ministry of War in October 1914 involved making very large purchases, albeit of a restricted number of aeroplane types. For Blériot there was the bitter-sweet compensation on 9 December 1914 of a huge order for 440 Caudron G3s, worth almost six million francs, after he had spent the autumn preparing for this – and building a few Blériots for which orders had somehow slipped through the embargo.

To build in the volume now required, the industry had to overcome major supply problems, as Emmanuel Chadeau has noted:

> The war effort was carried out in a country reduced by invasion: from the very first weeks of the war the coal mines, the metal industries and the textile works of the North/North-East, the industrial areas of the Aisne and Oise valleys were annexed, destroyed or paralysed.[7]

At Blériot's factory in the rue de la Revolte at Levallois the daunting task of overcoming unprecedented difficulties to produce an unprecedented quantity of aircraft of an unfamiliar design was placed in the ablest of hands – those of Alfred Leblanc.

★★★★★

Having delegated responsibility for current production, Blériot had freed himself to concentrate on what he was best at – getting out of desperate situations. His career as an aircraft manufacturer in his own right seemed to be at an end. Reduced to the role of subcontractor, with his famous monoplane declared obsolete and no new design to take its place, and committed to the construction of a large new factory on the bank of the Seine at Suresnes, Louis Blériot considered his position.

The near fatal flaw in his organisation was that he had no outstanding designer. Certainly he had competent engineers and draughtsmen, who had ensured the gradual development, and overall the immense improvement, of the Blériot XI, but when Raymond Saulnier had left in the autumn of 1909 there was a vacuum in creativity which had persisted for five years. Blériot had no one who seemed capable of bringing off a major innovation, and yet nothing less than a new and clearly superior design of aeroplane could enable his career to be re-launched. Such a designer, he knew, did exist, but recruiting him would necessitate making a massive investment.

One of the more dramatically successful, and certainly the fastest, aeroplanes in the pre-war years was the stylish and streamlined Deperdussin monoplane, winner of the Gordon Bennett Cup in 1912 and a repeated breaker of the world speed record, which it held when the war began with 203.60kph. The designer of these superb machines was Louis Béchereau, who by 1913 had earned a reputation at the top of his profession. He was associated with a particular *monocoque* type of construction. Three thin sheets of tulip wood were shaped and glued together to give a laminated fuselage which was strong and light, with smooth, uncluttered lines. An opportunity for Blériot to obtain his services arose just as the war began.

Béchereau had been employed, and his work had been grandly financed, by an extraordinarily successful self-made man of obscure Belgian origins who had become somewhat larger than life. When he was young, Armand Deperdussin earned a precarious living as a singer in café concerts in Brussels and then 'arrived' in Paris where he rapidly made a fortune from adventurous financial dealings as a silk broker. An aviation enthusiast, he set up Béchereau with a factory in 1910, first at Bétheny near Reims for a short time, and then in Paris in the aptly named rue des Entrepreneurs at

Grenelle in the 15ème arrondissement. At first the enterprise traded under the style of 'Aéroplanes A. Deperdussin', but sometime after March 1913 it was incorporated as: 'La Société de production des aéroplanes Deperdussin', a name later abbreviated as Spad, or SPAD.

Suddenly, in August 1913, Armand Deperdussin was arrested on suspicion of fraud, and he was eventually convicted, but with extenuating circumstances. His fraud had caused a bank to lose sixteen million francs. Deperdussin's transgressions related to silk not aeroplanes, but the sad and dramatic figure was ruined.[8] He was declared bankrupt and his aviation business passed into the hands of a court-appointed liquidator, who promptly prepared to sell it. Foreseeing the likelihood of war, the Ministry of War intervened and ordered the factory to be kept in full production.

Faced with this unaccustomed responsibility, the liquidator asked the court to appoint a suitably qualified person to help him. The court chose François Max Richard, an engineer who, by his own account, had already made a name for himself in the new industry, having been manager of the Astra company and having advised Henri Deutsch de la Meurthe to acquire the French rights to the Wrights' patents.[9]

It was made clear to Max Richard that the Ministry of War would be prepared to place large orders with the former Deperdussin factory – although not for their current model – but only if it was taken over by a new owner, because the Ministry would not deal with an insolvent supplier. On learning this, Max Richard went to Blériot and advised him to purchase the goodwill and the tangible assets of the workshops run by Béchereau, saying that the profit on the first order alone would more than cover the whole cost of acquisition.[10]

This was Blériot's great chance and he seized it. At the end of 1914 he led a group of businessmen in the purchase, taking up the majority of the shares himself, and becoming Chairman of the reconstructed company, with Béchereau as Technical Director and Max Richard as Managing Director, particularly responsible for the commercial side. According to Max Richard, Blériot also performed the role of private banker and technical adviser to Spad, which now stood for 'La Société Pour L'Aviation et ses Dérivés'.

The transformed company, with its new management and ample finance, would make Blériot, as the war went on, the leading aircraft producer on the Allied side, certainly in volume and frequently in renown. There would be more Spads than any other make, while in French hands the definitive versions had no superiors in the air. As the Supreme Allied Commander Marshal Foch declared, the Spads were indeed among *'les artisans de la Victoire.'*[11]

Spad was also, at least in the short term, an amazingly successful investment for Louis Blériot. In his personal balance sheet of 1 January 1916 he valued his 3,500 shares at 350,000 francs: twelve months later they appeared at a valuation of 2 million francs.

Max Richard proved to be an able general manager, acting in the same role in the rue des Entrepreneurs as Alfred Leblanc did at the new Blériot factory at Suresnes. He developed a deep admiration for Blériot, whom he considered: 'an engineer of the first rank. Beyond his technical competence, he saw clearly, he saw far, and never was the dictum "to manage is to foresee" better exemplified by anyone.'[12]

★★★★★

A Spad 7 having its machine gun adjusted, 1917 (MA 15426)

The first Spads to be employed on active service were the 'A' series, biplane two-seaters with the almost unbelievable feature that the propeller was positioned between the front and rear cockpits. Ahead of the fuselage proper, and attached to it by a single shaft around which the propeller rotated, was a small, separate fuselage cell, or *carlingue*, containing a cockpit for an observer/gunner who was provided with a swivelling machine gun mounted in front of him. The engine was a 110hp Le Rhône. The version principally employed in the field, the A-C2, was, just, the fastest French military aircraft when it was introduced in August 1915, with a maximum speed of 160kph. It took 11 minutes to climb to 2,000m and its ceiling was 4,000m.[13]

By the end of 1915 there were still only four A-C2s in service. Some more were delivered in the following year, but by April 1916 a new and altogether superior Spad was making its test flights. 'It was', J.M. Bruce has written, 'the first single-seat fighter to be powered by Marc Birkigt's brilliant new 150hp Hispano-Suiza engine, and was armed with a single Vickers machine-gun that was synchronized by a special mechanism also designed by Birkigt.'[14]

It was the increasingly effective and extensive use of aircraft in a variety of observation roles that led to the development of aerial combat and stimulated the construction of specialized aircraft, such as the new Spad, for that purpose. Quite simply, it was necessary to prevent enemy aircraft crossing over the Allied lines to carry out observations that would have deadly consequences, and conversely to protect Allied observation and bombing missions while behind enemy lines.

Hispano-Suiza aero engines were crucial to the success of the Spad marque, and their creator Marc Birkigt formed an alliance with Blériot which continued for the rest of

A Hispano-Suiza engine of the 1914-1918 war. (Royal Aeronautical Society)

Blériot's life. This is hardly surprising when we learn not only that Birkigt 'possessed an inspired genius for mechanical invention', but that 'his inventions were developed with absolute tenacity.'[15] Birkigt was an engineer from Geneva, who went to work in Barcelona in 1899 for a Swiss company called Vélino, developing electric vehicles. In 1904, when he was aged twenty-six, he founded the 'Fabrica La Hispano-Suiza de Automóviles' with the financial backing of Spanish industrialists. Two large four cylinder cars were prepared for the Paris Salon of 1906.

The motoring historian Ralph Stein has written that:

> Even the very early cars to come from Birkigt's drawing board were full of new ideas that became commonplace years later. The T-head, the cylinder cast as a unit (*en bloc*), the shaft drive with torque taken up by the rear springs.

199

By 1910 successful racing cars were being made, and from these was developed in 1912 what is regarded as one of the first production sports cars, the 'Alfonso XIII', named after the King of Spain who had become an enthusiastic and loyal customer.[16]

Then came the war. Neither Spain nor Switzerland was of course a belligerent, but by 1914 the company had a large factory in France. This had been specially built for car production at Bois-Colombes, near Paris. After various vicissitudes that factory became in 1915 the centre of Hispano-Suiza aero-engine production. This came about partly because Birkigt had already earned, if not an established reputation, at least certain credentials as a designer of aero-engines. In the previous three years he had taken out more than 100 patents relating to aero-engines in various countries. Prudently, Birkigt had set up a Swiss company to hold his patents and to collect licence fees from Hispano-Suiza, and later from other users as well. It was common at that time for leading inventors to hold 'their' patents for their own benefit and to charge 'their' companies for their use. Béchereau and Blériot did the same thing, for reasons which were partly fiscal.[17]

Birkigt's 1915 engine was a water-cooled V-8 of almost 12 litres capacity with many unusual and advanced features. For example, the cylinder blocks were cast in aluminium, overhead camshafts operated directly on the valves, the valve gear was fully enclosed, and there was force-fed lubrication.[18] The engine weighed 202kg and was rated at 150hp at 1,400rpm.

It was not so much in sheer speed, as in rate of climb and manoeuvrability that the Spad 7 outclassed its predecessor and most if not all of its contemporaries. The maximum horizontal speed at low altitude was 187kph compared to 160kph before, but reaching 2,000m took only 7 minutes, as against 11 minutes for the next best French aeroplane. Its ceiling was 5,000m.[19]

Here at last was a fighter which could satisfy, for the moment, the criteria laid down by Roland Garros in 1914: 'A machine which can fly higher and faster than any enemy aircraft, and by superior manoeuvrability place them in a position where they can best be attacked.'[20] Deliveries of the Spad 7 began prematurely in August 1916, in response to desperate pressure from the front to have at last a machine which could be a match for the dreaded Fokker E IIIs. But a full programme of tests had not been completed. The Hispano-Suiza suffered from lubrication problems at first, and there were persistent difficulties with the cooling system. Adjustable radiator shutters were developed, but they worked too well, in the sense that the engine was cooled excessively.

For a long time the quantities in which the Spad 7 could be produced were insufficient. The French army had only seventy of them at the front by February 1917. However, new production initiatives launched in the autumn of 1916 gave substantial results later in the following year. The measures taken included extending production of the new type from Spad's works in the rue des Entrepreneurs to Blériot's own factory at Suresnes. Blériot also created a formidable network of subcontractors, many making parts and some assembling complete aircraft.

Soon, the British Government also became a customer for Spad 7s. Although in the critical circumstances of the time it appears astonishing that France could spare even a single aircraft to another nation, such sales were in fact a well-established tradition. Right from the start of British military aviation in 1910, France had been a major source of both airframes and engines, and she continued to be a key supplier throughout the war, providing some 2,000 aircraft and some 12,000 engines.

Marc Birkigt, creator of Hispano-Suiza. (MA 4592)

At the start of the war the supply situation in Britain with regard to engines especially had been catastrophic. The then Chief Engineer of Daimler's in Coventry, A.E. Berriman, wrote:

> There were no aircraft engines in production in England when war was declared in the summer of 1914. The Daimler Company…arranged with Mr Holt-Thomas (who owned the English rights) to build the Gnome rotary air-cooled engine. But there were no drawings in England and no chance of getting them from France. An engine, therefore, was taken from an aeroplane at the Hendon Aerodrome and sent by road to Coventry. It was dismantled and measured in the Daimler tool-room. Drawings were prepared, also a printed list of parts, and I think we had the first engine running…in eight weeks.[21]

By April 1916 when the Spad 7 made its initial flights the British supply situation had been transformed, but the demand for aircraft was insatiable – Trenchard gave instructions on 12 May 1916 that all orders should be on the basis that aircraft would last only a maximum of two months.[22] Heavy purchasing from France was resumed in 1916 and 1917, especially of Nieuport and Spad fighters, and of Le Rhône and Hispano-Suiza engines. At first it was difficult for Britain to obtain French agreement to these new procurement programmes, but then the British offered the highly-prized Lewis, and later Vickers, machine-guns and Buckingham tracer bullets to France, and the two parties were able to deal on more even terms.

The Spad 7 impressed the Royal Flying Corps, and by October 1916 they had obtained three of them and wanted more. Thirty were ordered from Blériot's Suresnes factory, which delivered them between November 1916 and early 1917. Before the end of 1916 the British Royal Naval Air Service (RNAS) ordered 125 Spad 7s from two subcontractors in England. The RFC also ordered, probably in November 1916, 100 Spads from Blériot's new and only partly-built factory at Addlestone in Surrey, where Daimler's experience with the Gnome was virtually repeated, as a War Office letter of 4 December 1916 records:

> The Spad machine received as a sample by Messrs Blériot is now entirely dismantled in order that the firm may complete their drawings from the machine itself, those received from the French firm not being sufficiently complete to enable the machines to be built in England from them.

But still there were not enough Spads: 120 more were ordered by the RFC from the celebrated Parisian coachbuilder Kellner, temporarily transformed into the: 'Avionnerie Kellner et ses Fils', who would later secure a niche in automotive history by building the body for one of the seven Bugatti Royales. As with air frames, so with engines. Hispano-Suizas for Spads were made under licence by many firms, prominent among them in England being the Wolseley company.

The great ad hoc networks of constructors raised aircraft production to levels unattainable in any other way, but poor co-ordination caused many problems for the squadrons. There was chronic uncertainty about how complete any aircraft would be when received. Would they have engines, interrupter gear, guns, etc? Also, many practical difficulties resulted from faulty detailed design or manufacture. Even when these did not occur, aircraft maintenance in the field was hugely complicated by the multiplicity of sources of supply of the 'same' aircraft. Different contractors used different designs of radiator, different fabrics and, particularly awkward, different dopes and varnishes. At first, the maker of a particular aircraft could not always be identified, so detective work was carried out on fuselage construction, but it did not always reveal accurately which coating should be used in repair work. A wide variety of alternative products had to be obtained and stocked – and transported when the Squadron moved on. A useful innovation was to paint a small white 'K' on the Kellner Spads. Blériot's Spads made in England had a 'B' branded into the seat.

According to J.M. Bruce:

> The Spad 7 was, in the RFC, never quite the success that it was in French service. It seems that it was not regarded by the RFC as a particularly good dog-fighting aircraft, yet in the hands of individualistic French pilots it proved to be an outstandingly effective weapon…it remains one of the great classic types of the war.[23]

More than 5,000 Spad 7s were produced during the course of the conflict.

★★★★★

Aircraft were needed in such large quantities, not just to replace great losses, but because as the war went on new tactics were introduced progressively which depended on being able to deploy a large number of fighters simultaneously and for longer periods. After France had suffered the consequences of German air superiority in the early stages of the battle of Verdun, bold new tactics were introduced early in 1916 by Captain de Tricornot de Rose. He was a brilliant former pupil of the Blériot school at Pau, where he had arrived in 1910 and quickly displayed outstanding qualities as a pilot and as a leader. He was a cavalry officer in the tradition of Napoleon's Murat, who was afraid of nothing. Total offensive was de Rose's doctrine. This meant preventing all German incursions of French air space by occupying the sky continuously. To do this he introduced a highly organized system of rotation of group flying within defined sectors – the first fighter patrols. By April 1916 the Allies had recovered control of French air space, and observation flights across the enemy lines were resumed. The new tactic proved effective during the battle of the Somme in July 1916.

But the tide of the air war continued to swing this way and that, and it was driven as much by technology as by tactics. By the autumn of 1916 Germany had new and better aircraft, Halberstadts and Albatrosses of nearly 200hp which were very well armed. Then in the winter of 1916/17 two other remarkable developments occurred in German aviation: the number of fighters in service was tripled, and the successful system of patrolling in three layers was introduced by the von Richthofen circus.[24]

However, a French riposte was in preparation, because a new Spad was designed late in 1916. Designated the Spad 12, sometimes referred to as the 'Spad-Cannon', it was the result of particularly close cooperation throughout its development between Béchereau, Birkigt and the ace fighter pilot Georges Guynemer. The basic idea, it seems, was Guynemer's and it stemmed from his philosophy that:

> My aeroplane is neither more nor less than a flying machine-gun. One doesn't kill the Boche with aerobatics. One kills him by shooting at him as powerfully and as accurately as possible.[25]

Guynemer asked Béchereau for a fighter that could carry a 37mm Hotchkiss shell-firing gun. The new aeroplane resembled the Spad 7 in most respects except the power unit and armament. The engine was a 200hp Hispano-Suiza driving the propeller through reduction gearing arranged in such a way that the Hotchkiss gun placed between the cylinder banks could fire through a hollow propeller shaft. There was also a Vickers machine-gun installed conventionally on the fuselage at the pilot's eye level. Deliveries began in July 1917. Guynemer won four of his victories in the Spad 12. (An aspect of such 'scores' which is sometimes overlooked is that in the great majority of First World War aerial encounters there was neither victor nor vanquished. For example, Guynemer, in addition to his fifty-three victorious combats, and the one in which he in turn was killed, also took part in nearly 500 combats which were indecisive.[26])

Despite all the concentration on fighters, attempts were made from 1916 to develop a Blériot bomber. A young engineer called Touillet played an important role in designing four successive prototypes which were built at Suresnes. These aircraft were a total departure from all previous Blériots; they were four-engined biplanes, huge for their time. The last one, which was completed after the war ended, was the Bl 74, of 27m wing span. This, the *Mammouth*, had four Hispano-Suiza engines rated at 300hp each, two mounted on the upper wing and two on

Captain René Fonck with a Spad 12 cannon, 220hp Hispano-Suiza, 1917. One of the most effective Allied fighter pilots, Fonck testified that 'it was thanks to the Hispano-Suiza engine at the front line that we became masters of the air, and that we remained so.' (MA 1862)

the lower. None of these aircraft was considered entirely satisfactory and no production orders were given. However, theirs was a line of development to which Blériot would revert.

★★★★★

Efforts to provide the French squadrons with more and better aircraft began to bear fruit in the spring of 1917. Blériot and his men and women made their crucial contribution by producing the ultimate fighting Spad of the war, the type 13, built in staggering quantity, more than 8,000, making it the Spad of which most were built. The Spad 13 was designed in 1916, and appeared at the front in April 1917. As J.M. Bruce has explained, its appearance closely resembled the Spad 7, 'but could be distinguished by its more substantial fuselage, the curved trailing edge to its rudder, and the left-handed airscrew of its geared engine.'[27] At first it had a 200hp Hispano-Suiza engine, while later on 220hp versions were used.

For much of the remainder of 1917 many of the new power units did not work properly. The reduction gearing gave great trouble: units made by subcontractors seemed more prone to failure than those built by Hispano-Suiza. This apart, the Spad 13 had a remarkable performance, including a speed advantage over the Spad 7 of nearly 50kph.

Paradoxically, the improved performance of the latest fighters meant that even more of them were needed. They had a much increased ceiling, approaching 7,000m, and it was hard to master and defend so deep a slice of air. Experience showed that a fighter could not control an air space deeper than 2,000m, or even 1,500m during a large offensive. From this

André Herbemont, technical director and chief designer of Spad from May 1917, seen here at the age of 27, in 1920. (MA 1487)

1920 _ André HERBEMONT a 27 ans

Il vient d'être décoré de la Légion d'Honneur.

Il est Directeur Technique des AVIONS SPAD .

Le SPAD XX, dit "SPAD-HERBEMONT"a été commandé en grande série en 1918, à la fin de la Grande Guerre.

Ce même SPAD XX a battu, en 1920, le record du monde de vitesse, en dépassant 309 kms. à l'heure, avec le Pilote DE ROMANET.

came the idea of three or even four layers of aircraft, each protecting the one below.

With both sides now using similar tactics, equally extravagant in aircraft, supply became decisive. In this the Allies at last seized the advantage, so that by the spring of 1917 the war in the air turned tentatively in their favour. In 1918 the aircraft industry in France attained its war-time zenith in terms of the quantity and the suitability of its production.

Another innovation occurred as part of the crucial offensive in Champagne on 15 July 1918 when massive French bombing raids were made against German ground forces, one of them involving eighty-eight Breguet bombers plus their Caudron escorts. On the nineteenth the German army began to be turned back at the Ourcq: it was the beginning of the end. The ensuing four months of mobile warfare caused many problems for Allied air forces. Continually having to find new airfields was difficult, and there was never enough transport so that much *matériel* was abandoned, leading to renewed shortages at the ever advancing front.

★★★★★

An experimental Spad 13, 200hp Hispano-Suiza, fitted with a Rateau *turbo-compresseur in 1917.* (MA 23928)

The effect of aviation on the outcome of the war was, on the whole, neutral, with the possible exception of the closing phase when Allied air superiority permitted ground attacks without much risk of retaliation. Air superiority changed hands many times during the course of the war: a technical advantage or a tactical innovation would give one side the lead until it was imitated by the other. In the end success came from a greater capacity for mass production. Annual output of airframes in France rose from 541 in 1914 to 23,669 in 1918, and of engines from 900 to 44,560.[28]

Louis Blériot had played his part. According to his youngest son Jean, the grand total of all Spad production during the war was more than 16,000. 'At the end of the war, the factory at Suresnes turned out an aeroplane every 55 minutes.' The Spads rolling out of the door at Suresnes were taken across the Seine on a barge – a cumbersome and hazardous operation because of the volume of river traffic – to the race-course at Longchamp just on the other side. From there they took off and were flown to depots, prior to delivery to squadrons[29] – French, British and American. Blériot's market share in 1917 was 10%, and in 1918 sales in excess of 100 million francs placed him at the head of the list of French manufacturers.[30]

★★★★★

What aviation had done to the war was one thing, but what had the war done to aviation? One commentator, David Wragg, has written:

> It is a widely accepted belief that the 1914-18 war advanced aviation more in four years than would have been possible in more than forty years of peace. To accept this is to ignore not only the very real progress made between December

The Blériot 74 Mammouth, *with four Hispano-Suiza engines of 300hp. The aircraft was designed for use as a bomber, or alternatively for the transport of twenty-six passengers, 1919. (MA 2567)*

1903 and August 1914, but also the fact that the developments of World War I were made possible by stretching existing technology to its limits, rather than by any vast technological strides forward. For the most part engines and airframes were developments of designs available before the start of the war…[31]

For *military* aviation, however, there is no doubt that the 1914-18 war was its real birthplace. The condition, and the status, of military aviation in 1913 and 1914 were clearly such that nothing other than a major war could have taken them forward. But the effects were different in different countries, and they remain matters on which opinions differ. J.M. Bruce has written:

Whatever harm the first World War may have done to the development of British Aviation, there can be no doubt that it gave a tremendous impetus to the development of British aircraft. During those four years of conflict the advances which were made under the urgent spur of relentless necessity were of a magnitude which has not been surpassed in any subsequent period of equal length. Techniques of design, construction, production, operation and combat did not merely have to be improved; they had to be devised.[32]

Commandant Caquot, the head in 1918 of the *Section technique aéronautique*, when asked later to express his opinion on the general influence of the war on technical progress in aviation replied: 'Very little. It simply meant that technical advances would take place

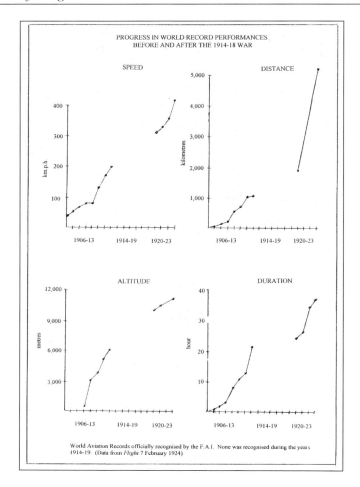

PROGRESS IN WORLD RECORD PERFORMANCES
BEFORE AND AFTER THE 1914-18 WAR

World Aviation Records officially recognised by the F.A.I. None was recognised during the years 1914-19. (Data from *Flight* 7 February 1924)

because money was available. It was a question of money...'[33]

A limited analysis of performance data suggests that the truth is more mundane than some of the opinions cited above. While record-making performances are obviously not indicative of every-day capabilities, the trends they show over a long period of years are of some significance as objective measures of progress. An analysis of the world records for speed, distance, duration and altitude set in the eighteen year period from 1906 to 1923 inclusive, reveals that the rates of progress were rather constant, apparently unaffected by whether the world was at war or at peace.[34]

Whatever may have been the 'progress' made in the 1914-18 war, not everyone in aviation welcomed the way it had been achieved. Alberto Santos-Dumont was so appalled that he never got over it. His feelings about the war were thought to have contributed to the state of mind that led him to suicide. As for Orville Wright, towards the end of the war he wrote simply: 'What a dream it was; what a nightmare it has become.'

16 Vision and realism

Although the Blériot marque disappeared after the early banishment of the type XI, primarily because it gave poor visibility, by the end of the war Louis Blériot had again become the leading aircraft manufacturer in France. This achievement was of course due to the outstanding successes of the Spad designs and to his ability to greatly supplement Spad's own production capacity by using his large modern factory at Suresnes, and later an additional factory built on land he bought near Bordeaux.

When peace came Blériot stood poised to become the victim of his spectacular, if in a way surprising, business success. Like other successful aircraft manufacturers he was the possessor of vastly excessive capacity, and like them, he was faced by an uncertain future exacerbated by the huge surplus stocks of aircraft and engines which would overhang the post-war market for several years. Those stocks, which early in 1919 amounted to nearly 10,000 aeroplanes and some 23,000 aero engines, were eventually liquidated in an orderly way over the following six years. This was achieved by the 'Société des Stocks', a combined endeavour by the industry, managed initially by Alfred Leblanc.[1]

What peacetime aviation would consist of was quite unclear at the end of 1918. It was obvious that there would be no military market for some years in any of the major previously belligerent countries. There was no civil market either. The demand for individual 'sports' and 'touring' machines, on which Blériot and others had once set great store, had effectively dried up well before the war had started. Civil air transport, for long in Blériot's view the true future of aviation, still did not exist. It would now have to be created, for there was no alternative. Unless markets could be established for the carrying of letters, parcels and passengers, aviation would be finished until next there was a war.

As if Blériot did not have enough to worry about in the spring of 1919, fate dealt him the first of a long series of cruel blows. The patent litigation which had been put aside during the war was resumed. On 8 March the court gave its verdict in favour of Robert Esnault-Pelterie, annulled Blériot's 1907 patent for the famous *cloche*, and awarded damages against him of 780,000 francs. 'Failure over the Channel would have done less harm to the firm than the loss of this case', Blériot is reputed to have said on hearing the news.[2] The trial had reached back over the events of his career, to the time when he had first flown. What hurt above all was the feeling that his reputation as a pioneer was somehow diminished, and that credit for an idea so valuable to aeronautics had been taken from him. (However, there is a mystery here, because the statutes of Blériot-Aéronautique drawn up three years later refer to that patent (No.374494) as if it were valid at that time.)[3]

As well as regret, there may have been a sense of release, in as much as a long-running cause of worry had at last been removed, however unsatisfactorily. If so, the relief was short-lived, for one chronic anxiety would quickly be replaced by another. Blériot's tax affairs, it soon became apparent, were in disarray, and his struggle to resolve them would drag on almost until the end of his life, the dispute with the authorities being about alleged war-time profits.

★★★★★

Nothing could distract Blériot for long from the pursuit of his passion. His determination to succeed as an aircraft manufacturer never wavered, but he knew only too well that the priority now was to survive, and for this he adopted a three-pronged strategy. He would help create a civil market by joining with others to found an airline, he would develop two distinctly different transport aircraft from some of his war-time designs, and he would launch a great diversification programme to keep his cherished factory at Suresnes intact for a better future.

On 6 April 1919 Messrs Blériot, Breguet, Caudron, Farman, Morane, Saulnier, Weiller and Renault set up the 'Compagnie des Messageries Aériennes' (CMA), and appointed Alfred Leblanc as managing director. Using Breguet's successful war-time bomber, the type XIV, regular services were quickly started between Paris and Lille, and between Paris and Brussels. That choice of routes was determined by the opportunity, however temporary, presented by the extensive destruction of roads and railways in those regions. By June 1919 a link between Paris and London was in tentative operation in order to ascertain the costs of providing a service between the two capitals.[4]

CMA had Alfred Leblanc at its head for less than three years, because he died in November 1921, at the age of fifty-two. He was worn out, it was said, by his labours throughout the war as general manager of Suresnes, swiftly followed by the dual task of launching and running two enterprises for which there were no close precedents, both essential to the future of aviation in France – the Société des Stocks and CMA. Leblanc's early death was a heavy blow to Blériot, who had felt able to depend on him as he did on no one else, and to accept his commercial judgement which was probably superior to his own.

In 1919, Blériot, then a fighter specialist, had of course no suitable aircraft to offer CMA, but he planned to rectify that soon. First, he put the Spad company into liquidation, so shedding some capacity by disposing of its factories in the rue des Entrepreneurs and at Juvisy, and brought Herbemont (who had succeeded Béchereau as chief designer in 1917) with key members of his staff to Suresnes, where all work in France would from now on be concentrated.

André Herbemont, born in 1893, was a graduate of the Ecole des Arts et Métiers at Chalons-sur-Marne who went to work as a joiner for Deperdussin in 1912. The next year he moved into the drawing office under Béchereau. He became technical director of Spad in May 1917, after Béchereau's departure. 'In a quarter of a century, Herbemont was responsible for the design of 140 prototypes, of which 123 were flown, and almost 1,200 production aircraft, many of which were exported'[5]

At Suresnes, the men from Spad mightily reinforced a small design team which included Touillet. His bomber prototypes had not found favour during the war, but Blériot now saw a future for them. They were biplanes and they had four engines, two on the upper wing, and two on the lower. In early versions the fuselage was suspended equidistant between the upper and lower wings, a layout which required an amazing array

The Blériot 75 Aérobus *for twenty-six passengers, 1920. (P 110170)*

of struts and wires. The complicated appearance was accentuated by an eight-wheeled undercarriage. Trials of one of the prototypes, with a fuselage by then resting on the lower wing, continued until 22 January 1920 when it broke up in the air, killing its pilot.

Such was the unpromising precursor from which Blériot grandly proposed in 1919 to develop an airliner to carry the unheard of number of twenty-eight passengers. The task of converting the *Mammouth*, as it was aptly named, into the *Aérobus* was given to Herbemont. He strengthened the wings, and altered their shape and section. The resulting aircraft, the Blériot 75, was shown at the Salon of 1919, and late in 1920 several good flights were made by one of the firm's test pilots, Jean Casale, but no orders were obtained from CMA or anyone else. Two improved versions were designed but found no buyer and were never built. While the *Mammouth* had been funded by the Ministry of War, apparently its transformation into the *Aérobus* was undertaken by Blériot at his own expense.[6] With hindsight it seems obvious that the project was over-ambitious, stretching obsolescent technology beyond its limits.

True to his investor's approach to aircraft development, Blériot had hedged against the failure of the *Aérobus* by pursuing another venture in parallel. At the end of the war Herbemont had designed a two-seater fighter, the Spad XX, with which he arrived at a set of definitive design principles from which he rarely departed throughout the rest of his long career. These included: monocoque fuselage in moulded tulip wood, V-shaped upper wing for better visibility and speed, straight lower wing, a single strut between each pair of wings, ailerons on the lower wings, and wooden construction throughout with fabric covering.[7] Herbemont now designed a *limousine* version of the Spad XX. Seats for two passengers were provided in a closed cabin within the fuselage, just behind the pilot who continued to occupy an open cockpit. This, the Spad 27, first flew in November 1919. Small, fast and practicable, with its 300hp Hispano-Suiza engine, it appealed to CMA who purchased ten which were used on its Paris-London service.[8]

Spad XX, 300hp Hispano-Suiza, a two-seater fighter, 1920. (MA 25688)

★★★★★

With no aircraft in production in 1919, and two costly development projects to fund, Blériot had really no alternative but to diversify production if he was to stay in business and keep his factory and a nucleus of his skilled labour force in readiness for the time when, somehow, aircraft manufacture could start again.

For the next few years a chaotic variety of unrelated products poured, or more often trickled, from Suresnes. It was as if their selection had been inspired by a toy cupboard. There were ships, sand yachts, motorcycles, cars, furniture and pre-fabricated houses. To some extent at least, the need for and the nature of such a programme had been foreseen before the war ended. In the summer of 1918 Blériot had recruited a *centralien* and war-time pilot named Jean Brun to reorganize the factory and equip it with the metal-working machinery the new product range would require. Brun found when he started that there were only wood-working machines, and a large clear space used for assembling aircraft.

There were difficulties right from the start, provoked by Blériot's opportunistic acceptance of a government contract to build tuna fishing boats for the Boulogne fleet, to replace vessels lost in the war. These were substantial small ships, with wooden hulls, and their construction was a task for which the factory could hardly have been less appropriate, except perhaps that only the width of a road, the Quai Gallieni, separated it from the Seine into which they could be launched. The fact that Blériot went into such an incongruous and risky venture shows the peril of his situation.

Jean Brun later reminded him ruefully of those days:

> ...you asked me to produce boats in a workshop that was totally unsuitable
> for the job. After going through endless contortions we built, launched,

Spad 27 Limousine, 300hp Hispano-Suiza, which carried two passengers seated side-by-side in a closed cabin behind and below the pilot, 1919. These aircraft were used on the Paris-London route by the Compagnie des Messageries Aériennes. (MA 28364)

rigged and delivered thirty vessels, then we had great trouble in winding up this laborious and painful venture.

At the same time you asked me to produce a motorcycle which had been designed, before I was recruited, by Touillet and that sinister[…]. Once again I threw myself into the job and, with the help of my brother in this thankless task, I succeeded, despite having to stop production on four occasions, in getting that ill-conceived machine to work, while being prevented from changing it very much because large stocks of components, for which I was not responsible, had already been built up.

You thought the development of the motorcycle took too long, but you had never done any mechanical engineering at the factory, and it was necessary first to set up all the facilities for metal-working, namely to recruit skilled people, oversee the choice of steels, establish departments for heat treatment, assembly, quality control, etc. and to do all this with imbeciles like […] and […], whom I did not then dare to dismiss…[9]

In fact, the motorcycle that emerged from these fraught beginnings was no discredit to the name it bore. Immaculately enamelled in *bleu de France* – the one colour offered – the Blériot *Touriste* was a sound, workmanlike job, if a little on the heavy side. Disc wheels front and rear were its most striking feature. There was a 500cc four-stroke air-cooled vertical twin engine (bore 60mm, stroke 88mm), going up to 3,500rpm. Precociously, clutch and three-speed gearbox were integral with the crankcase. Final drive was by belt. There was no front brake, but two brakes on the back wheel: one was actuated by a foot pedal and operated on the rear belt pulley, while the second was a drum brake worked by a lever on the handlebar. Both wheels were suspended with systems using enclosed spiral springs: greasing of the suspension joints was recommended every 400km. A variant on the basic design, called the *Sport*, was also available. Here weight was saved by dispensing with rear suspension and by machining surplus metal from the frame, and a racing-style riding position was provided. A maximum speed of 80kph was claimed, against 70kph for the touring model.[10]

As might be anticipated, a publicity poster depicted the Blériot *Touriste* flying through the air at an impressive angle of climb, above the caption: *Elle ne roule pas elle vole!* That was all very well, but it is unlikely that the marketing effort extended much beyond a few posters, an illustrated catalogue, and a little press advertising. The lack of a distribution network, the not outstanding qualities of the product, intense competition from far too many suppliers for a much over-estimated demand for motorcycles in the early 1920s, all these factors spelt the commercial failure of Blériot motorcycles, for few were ever sold.

The extent of the failure is suggested by the fact that in 1922 the entire stock of unsold motorcycles remaining, which had cost 550,000 francs to make, was written off as worthless. Surprisingly, engine parts had been machined in-house, necessitating a substantial investment in specialized machine tools for which there was no further use. In May 1923 Jean Brun hoped to realize 200,000 francs by their disposal, but he had difficulty in getting Blériot to make up his mind whether to sell them.[11]

There was one part of the diversification programme where Blériot and his people knew perfectly well what they were doing, but unfortunately its potential to contribute to the programme's success was not significant. Long ago, before the turn of the century, while still in his twenties, Blériot had become an enthusiastic sailor of sand yachts on the Normandy beaches. Characteristically, while on holiday he threw his engineering energy into improving the design and construction of these wheeled craft.

There is a report that as early as 1900 he supplied a *chariot à voiles* to the painter Michel Cazin who used it at Hardelot (where Blériot had a summer villa) and was later regarded as one of the pioneers of the sport.[12] By 1913 Blériot was advertising, along with aeroplanes, his *aéroplages*, this being the elegant and evocative term which he coined (and cannily registered as a trade name). Fellow aviators were among his customers, and interest was stimulated by organized races. His salesmanship was persuasive:

> Sailing on land is an excellent preparation for sea-sailing, for it reproduces all its difficulties without any of its dangers. It is also very much less expensive.
>
> It is an extremely healthy sport, with the intoxicating speed of the motor car, but in sea air free of all dust. Young people, children even, can learn easily, and virtually without risk. These models, mounted on four pneumatic tyres spaced far apart, are very stable and run smoothly. When wind and sand conditions are favourable speeds of 60kph and more are attainable. At low tide especially, real voyages can be made: the return trip is easy because Aéroplages are docile when tacking and, thanks to their light and sophisticated construction, they are responsive to the slightest wind.[13]

Blériot's standard model, his *Aéroplage Populaire*, sold in 1920 for about 600 francs. For this the customer got a two-seater yacht, weighing about 60kg, with a wheelbase of 2.50m and track of 1.50m, and carrying 8sq.m of sail on a single mast. Never more than a marginal side-line, the *aéroplages* were susceptible to little further development – their successors today look remarkably similar – and their market was minimal, because few beaches, in reality, could offer them worthwhile scope.

No attempt seems to have been made to revive another of Blériot's pre-war hobbies, hydroplaning, for the diversification programme (he had built experimental hydroplanes, which he called *Pnydres*, in 1913). However, sensible use was made of existing wood-working skills and machinery, with minor ventures in pre-fabricated housing and furniture. But the culmination of the firm's efforts to diversify was, unquestionably, the Blériot car.

No sooner had the versatile and energetic Jean Brun solved the production problems of the motorcycle than Blériot gave him another assignment:

> You asked me to make a 'cyclecar', by copying that *amalgame antimécanique* which constitutes the English cyclecar (air-cooled engine, belt-drive, wooden chassis). We made a four-stroke engine and a gearbox, but we had hardly finished before you were complaining that it was all too complicated. Then we made a two-stroke engine and took a lot of technical decisions which were very difficult to put into practice and which horrified the public. You stopped it, and I told you at the time that you were right, because we hadn't got a car of the sort customers wanted, and neither the commercial muscle nor the financial strength to compete with rivals like Amilcar, Salmnson, Peugeot or Citroën.[14]

★★★★★

It was not however at Suresnes but at Addlestone in Surrey that much of the drama of the Blériot car would be played out. Since the engineering heresies it exemplified were allegedly English in origin, this was perhaps appropriate.

First, Blériot would spend a holiday in England. Despite all the industrial turmoil of 1919 he managed to get away for a much needed break. He was particularly anxious to take his family to England because he had bought a house there in 1916 which they had never been able to use. This was 'Riversdale', an elaborate neo-Tudor mansion standing in twelve acres on a lovely reach of the Thames at Bourne End in Buckinghamshire. The house had twenty-one bedrooms, five reception rooms, and its many other attractions included a winter garden and superb grounds running down to the water's edge, where a boathouse stood.

Life there that summer had an Elysian quality, as Alice Blériot remembered:

> It was lively and amusing, with servicemen back from the war organising boating parties to go up the Thames. Our house was well known, and people knew that Blériot was there, so they came and serenaded him under our windows. A party of English airmen had rented a cottage on one of the nearby backwaters, and they came to dine or play tennis or bowls several times a week...
>
> We had an electrically driven boat that could take twenty or thirty people. We would set out in the afternoon and have tea or dinner on board. The

men wore bathing costumes under their clothes, and late in the evening they would go to the stern and jump in, then follow us home swimming…these young men brought a great deal of gaiety and entertainment to our stay over there… they were all aces of 1914-18.[15]

Apparently, Blériot had not been in England since before the war. He recalled later that his war-work in France: 'occupied sixteen hours a day and left me little time to be involved in the running of my foreign factories.' Nonetheless his aircraft works at Addlestone had done well, both for the war effort and for its shareholders. Shortly after the war began, he felt obliged to give this establishment what he called a *façade anglaise*, by changing its name and bringing in British nationals as substantial minority shareholders. Thus 'Blériot Aircraft' became 'The Air Navigation Company Limited', with Blériot holding 150,000 of the 240,000 shares issued. He noted later:

> This was a very substantial enterprise, with net profits of more than £53,000 in 1915. Those profits were used partly to enlarge the factory and partly to buy another property [Riversdale]. The business was then at its peak… my net assets in England at that period amounted to some £200,000.[16]

The collapse at the end of the war was total. Frantic efforts were made to obtain a share of the very few orders for military aircraft placed by the British government in the immediate post-war years, but despite Blériot's contribution to the war effort, his *façade anglaise*, and his willingness to go even to the length of resigning from the board of directors (which he did in December 1923), the national constructors were able to squeeze him out: 'I soon learned to my cost that those who are absent are always in the wrong. [The Society of British Aircraft Constructors] refused to accept me as a member. That decision meant the end of any chance of government orders and amounted almost to an expulsion.'[17]

Even before this, the business, or a part of it described as the 'Blériot Manufacturing Aircraft Co.', had been put into liquidation. The creditors were paid in full and by the end of January 1919 the shareholders had received back just over 75% of their original investment.[18]

Blériot's feelings about England and the English must have been bitter-sweet that year. Simultaneously idolized and, as he saw it, conspired against, he refused to accept defeat and decided boldly, not to give up Addlestone, but to build his car there.

The Blériot 'Whippet', for so it was called in England, was a two-seater open touring car, of which two examples survive in a private collection in France. It possessed several unorthodox, not to say idiosyncratic, features but the result was only moderately impressive. The factory's expertise was with wood, and thus they used it as much as possible. The chassis was almost entirely made from that material, as was the body, the latter being protected from the elements by a covering of leathercloth. Suspension was by four quarter-elliptic leaf springs, apparently undamped. Power came from an air-cooled V twin Blackburn motorcycle engine with belt drive to the solid rear axle. A handbrake operated through the drive belt, but otherwise there were apparently no brakes, on early versions at least. What looked like a radiator cap was in fact where the petrol went in, but apart from that one comical detail the general impression given by the car is not terribly

Blériot Whippets in full production at the Addlestone factory in the early 1920s. (Author's Collection)

attractive. Looking today at the Blériot motorcycle, it is easy to feel sorry that it was not more successful. But sight of the Whippet does not evoke similar regrets. It is strange to think that while Blériot was making this, his ally Marc Birkigt was turning out some of the very best cars ever made. The Hispano-Suizas of the 1920s have few peers.

Nevertheless, the Whippet had its partisans, and none was more fervent and consistent than Norbert Chéreau, who for so long had been Blériot's manager in England. Of course, Chéreau knew there would be no job for him if the car project failed, as frequently seemed imminent. By 1921 much of Blériot's remaining fortune in England had been invested in its development, and he was doubly reluctant to send further funds from France, being pessimistic about his longer term prospects in England and wanting to stick to his principle that each business should function independently. However, there were times when he had to make an exception, as on the occasion in January 1921 when Chéreau reported that he had ninety-two unsold cars in the showroom, and a stubborn array of creditors who would supply no more materials until they were paid. Blériot sent his finance director, J.B. Antelme, to Addlestone to investigate, but he could only confirm that Chéreau's request for funds was well-founded.[19]

By the end of the year, although Blériot was certainly weary of the car project, some slight degree of confidence reigned again at the English company, which was now called 'The Air Navigation & Engineering Co. Ltd' at the 'Blériot aircraft and motor car works…adjoining Addlestone Station (L.& S.W.Ry.)'. (With more optimism than accuracy the company's letter heading also asserted that they were: 'Contractors to H.M. Government'.) Chéreau was in the habit of writing to Blériot at least once a week to keep him up to date with current events in the factory. His neat, handwritten letters were usually received at Suresnes the next day, such was then the speed of the post. In one, written on 17 December 1921, he made a remarkably argued plea:

Voiturettes: This week we received four new orders and numerous requests for information from England and the Colonies. Since you would like to stop car production, after allowing for those ordered already, I want to give you the following information, in addition to what Monsieur Antelme has noted already. If we stop production we will make our large stocks of parts completely worthless. If on the contrary we go on using those parts we shall obtain substantial value from them each time we sell a car.

I have in fact calculated that each car which we sell to the agents for £182, our cost for all components and labour is £130, so we are left with £52 per car. If we produce 150 vehicles, which I have no hesitation in saying could easily be sold between January and the end of July, that would give us £7,800. If we spent £800 of that on advertisements we would still have £7,000 to put towards our general overheads. Such a sum would be a very appreciable contribution, and it would prevent the catastrophe of closing down completely, which would damage our reputation so much with the Ministry of War as well as in the eyes of the public. You will say perhaps that we cannot be certain to sell these 150 cars, but I am convinced that we would sell them easily, judging by what is happening at present. Both the agents and the general public are very pleased with the new model, and I believe the demand for it will grow in the new year. It is much more attractive than the old one whose belt-drive, we have to admit, stopped sales last season…

In all sincerity, I know that we now have a small car that is really astonishing: almost 7,500km without having to touch anything; 106km per gallon of petrol; 1,200 km per gallon of oil, all that on top of its other good points you already know about, and we guarantee that it will climb any hill. Basing myself on these facts, I am compelled to say to you that without any fanciful hopes for sales, even the conservative forecast I have given you makes it worthwhile to continue instead of abandoning everything.

But abandoned it all had to be. Production stopped in mid-January 1922 and sixty-two employees were dismissed. Seven cars were delivered from stock in January and eight in February: then the agents reported that there was no demand. There were many better buys available than Blériot's Whippet: it was never good enough, and stood little chance in a British market overcrowded by almost 100 manufacturers. His own matter-of-fact account of the end in England speaks for itself:

When the war was over I went to London and saw that the factory could get no orders for aircraft and must try to live off something else. We began making cars, but the development costs used up all the money I still had available.

By 1922 I considered liquidation because the English tax authorities were demanding large sums in respect of the company's profits during the war. The situation became hopeless and the factory was seized by creditors in 1926 and sold without me receiving a penny. It was the same with 'Riversdale'… sold for £2,000 to pay creditors in 1927.

Finally, my fortune in England, which in 1914 and 1915 had been about £200,000, had now completely gone.[20]

Fortunately for Blériot his other foreign venture, in Italy, had finished 'a little better.' He once explained how:

In 1916 the Italian government, needing aircraft, obliged me to hand over SIT, in which I owned most of the shares, to an Italian firm, the Ansaldo shipbuilders of Genoa. They paid me in cash for my 5,900 shares, at 250 lira, plus other compensation. It was therefore a sum of about two million gold francs which was paid to me at that time. I took them with me to the Principality of Monaco where I purchased the Hôtel de la Méditerranée and the villa called 'Le Nid', both of which I still own [in 1932].[21]

By the end of 1922 the diversification programme was over. It had run its course, with none of its products able to sustain it any longer. In one sense it had been a chapter of disaster, but that should not disguise its complete success in achieving its central objective, the survival of Suresnes. It was the end, not the means, that Blériot cared about. According to one of his senior managers at the time, J.B. Antelme, Blériot took no interest in the non-aeronautical products, and his technical and design staff seem to have largely followed his example, because Antelme complained that he could never get the support from them that he needed.[22]

If so, it was because the design and technical staff had better things to do. In 1920, just when the diversification initiatives were most in need of concentrated attention, a distraction was caused by an apparent revival of the aviation business. Quite suddenly, several variants on Herbemont's basic theme were in demand and, reassuringly, interest came from both military and civil sources. The benchmark Spad XX, ordered before the end of the war, still had such appeal for the Ministry of War that 100 more were ordered, while orders for a new two-seater side-by-side trainer, with dual controls, the Spad 34-2, would ultimately total 150 (some of them stayed in service until 1936). Spirits were lifted too by a new record for the firm. On 5 November 1920 a Blériot test pilot, Bernard de Romanet, broke the world speed record with 319.012 kph in a Spad XX.

At the same time, Herbemont's policy of evolutionary design led, on the transport side, to a successor to the two-passenger Spad 27 which had been well-received by CMA. This was the Spad 33, which first flew in December 1920. A cabin for four passengers was placed in the forward half of the fuselage, in front of the pilot's open cockpit and just behind the Salmson nine cylinder radial engine of 260hp. Altogether forty-one of these aircraft were built, including fifteen for the Compagnie des Messageries Aériennes and twenty for the Compagnie Franco-Roumaine. The type 33 played an important role in airline development until 1927, opening up many new routes.

The Spad 33 was followed within six months by a variant, the Spad 46, which used the same fuselage but larger wings and a more powerful engine, a 370hp Lorraine. In December 1921 a Spad 46 attracted attention by flying from Paris to Istanbul and back, a distance of 5,054km. From 1922 the Compagnie Franco-Roumaine bought thirty-eight of

Cabin of a Spad 33, a Berline *with one 260hp Salmson engine. The cabin contained seating for four passengers, while a fifth sat in the open cockpit beside the pilot. 1920. (MA 8703)*

these machines, at 60,000 francs each. One of the more celebrated Spad *Berlines*, they were in use on the Paris-Warsaw and Paris-Istanbul routes until 1930.[23]

Encouraging as the new business was, some of it was not profitable, and the volume of aircraft manufacture was still far below the capacity of Suresnes, 'this too big and too beautiful factory', as Jean Brun described it. By 1922 the revival had flagged and Blériot was sub-contracting for Nieuport, building 270 machines for them that year at prices forced down by fierce competition from other constructors also afflicted by under-use of their facilities.

It was also in 1922 that Blériot took the defensive step of turning his aviation business into a limited company. Although the original business designation of 1906: 'L. Blériot, Ing. ECP – Recherches Aéronautiques' had given way to the modern name of 'Blériot Aéronautique', the business had throughout those momentous sixteen years had been carried on by Louis Blériot as sole proprietor with unlimited personal liability. The newly formed company, Blériot-Aéronautique S.A., had a nominal capital of 6,000,000 francs and to it, in return for most of the shares, Blériot handed over virtually the entire business as a going concern. The brand names of 'Blériot' and 'Spad', the premises, the stocks and work in progress were ceded. He gave the company a licence to use his aeronautical patents in France, while retaining for himself the ownership of these, as well as of all rights in his foreign patents.[24]

There was a substantial loss in 1922. Such profits as were earned by some of the new Spads were insufficient to cover the losses incurred in building Nieuports, write-offs on the termination of motorcycle and car production, and last but not least the writing off of

The Blériot 115, with four 180hp Hispano-Suiza engines and a cabin for eight passengers, 1923. (P 116115)

the development costs of unsuccessful aircraft projects, notably the *Aérobus* – which he had undertaken as a private venture with no external funding.

★★★★★

In the face of all the disappointments and dramatic business difficulties heaped upon Louis Blériot in the early 1920s, his faith in the future of aviation did not flinch, and his conviction that he still had a role to play in it seemed as unshakeable as ever. But it was his actions that made this plain, not his words. Indeed, of words there even fewer than before. Reserved and taciturn he had always been, but under the terrible pressures of the times, he became still more withdrawn. Jean Brun complained that he was difficult to work for:

> Your extremely reserved character means that I am never fully in the picture about the current position, and I never know what your plans are… I hope you will forgive me for this letter, and understand that it has done me a lot of good to write to you so freely…[25]

Nevertheless, Blériot's resilience remained a byword, and it was undoubtedly a factor in retaining the respect of men like Brun, who stayed with him until 1926, then becoming chief executive of the Farman airline, and later a director of Air France. Never was that resilience more vividly demonstrated than by his resolve, when all seemed hopeless in 1922, to launch a new project on the grand scale. It was time, he decided, to build another four-engined airliner.

The idea came from a new designer recruited in February 1922, Léon Kirste, an Austrian who had worked for Breguet in England. Kirste's Blériot 115 was a biplane with two Hispano-Suiza 180hp engines on each set of wings. Although its overall dimensions were little different from those of Herbemont's *Aérobus*, Kirste's design was by comparison simple and clean-lined. There was a cabin for the realistic number of

The Blériot 115: the pilot's elevated seat, and part of the passenger cabin. (MA 29062)

eight passengers, lit by triangular windows, and at the front of this was a 'glazed balcony' giving the crew of two good visibility, although they sat one behind the other. The Blériot 115 was capable of taking off on two engines. The prototype was built in just four months and made its maiden flight at Buc on 9 May 1923, in the hands of Jean Casale, the firm's chief test pilot. On 1 June he took it up, with a one ton load, to 5,600m setting a new world record for that particular feat. Tragedy intervened in this meteoric progress on 23 June when in a high wind and at the low altitude of 600m an aileron cable jumped a pulley and jammed. In the inevitable crash Jean Casale, marquis de Montferrat, lost his life.

By September a second prototype was ready to take part in an important, and complex, series of competitive tests at Le Bourget called the 'Grand Prix des avions de transport'. With 500,000 francs in prize money, the event attracted eight entrants. A bizarre and much criticised rule of the competition was that participants had to demonstrate their ability to replace sparking plugs while in flight. The Blériot 115 finished third in the overall classification, a remarkable performance in view of the short time that had been available to develop it.

Thus 1923 came to an end on a note of some optimism, although it had been another year of factory under-performance, with the firm surviving by building and marketing seaplanes for Maurice Blanchard, a designer who, perhaps wisely in those days, preferred to contract out his construction and marketing rather than set up facilities of his own.

17 The hard years

In 1924 and 1925 the affairs of Blériot-Aéronautique seemed to take a dramatic turn for the better, and of the company's two marques, Blériot and Spad, it was the latter which was prominent. For the first time since 1920 substantial aircraft orders were obtained, and it was to the traditional André Herbemont rather than the more radical Léon Kirste that these successes were due. What Jean Liron has described as Herbemont's industrious way of pushing his basic design principles to their limits, while cautiously accepting a few of the more modern construction techniques, bore fruit in three new Spad fighters, all of which were sold in significant numbers.

The Spad 51 first flew in June 1924. While its fuselage was of the classic moulded wood monocoque type, the wing structure was of metal, although fabric covered. There was an all-metal undercarriage. The Polish government purchased fifty in 1925. Secondly, there was the all-wood Spad 61, of which 250 were sold to Poland and 100 built under licence in Romania. Thirdly, the Spad 81, with straight wings and four ailerons, and some metal in the wing structure, appealed to the French government to the extent that eighty were ordered.[1]

Although this new business had its value, it did not herald the resurgence of the Spad marque, for while Herbemont continued to design, and sometimes build prototypes representing still further variations on his theme, no more batch orders for Spads were obtained during the next ten years. The commercial successes of 1924 and 1925 were a flash-in-the-pan, not a revival.

Nevertheless, the episode was some vindication of Blériot's policy of continuing to support Herbemont, and treating Kirste not as a replacement but as a new and additional source of design inspiration – one with a particular focus on civil air transport. Consistently with that policy, Kirste's promising airliner, the four-engined Blériot 115, of which the second prototype, as noted earlier, had performed more than creditably in the 1923 Grand Prix, was developed energetically throughout 1924 while the Spads occupied the headlines. A third version, with the crew now sitting side-by-side and making room for two more passengers (twelve in all), was tried out by Air Union on the Paris-London service, once making the flight in a remarkable 1 hour and 47 minutes. (Air Union had been formed in 1923 by the merger of the Compagnie des Messageries Aériennes and the Compagnie des Grands Express Aériennes.)

Such a journey time brings us within reach of the experience of travellers at the beginning of the twenty-first century. So too does Air Union's brochure of those days, in some ways if not in others. Sumptuously produced, this stylish publication by 'the first airline in the world' is full of advertisements for luxury goods and reassuring statements about safety. Such was the perceived propensity of aviators for getting lost, that great emphasis is placed on assertions that Air Union's pilots knew the way, being capable of identifying on sight virtually every tree, hedge and ditch between Le Bourget and Croydon. Landmarks of a kind likely to interest passengers are enumerated in the manner of a tourist guide, ostensibly to make the journey more interesting but also no doubt to help people see for themselves that the pilot was going the right way. There is also an impressive statistic – Air Union claimed that 15,000 passengers flew between the two cities in 1925.

The dependability desired for airline operations was further tested within France in 1924 by a Salmson-engined version of the 115, designated the Blériot 135. This aircraft took second place in that year's Grand Prix for transport machines, winning prize money of 300,000 francs. One of the tests it successfully accomplished was a daily flight on seven consecutive days from Le Bourget to Bordeaux and back, with the stopover at Bordeaux never once exceeding forty-five minutes.

It was time for Blériot to strike another of his *grands coups*. In January 1925 two specially built Blériot 115s took off from Buc and turned south. The object was to study the feasibility of establishing an air service between France and Chad, as a first step towards a line to Madagascar. This ambitious and highly scientific project came to a tragic and premature end when one of the aircraft crashed immediately after take off from Niamey on the last stage of the journey to Lake Chad. The primary cause was probably an excessive load at the rear of the fuselage – the wheels left the ground before the tail skid. At thirty metres the machine lost speed and slipped sideways to the ground, killing its radio operator. Orders came from Paris to abandon the project. Of the planned 13,000km, only 4,237km had been covered. The surviving Blériot 115 was partly dismantled on the airfield at Niamey, where its remains could be seen for many years.

Nothing lightened the gloom at Suresnes until the spring of 1926, when a twin-engined monoplane designed by Kirste began to fly. This was to be a multi-purpose military aircraft with a crew of four, including two gunners, and it would become the only Blériot since 1913 to be produced in any quantity. From 1928, a total of forty-two Blériot 127s were ordered by the French government. It was then faster than other French fighters, but in a cruel echo of history a series of fatal accidents occurred when its wings broke, and at the end of 1933 the surviving 127s were permanently grounded.

That dismal ending was hidden in the future in 1926, and the optimism engendered by the 127s encouraging debut was increased, but again only temporarily, when in August a Spad 61 set a new world altitude record at the remarkable height of 12,442 metres. This feat was achieved by a test pilot specializing in high altitude flight who had recently joined Blériot-Aéronautique from another firm. Then Blériot received a telephone call from the previous employer who said: 'If I were you I would be suspicious, because when he was with me he went much higher than the ceiling of his aeroplane.'

When the next record attempt was to be made Blériot had a second barograph (self-recording barometer) secretly installed in the rear of the Spad's fuselage. The instrument carried in the cockpit duly recorded a maximum altitude attained of over 12,600 metres, but the second one showed only 4,000 metres. The culprit, who had discovered a way of falsifying the official barograph, had first to face Blériot's wrath, then see all doors in aviation closed to him, and finally suffer expulsion from the Legion of Honour.[2]

Everything seemed to be going wrong, yet the design and development functions at Blériot-Aéronautique were working flat out on a multitude of new or derived designs and on several prototypes. One such, one of many, was the 1927 Herbemont designed Blériot 111, described as a forerunner of the modern 'executive' aircraft. It was a low-wing semi-cantilever monoplane for four passengers and a crew of two. In the next seven years five further versions were built as prototypes, each with a different engine, and two with retractable undercarriages, but despite these great and sustained efforts not a single one was sold.[3]

★★★★★

All this activity was continually overseen by Blériot when he was in Paris. He believed in management by walkabout. His second daughter, Ginette, who went to work at Suresnes in 1927 as an additional secretary to her father, later wrote of that time:

> His days were very full. He arrived at the factory at 8.00 a.m. and worked all day except for lunch-time when he almost always went home – he had few business lunches. After a quick meal he took a siesta for a quarter of an hour, which he found essential. In the evenings he generally left around 6.30 p.m., but stayed later if there was work he wanted to finish. His only recreation was the occasional game of bridge. He never went to the theatre or the cinema. He did not read, except for aviation books…He was always analysing, looking for something. Apart from technology, I never saw my father with a book in his hand.
>
> At the factory his predilection was for the drawing office – that was his life. Sometimes, but not often, he would get up a shooting party. He loved Sologne…he detested social engagements like dinners or dances…His life was aviation and his family. His was not a cheerful disposition, he was very austere, and one would rarely see him laugh. We were all highly delighted when it did happen, but that wasn't often.[4]

The arrival in Paris of Charles Lindberg on 21 May 1927 provided a happy interlude in Blériot's grim struggle to stay in business. By completing the first solo non-stop flight across the North Atlantic, and the first direct flight from New York to Paris, the American brought to an end the series of unsuccessful and sometimes fatal attempts by Frenchmen that had been made in the long interval since the first non-stop crossing of the Atlantic had been achieved by Alcock and Brown in 1919. Only eleven days before Lindberg's arrival, the French pilots Nungesser and Coli had disappeared without trace over the ocean, last seen when they flew west over the cliff at Etretat where Levavasseur had walked so long ago.

The warmth and vigour of Lindberg's welcome in France, like Blériot's in England back in 1909, did much to ensure that his feat would be given its due credit in his own country. Indeed, it is arguable that whole-hearted interest in aviation in the USA dates from Lindberg's flight in 1927.

It is said that Lindberg, when asked after he landed whether there was any Frenchman he particularly wanted to meet, replied simply: 'Louis Blériot.' A grand luncheon was duly given at the Blériots' apartment in the Avenue Kléber, when Blériot made a presentation to Lindberg, saying:

> So that you may not forget me I present you with an ordinary piece of wood, of no value to anyone, but which is very dear to me, a fragment of the victorious propeller of the Channel. Kindly accept it as a souvenir of this day that you have so affectionately devoted to me. Lindberg, I raise my glass to you, to your country, and to all who are dear to you.[5]

Afterwards, the two men stepped out onto the balcony, accompanied by Blériot's eldest daughter Simone who acted as interpreter and remembered this exchange:

> Blériot: 'I admire your courage in this marvellous exploit because you risked your life for thirty-six hours, while I risked mine for only thirty-seven minutes.'
> Lindberg: 'No, Monsieur Blériot, I don't accept what you say, for I wouldn't go up in your aeroplane even for one minute.'[6]

Blériot was soon drawing up plans for an airmail service across the North Atlantic via Iceland and Greenland, and within months of Lindberg's triumph Kirste was busy designing a four-engined monoplane for this purpose. There was a tendency to see this grand scheme as a French response, in the opposite direction, to Lindberg's 'challenge', and it was intended that Blériot's eldest son, also called Louis and then twenty-three years old, should be a co-pilot on the proving flight. The second son, Marcel, had no leanings towards aviation, but his elder brother was not only a good pilot, who had also trained as an electrical engineer, but was 'brilliant and very able in every way'[7] Clearly, the young Louis was intended to succeed his father at the top of the firm one day.

Work on Kirste's project, the trans-Atlantic Blériot 195, proceeded throughout 1928, although interrupted several times by cash shortages. It was in the midst of this depressing period that Blériot made another of his bold, or rash, decisions. Never able to resist new ideas, he was captivated by some preliminary designs for aircraft shown to him by Filippo Zappata, an engineer who had trained at the School of Marine Engineering at Genoa. Zappata was especially interested in improving the shape of flying-boat hulls.

Blériot promptly recruited Zappata, who began work for him towards the end of 1928, just before the construction of the Blériot 195 was finally completed in January 1929. Perhaps Blériot had some premonition of the future reserved for this machine, and wanted to acquire capacity to develop an alternative. If so, he was absolutely right, for the 195 was never satisfactory, either as a seaplane or a land plane, and in due course suffered the ultimate indignity of failing to obtain a certificate of air-worthiness.[8]

However, Zappata's first task, as things turned out, was not to design a seaplane for

The Blériot 110 Joseph Le Brix which Codos and Rossi flew non-stop from New York to Rayak in Syria, a distance of 9,104km, at an average speed of 165kph in August 1933. (MA 9130)

Blériot, but a land-plane and a very odd one at that. Early in 1929 the Air Ministry resolved that, as a matter of national prestige, the world records for distance and duration should be recovered by France. To that end three prototypes were ordered from different constructors, one of them Blériot-Aéronautique. Zappata's design, designated the Blériot 110, was approved by the authorities in March 1929, and its construction was completed in May 1930.

At this time, Blériot was able mostly to contain his anxiety about the total absence of batch orders, and his descent into the role of a prototype builder. He worked at the things which were to him much more important. Full of ideas about how to run regular services across the Atlantic, he worried about whether Kirste's plane would be good enough for that task – good enough too to carry another Louis Blériot across the ocean as twenty years before the faithful type XI had borne him to Dover, fame and fortune – and he shared in Zappata's excitement as they laid their plans to win the endurance records for France. Business was bad, but new and glorious prospects beckoned.

Then, on 20 February 1929, his son Louis died, carried away very suddenly in his twenty-fifth year by a violent attack of appendicitis.

★★★★★

'These were the hard years, the bad years', wrote Blériot's youngest son Jean, 'saddened moreover by the death of my elder brother, which deprived my father of all hope of the relief that he so desperately needed.'[9] Jean was himself only eleven years old when his brother died.

At the age of fifty-six, but looking ten years older, Blériot now knew that he would have to go all the way alone. He was too uncommunicative to be able to share with anyone the major decisions on the future of Blériot-Aéronautique, and his excessive reserve placed him at a disadvantage in dealing with the Air Ministry, with whose officials and technical staff his relations were strained. As his grandson has put it, he 'sometimes lacked *souplesse'* in those relationships. When he saw that something was seriously wrong, he was likely to say so, unambiguously:

> He most notably brought upon himself the enduring hostility of the [Air Ministry's] Service Technique de l'Aéronautique by publishing, in 1924, a pamphlet which was widely distributed throughout the industry. In it he fiercely criticized that department's working methods, its offensive attitude to constructors and its total ignorance of industrial realities. Although these criticisms were not without justification, the least one can say is that, from then onwards, whenever a Blériot project was submitted to the department, there was no presumption in its favour![10]

For the moment he had no choice but to soldier on as best he could. He strove to maintain a nucleus of production capacity by building and marketing aircraft for Jean Guillemin, like Blanchard an independent designer without manufacturing or marketing facilities of his own, while devoting most of his attention to Zappata's projects.

Zappata's Blériot 110 was built to fly further and for longer than any aeroplane before it. Resembling a large glider, it was a high-wing monoplane made of wood. The fuselage was exceptionally tall and narrow, formed of a keel and two longerons covered by a monocoque skin made from three layers of tulip wood laid in strips 50mm wide, crossed at 45 degrees, then covered with fabric and varnished. There were six fuel tanks in the wings and four in the fuselage. The cabin was only 1.05 metres wide inside, and contained two pilots' seats in tandem, with dual controls. While windows gave the crew side views, the view ahead, like Lindberg's had been, was through a periscope only – any other arrangement would have occupied space needed for fuel. Behind the seats was a couch where the crew could take turns to sleep, although that hardly seems possible with a 600hp Hispano-Suiza, the single power-unit, located a few metres in front. The dry weight of the Bleriot 110 was 2,800kg, and this for an aircraft with a wingspan of 26.50m and a length of 14.50m. Amazingly, it was capable of carrying a load of some 6,200kg, more than double its own weight.

Lucien Bossoutrot, a former Farman works pilot, was the test pilot for the type 110. Between May and September 1930 he clocked up a total of 150 hours flying time with it, enormous for those days, and then he was satisfied that the machine was ready to go for the endurance records. But it was then too late in the year to make an attempt in the

French climate, so the 110 was flown to Oran in Algeria on 5 November 1930.[11]

The attempt was to be made over a closed circuit starting and finishing at La Senia aerodrome near Oran. The world duration record stood at 67 hours 30 minutes, and to set a new official record it would be necessary to exceed that time by a margin of one hour. On 15 November all was ready: Lucien Bossoutrot was to be chief pilot, with Maurice Rossi as second pilot and navigator. The weight of the aeroplane and everything it carried were meticulously noted by Bossoutrot as follows:

The aircraft fully equipped but empty	2,767kg
Two pilots and their parachutes	190kg
Water	12kg
Food	30kg
Oil: 220 litres,	211kg
Fuel: 5,865 litres	4,294kg
Total weight	7,504kg

Taking-off with such loads of fuel was what pilots dreaded most about flights of this kind. An agonizingly long run was essential, perhaps *five times* as long as a normally loaded aircraft of similar power would need. Even to get the tail wheel up took a considerable distance, so the Blériot team decided on this occasion to give themselves some help by using a detachable trolley to hold up the rear of the fuselage in the flying position right from the start. Bossoutrot described the flight in a letter written to Louis Blériot a few days later:

> The take-off was fairly easy, helped by very flat, firm ground. After travelling 150 metres I released the trolley which caused loud banging noises in the fuselage. The tail was still heavy and it dropped a little, but soon the aircraft lined itself up properly. At the 1,000 metre marker, when the speed reading was 140kph, I put the question gently and got an immediate response. After a run of about 1,180 metres in distance and 47 seconds in time, we took off. A few moments later, with the engine running at 1,950rpm and an airspeed of 175kph, at a height of 20 metres, the wing began to vibrate… I immediately closed the throttle a little and the shaking, which had only lasted a few seconds, stopped at once… During the first part of the flight in calm conditions there was no difficulty in flying the aircraft, except that the rudder was rather heavy, but when it got bumpy the controls felt terrible and the aircraft seemed as if it were made of rubber… but as the load was gradually reduced the handling improved…
>
> I thought the first day was very much the most tiring, because of the nervous strain of the take-off, the unpleasant sensations when conditions were bumpy, the difficulty of making turns without banking – in accordance with Zappata's instructions – the bad visibility in front, the too-short circuit with frequent turns, not being able to move from our

seats, and the length and total darkness of the night which meant that we had to fly on instruments alone for twelve consecutive hours...

The second twenty-four hours and the third day were less tiring, the plane flew better in the turbulent patches (which also were less intense) the turns were banked and tighter, but we suffered the effects of intoxication by the exhaust gases – Rossi in particular. As a result of this we were unable to eat as we should have done. We were able to get some rest in our seats, but never to use the couch, because it was constantly necessary for both of us to fly the aircraft, especially at night, with one doing the steering and the other doing everything else. The last night was very hard, the atmospheric conditions were distinctly worse, the already poor visibility deteriorated further, and our emergency lighting began to give cause for concern...

There was never a boring or empty moment, nor the time to sleep, busy as we were with monitoring the fuel and oil consumption, seeing to the engine, and flying the aircraft.

Never did I think that we would be forced to land because of fatigue, and when we did land it was perfect in every way, although in the worst possible conditions: in pitch dark, with obstacles on the runway, and with the engine off. When we got out we staggered like drunk men for a few minutes, but soon we felt perfectly alright...[12]

Bossoutrot and Rossi had taken the difficult decision to terminate the flight, at the very moment when success appeared to be within their reach, because of dangerously excessive oil consumption. They had covered 7,701km and had flown for 67 hours 32 minutes, exceeding the old record by two minutes. It was a moral victory, although they were of course short of the margin of one hour needed to establish a new record officially.

The fact that they had had enough fuel left in their tanks for another twelve hours flying added to their confidence as they immediately set about preparing to try again. Bossoutrot wrote to Blériot:

Our experience has shown that for the next attempt the circuit should be 150km long instead of 91 km, so gaining 300 or 400 km lost in an excessive number of turns. [in fact a compromise was reached, with the original circuit being used at night and a longer one of 164km by day] By then also there should be moonlight, and our ground lighting should be better. We have to improve forward visibility and re-route the exhaust...[13]

But fate in the form of violent storms intervened to cause two further attempts to be abandoned, one after twenty-seven hours, the other after fifty-six hours, and it was not until their fourth attempt, begun on 26 February 1931, that the Blériot 110 finally succeeded in establishing new world records of 8,822km and 75 hours 23 minutes.[14]

'Nothing is more ephemeral than a record', Louis Blériot had written in 1927,[15] and so it was for Bossoutrot and Rossi, because only one month later they saw one of theirs

Charles Lindberg and Louis Blériot in Paris on 22 May 1927 (MA 8641)

fall to two other French pilots who flew 8,960km in a closed circuit. The Blériot team quickly organized a new attempt, again at Oran, and flew for fifty-seven hours until a sandstorm forced them to give up. They then learned that while they had been in the air yet another French team, Doret and Le Brix, had flown 10,342km. Soon afterwards Joseph Le Brix was killed on a flight over Russia, and as a tribute the Blériot 110 was given his name. So it was the *Joseph-Le-Brix*, after two further abortive attempts, that in March 1932 again took the endurance records for Blériot, with 10,601km and 76 hours 34 minutes.

Although the state had paid the capital cost of the *Joseph-Le-Brix*, its contributions towards the running costs for these record attempts were parsimonious. Yet the expenses were various and substantial, for example the provision of ground lights to mark out the shorter night circuit cost 65,000 francs. Altogether the programme of eight attempts in seventeen months had cost Blériot at least one million francs, and after taking the records for the second time, in March 1932, he decided to stop.

However, in 1933 a press campaign persuaded the Air Ministry to put up more money, and a daring project in the pure Blériot tradition was conceived – to cross an ocean *and* a continent without stopping. In June the *Joseph-Le-Brix* was shipped to New York. At 9.41 GMT on 5 August with Paul Codos as pilot (Bossoutrot was busy elsewhere, as will be seen) and Maurice Rossi as navigator, carrying 6,300 litres of fuel, it took off from Floyd Bennett field after a difficult run of 1,000 metres. Thirty hours later the aeroplane was sighted over Cherbourg. Codos and Rossi flew on, over Le Bourget – making the point that they were going on where Lindberg had stopped – then

Strasbourg, Vienna, Rhodes, Cyprus, Beirut, and finally on 7 August at 18.10 GMT they landed at Rayak in Syria.

They had flown from America to Asia across Europe without pause, covering 9,104.7km, a new world distance record from point to point which would stand for four years, in 55 hours 29 minutes. After a few days rest Codos and Rossi flew the *Joseph-Le-Brix* back to Paris where it was grandly displayed in the Tuileries gardens for a week, an exceptional honour for an aeroplane.[16]

★★★★★

On these laurels Blériot had never intended to rest. Throughout the period of the record attempts he had been preparing, at huge technical and financial risk, what would turn out to be his last great adventure in aviation, the nobly-named *Santos-Dumont* trans-Atlantic flying-boat. But first we should consider a bizarre design which he allowed to distract him, and also to try to understand something of his deepening financial predicament.

As far back as 1924 Kirste had imagined an aircraft with twin fuselages and other features sufficiently radical to be irresistible to Blériot. This finally saw the light of day in 1930, as the Blériot 125. Each fuselage contained a luxuriously appointed cabin for six passengers, a toilet and a baggage hold. The fuselages were 5.60 metres apart, joined by a monoplane wing and a tail-plane which sported four fins and four rudders. Two 500hp Hispano-Suizas, one with a tractor propeller and one with a pusher, were mounted 'back-to-back', with a space between them in and above which was located the crew's cabin. This tandem engine layout was intended to enable flight to continue on one engine if necessary. Two tandem undercarriage wheels were recessed into each fuselage.

The type 125 was shown at the Salon of 1930. With a wing span of 29.40 metres it was the largest Blériot built so far. Test flights began in the spring of 1931 and continued until the end of 1932, but the concept was too novel for the airlines, and no production orders were obtained.[17]

When Codos and Rossi had returned to Paris 'victoriously and gloriously', Jacques Breguet, friend and rival for nearly thirty years, congratulated Blériot: 'an old name in aviation, perhaps the oldest, has shown that it is still there…'[18] It was, just, still there, but at a cost that only Blériot rightly knew. Early in 1934, however, the time came for the French government to know also, and when Blériot told them he did so with poignant pride:

> No production orders have been given to me for the past five years. I have had to make great efforts just to keep my design office going and to maintain my factory buildings in good condition.
>
> The financial sacrifices I have had to make are shown by the annual accounts as follows:
>
> Loss in 1929   F2,076,187
> Loss in 1930   2,369,111

The Blériot 125, with two 500hp Hispano-Suizas mounted in tandem between the twin fuselages, each of which had a cabin for six passengers. 1931. (MA 6378)

Loss in 1931	3,288,593
Loss in 1932	1,100,689
Loss in 1933	2,500,000 at least (accounts not yet closed)

To these losses must be added an advance of more than 8,000,000 francs to bring the Blériot 5190 *Santos-Dumont* to its present stage. Without the help of the leading banks, notably the Société Générale, I would not have survived the past three years. I pass over in silence all the businesses that I've had to withdraw from after creating them: Phares Blériot, Messageries Aériennes, Air Union.

I have however a clear conscience that I have given myself body and soul to aviation, and without greed for money, before, during and after the war. I have always lived for aviation and not by it: it has dominated the whole of my life.

Before the war, the Blériots of Garros and Pégoud astonished the whole world. During the war, the Spads, whose factories and offices I ran, were built in numbers exceeding 16,000.

History will record - or so I hope and it will be my finest claim to fame - that they supported victoriously the heroism of our pilots.

After the war, a highly developed technology has again shown its superiority, despite a five-year break in production... [here he cites the records broken by the type 110 and other feats] Is all this effort to be wiped out? Can I hope to go on? Will you give me the chance to use this

The Blériot 5190 Santos-Dumont which made thirty-eight successful Atlantic crossings in 1934-37. (MA 31096)

marvellous tool which has been created by twenty-five years' work: the firm of Blériot- Aéronautique?

The works at Suresnes, situated between the railway and the Seine, opposite the Longchamp aerodrome, are a major asset for national defence. The fire service, which is exceptionally powerful, is supplied by the river, while diesel generators make the factory independent of the electricity grid. They cover five hectares, and they are backed up by the test ground at Buc (60 hectares) and its school, as well as by the Tartifume works at Bordeaux, even better placed perhaps than those at Suresnes, since they are on the edge of a sixty hectare airfield…

All this has not been brought together out of personal ambition. Every time the State has asked me to make aircraft of other marques, such as Potez, Nieuport, Breguet or Caudron… these great industrial resources have willingly set to work.

I ask to be allowed to consecrate in one final effort all the technical and industrial experience that I have acquired by thirty years of life on aerodromes and in the air, and by the finest sporting victories.[19]

The fervent plea was in vain. Blériot's last chance was denied to him. The cup was dashed from his lips at the very moment when he had succeeded in filling it again. The story of the end is the story of the *Santos-Dumont*.

Its beginnings had been promising, though full of uncertainty. In 1928 the Air

Ministry issued specifications for flying boats to carry mail across the South Atlantic, between Dakar in Senegal (then French territory) and Natal in Brazil. These machines preferably were to be four-engined, and had to be able to carry one tonne of mail and a crew of four. In an example of the 'policy of prototypes' at its most munificent, the Ministry grandly ordered six different aircraft from five constructors for a total of 36 million francs.

The most expensive, at 10,720,000 francs, was the Blériot, the type 5190 designed by Filippo Zappata. What he proposed was a very large flying-boat of no less than twenty-two tonnes laden (including eight tonnes of fuel and one tonne of mail). The fuselage would be made entirely of metal: the wings and tail-plane would have metal structures and fabric coverings. This was at a time when no aircraft of more than ten tonnes (fully laden) was in service anywhere and before 'all-metal' construction had become commonplace.

It was a project 'heavy with risks', as an internal memorandum of Blériot-Aéronautique emphasized, but one which after great efforts in the end succeeded 'at least from the technical standpoint, for it is pointless to stress the magnitude of the financial cost of those efforts.'[20] More than eighteen months were taken up by testing models in pools and wind-tunnels, and in planning how to actually build the aircraft. A lot of special plant and machinery was needed, much of it having to be designed and made. By May 1933 the construction of the *Santos-Dumont* was completed. Blériot named it after his old friend, who had died by his own hand the year before: Alberto Santos-Dumont had never recovered from his horror at the use made of aircraft in the war.

It was a high-wing monoplane of 43m span, with a fuselage 26m long and 3.65m wide. The wing was mounted on top of a large 'chimney', as it was called, which contained a spacious cabin for the entire crew. Having the whole crew in the same cabin was thought to be a good idea, but it was marred by the noise and vibration from two engines mounted in the cabin roof. These power units were laid out in tandem, back to back, one with a tractor propeller and the other a pusher. The third and fourth engines were conventionally placed on the wing, with tractor propellers. All four were twelve cylinder Hispano-Suizas of 650hp with reduction gearing. An auxiliary Bristol engine was used for starting them. All engines were accessible in flight.

The flying-boat was taken down the Seine on a special, very large barge to Caudebec below Rouen, where there is a relatively open stretch of water seven kilometres long, with an average width of 350 metres. There was normally heavy traffic on this part of the river, but when Bossoutrot, Zappata and a mechanic took their places in the cabin for the maiden flight on 3 August 1933, the authorities had been asked to clear it of shipping. The take-off has been described by Jean Liron:

> The flying-boat, at 160kph, had just risen onto the step of its hull when there appeared straight in front of it, going in the same direction at some ten knots, a long ship flying the Swedish flag. In little more than 200 metres, five seconds in time, Bossoutrot got the nose up, wrenched the plane off the water and, skimming the ship's funnel, found open space. In the cabin, not a word had been spoken…[21]

The *Santos-Dumont* rapidly confirmed this dramatic demonstration of precocious ability in further test flights throughout August. Then a small fire on board necessitated an overhaul that took several months, and by the time the work was finished the Seine had frozen over, in the winter of 1933-34, immobilizing the aircraft at Caudebec. However, by the end of the following summer all the official tests were passed and the time had come for the flying-boat to take up the task for which it had been made.

Put into the hands of Air France, but with Lucien Bossoutrot still as chief pilot for the time being, the Blériot's first flight from Dakar to Natal (3,200km) was made on 26 November 1934 in 16 hours 10 minutes, gaining the huge margin of four hours on its rival the Latécoère 300 which had made its first crossing on 3 January 1934. In the next fifteen months the *Santos-Dumont* crossed the ocean thirty times, never once having to turn back, and made six trips between France and Senegal. Such dependability and regularity were astonishing, and absolutely unprecedented over the Atlantic.

The *Santos-Dumont* carried mail but no passengers. The primacy of letters over people on long routes in the mid-thirties has an explanation in part economic. Blériot said in 1935 that the tariff for mail between France and South America was 2,000,000 francs per tonne, a rate many times more than the highest imaginable passenger fare could yield. But he was well aware that air-mail was enjoying a honeymoon period:

> This mail will become lighter, for soon it will be divided among the countries located on the same route, and more and more it will be subject to the competition of the radio.
>
> It will therefore be necessary to consider a less remunerative freight. The difficulty for the great ocean routes will then be to reserve for this freight at least twenty per cent of the weight of the aircraft. In this case, as it is necessary to count on about sixty per cent for the weight of the airframe, its motors and equipment, there would remain therefore only twenty per cent for the weight of the fuel. This would limit the range to about 1,500km…[22]

The refuelling facilities on ocean flights that this implied could best be provided, Blériot argued, by 'floating islands'. In embracing this solution he was careful to distance himself from designs for such islands proposed by different French architects, which he described as 'unfortunately somewhat fantastic', and instead advocated 'Seadromes' huge anchored floating structures, on tall legs, on which wheeled aircraft could land and take off. These were the work of the American engineer Armstrong, who had been studying the problem in depth, with models and laboratory experiments, for about fifteen years. Blériot envisaged four Armstrong Seadromes spread across the North Atlantic, to be used in conjunction with a bi-fuselaged aircraft that could be derived from his Blériot 125.[23]

All this did not mean that he had no plans for developing the highly successful *Santos-Dumont*. That he intended to do in several ways. First, pay load could be increased by improving fuel consumption as a result of using a system recently invented by Blériot-Aéronautique for varying the pitch of propellers in flight. Then there would be several derivative aircraft, each carrying passengers and fuel in different proportions over a different range, for example a ten passenger version for the South Atlantic, a forty

Alice and Louis Blériot in 1934. (MA 28830)

passenger one for Marseilles-Algiers, and a sixty-man troop carrier for the same route.[24]

While Blériot was dreaming these dreams, the prototype continued its regular progress as if governed by a giant metronome in the sky. When it had completed its twelfth ocean crossing the government acted: they ordered three more type 5190s. As if that was not enough, at the same time the Ministry asked Blériot-Aéronautique to construct thirty Potez 540s. The combined value of these orders was some 40 million francs, and the authorities emphasized their desire for very rapid delivery of all the aircraft.

Something of what this meant to Louis Blériot can perhaps be imagined. Suddenly, all the years of stubborn perseverance were vindicated, the prolonged financial sacrifices promised now to have their reward. The moribund production shops at Suresnes came joyfully to life and, despite shortages of skilled labour, a workforce of 500 was soon assembled – all thanks to heavy borrowing from the Société Générale. Within a very few weeks actual construction of the new aircraft began, with hope reborn at Suresnes.

Then on 14 June 1935, six weeks after it had been placed, the order for the three flying-boats was summarily cancelled. In taking this extraordinary and abrupt action the Air Ministry cited vague 'operational reasons', but did take some pains to point out that its decision in no way reflected on the quality of the *Santos-Dumont*. Two months later the

237

thirty Potez were cancelled as well.[25] These were times of political turmoil in France.

It was too much. It was too much for the Société Générale which, despite having given support over a twelve-year period, immediately suspended further credit. Above all it was too much for Louis Blériot, now weakened by an intensification of the heart condition that he owed to the crash at Istanbul nearly thirty years before.

It did not really matter that the cancellations were swiftly followed by an order worth 14 million francs for sixty Spad 510 single seater fighters. It did not really matter that it became apparent that most of the French aircraft industry was about to be nationalized. The damage was done, and it was irreversible.

On 1 August 1936, at ten o'clock in the morning, Louis Blériot died at home from a heart attack. He was sixty-four. Fifty years before he had written to his parents: 'Yes, I see how necessary science is for man…Well, this science I will work to learn.'[26]

He had kept his promise.

Epilogue

Louis Blériot was given a funeral with military honours at Les Invalides, and was buried in the family vault at the Gonards cemetery at Versailles, not far from his beloved Buc.

Pressure to re-arm led France in 1937 into a chaotic programme of nationalization of most of her aircraft industry into which Blériot-Aéronautique S.A. was drawn. Compensation of F12,423,400 was ultimately paid for the property and fixed assets.[1] The factory at Suresnes and the aerodrome and workshops at Buc, after various amalgamations, became in 1957 part of Sud-Aviation which in its turn was eventually absorbed into Aérospatiale. The Compagnie des Messageries Aériennes (CMA) had merged in 1923 with the Compagnie des Grands Express Aériennes to form Air Union which, in its turn, became part of Air France in 1932.

Paris honoured Blériot's memory in the traditional way by re-naming the Quai d'Auteuil the 'Quai Louis-Blériot' in May 1937. The people of Les Baraques had moved more swiftly, too swiftly for the liking of higher authority: immediately after Blériot died they began calling their village 'Blériot-Plage', but it was not until 1959 that the new name was recognised officially.[2]

Alice Blériot died in 1963.

★★★★★

The Blériot XI which flew the Channel was soon given a permanent home at the Conservatoire des Arts et Métiers to which it was brought in triumph, wheeled by the mechanics Ferdinand Collin and Julien Mamet through massed crowds lining the boulevards, with a mounted escort of the Garde Républicaine. Although temporarily removed for restoration at the time of writing, it is normally on display in the museum attached to the Conservatoire, the Musée Nationale des Techniques.

As it always did, the aeroplane impresses by its smallness. It really is quite tiny, and looks so frail that the thought of a man trusting his life to it over the sea catches at the heart for a moment. Unlike those who first saw it, we can compare it with others made since. Immediately it is apparent that this, and not any contemporary Wright, Voisin, Farman, Antoinette or Santos-Dumont, was the machine which settled the question of what the aeroplane was going to be like.

Source notes

Abbreviations:

BA – The Blériot family archives in the Musée de l'Air et de l'Espace, Le Bourget

MA – The Musée de l'Air et de l'Espace

Note: Printed works in French were published in Paris, and those in English in London, unless otherwise stated.

INTRODUCTION

1. *The Daily Mail*, 27 July 1909.
2. *The Times*, 3 August 1936.

CHAPTER 1

1. Prize list, Institut Notre Dame, Cambrai, in BA.
2. Dossier de l'étudiant L. Blériot, Ecole Centrale des Arts et Manufactures, Paris.
3. *Mémoires d'Alicia Blériot*, typescript, (1959), 72pp, in BA.
4. Text of commemorative address given by Jean Blériot in 1972, in BA.
5. J.M. Laux, *In First Gear: the French automobile industry to 1914*, Liverpool, 1976, p20.
6. Ibid., p7.
7. Ibid., p50.
8. Ibid., p209.
9. L. Baudry de Saunier, in preface to catalogue of the Société Anonyme des Etablissements L. Blériot, 1 July 1906.
10. *Catalogue L. Blériot*, 1906,
11. L. Baudry de Saunier, *op cit.*
12. *The Car Illustrated*, 1 March 1905.
13. *Catalogue L. Blériot*, 1906.
14. *Mémoires d'Alicia Blériot*, *op cit.*
15. Ibid.
16. Simone Rubel-Blériot in *Icare* No.89, 1979, p99.
17. F.T.Jane *All the World's Aircraft*, 1912, p362.
18. *Mémoires d'Alicia Blériot*, *op cit.*
19. *Catalogue L. Blériot*, 1906.
20. *Mémoires d'Alicia Blériot*, *op cit.*
21. *Catalogue L. Blériot*, 1906.
22. Ibid.
23. *Catalogue Recherches Aéronautiques L. Blériot*, 1909, p2.

24. Statuts des Etablissements L. Blériot, 1905.

25. E. Chadeau, *L'industrie aéronautique en France 1900-1950*, 1987, p60.

CHAPTER 2

z1. J. Mortane, *Louis Blériot*, 1939, p16.

2. Nadar, *The Right to Fly,* 1866, tr. J.S. Harry, pp18, 74, 78.

3. *Mémoires d'Alicia Blériot, op cit.*

4. Letter from Louis Blériot to Robert Esnault-Pelterie dated 30 January 1918, in BA.

5. *l'Aérophile*, November 1902, p292.

6. G. Houard, 'Louis Blériot pionnier incomparable de l'aviation française', in *Le Pionnier No.2*, p9. See also C. Dollfus in *Icare* No.89, p89.

7. *Mémoires d'Alicia Blériot, op cit.*

8. G. Voisin, in preface to *Parmi les Précurseurs du Ciel*, by F. Collin, 1948, pp9-10.

9. G. Houard in *Le Pionnier No.2*, p9.

10. Letter and annexe by Alicia Blériot to the Ministre de l'Air, dated 17 February 1937, in BA.

11. Author's conversation with MA staff in December 1987.

12. C. Dollfus in *Icare* No.89, pp89-90.

13. C.H. Gibbs-Smith, *A Directory and Nomenclature of the First Aeroplanes 1809-1909*, 1966, p39.

14. *Mémoires d'Alicia Blériot, op cit.*

15. Information mainly from G. Voisin, *Men, Women and 10,000 kites,* 1963, tr. O. Stewart; G. Voisin in preface to *Parmi les Précurseurs du Ciel, op cit,;* and *l'Aérophile*, July 1905.

CHAPTER 3

1. *l'Aérophile*, February 1908, p58.

2. R. Gastambide, *L'Envol*, 1932, p20.

3. M. Matteucci, *History of the Motor Car*, 1970, p103. See also C. F. Caunter, *Motor Cycles: a technical history,* 1982, for an excellent summary of the early history of the internal combustion engine.

4. C. Dollfus and H. Bouché, *Histoire de l'Aéronautique*, 1932, p209.

5. Lord Brabazon of Tara, 'Forty Years of Flight' the Romane lecture, delivered at Oxford on 17 May 1949.

6. R. Gastambide, *l'Envol, op cit,* p44.

7. Technical details of the Antoinette engines are mainly from the author's conversation in April 1987 with the aeronautical engineer and historian M.P. (Bill) Sayer, who died in May 1988. Through long and painstaking study Mr Sayer had acquired an exceptional, intimate knowledge of these engines: he personally repeated the stress calculations referred to here. Information has also been taken from F. Ferber's 'Histoire du moteur Antoinette', in *l'Aérophile*, 15 February 1908, pp58-61.

8. M. Calderara and P. Banet-Rivet, *Manuel de l'Aviateur Constructeur*, 1910, p196.

9. *Louis Blériot in The Aeroplane: Past, Present and Future*, ed. C. Grahame-White and H.

Harper, 1911, p215.

CHAPTER 4.

1. G.Voisin in preface to *Parmi les Précurseurs, op cit,* pp17-18.
2. *l'Aérophile*, 15 May 1909, p227.
3. F. T. Jane, *All the World's Airships*, 1909, p158.
4. G. Voisin in *Parmi les Précurseurs, op cit,* pp17-18; and in *Men, Women and 10,000 kites, op cit,* p142.
5. Text of agreement dated 7 January 1906, in BA.
6. *l'Aérophile*, October 1906, pp250-1, and December 1906, p295.
7. Ibid., December 1906, p295.
8. Letter from S. A. Antoinette to L. Blériot dated 17 October 1906, in BA.
9. *l'Aérophile*, December 1906, p295.
10. G. Voisin in *Parmi les Précurseurs, op cit,* p19.
11. C. Dollfus in *Icare* No.89, p90.
12. L. Blériot in *Le Matin*, July 1909, quoted *in La Gloire des Ailes: l'aviation de Clément Ader à Costes*, by L. Blériot and E. Ramond, 1927, pp95-6.
13. *l'Aérophile*, April 1907, p98.
14. J.W. Dunne in the *Aeronautical Journal*, April 1913, pp83-4.
15. *l'Aérophile*, April 1907, p98.
16. Ibid.
17. Ibid.
18. Ibid., May 1907, pp126-7.

CHAPTER 5

1. *l'Aérophile*, June 1907, p167.
2. H. Fabre, *J'ai vu naitre l'aviation,* 1980, p81.
3. *l'Aérophile*, July 1907, pp194-5.
4. Ibid., August 1907, pp230-2.
5. L. Blériot and E. Ramond, *La Gloire des Ailes*, p96.
6. *Mémoires d'Alicia Blériot, op cit.*
7 *l'Aérophile*, September 1907, p262.
8. L. Blériot and E. Ramond, *La Gloire des Ailes*, p96.
9. *L. Blériot in The Aeroplane, Past, Present and Future, op cit,* pp204-6.
10.G. Voisin in *Parmi les Précurseurs, op cit,* p20.
11. *l'Aérophile*, November 1907, pp318-9.
12. Ibid., 1 January 1908.
13. Quoted by G. Cullingham in *Patrick Y. Alexander*, 1984, p173.
14. J. Devaux and M. Marani in *Pégase* No.54, p15.
15. *l'Aérophile*, 1 November 1908, p434.
16. Ibid., 15 November 1908, p460.
17. A Berget, *The Conquest of the Air*, 1909, p252.

CHAPTER 6

1. R. Gastambide, *L'Envol, op cit,* p143.
2. F. Collin, *Parmi les Précurseurs*, *op cit,* pp49-50.
3. M. Degoul in *l'Aérophile*, September 1906, pp190-1.
4. O. Curti, 'Alessandro Anzani: un grand italiano sconosciuto', in *Museoscienza no.4*. See also Anzani's catalogues of 1910 and 1911.
5. M. Bourduriat, manuscript note dated 15 May 1973 in dossier Anzani, MA.
6. General Salinas Carranza in *Air History*, 1959, pp94-6.
7. O. Curti, Alessandro Anzani, *op cit.*
8. *l'Aérophile*, 15 December 1908, p521.
9. Letter from G. Fouillarat to Alicia Blériot, dated 1956, in BA.
10. *Mémoires d'Alicia Blériot, op cit.*
11. *l'Aérophile*, 15 July 1909, p319.
12. E. Picard, *Rapport sur le Prix Osiris*, Institut de France, 1909.
13. Ibid.
14. *Mémoires d'Alicia Blériot, op cit.*

CHAPTER 7

1. R. Gastambide, *l'Envol, op cit,* pp143-7.
2. Ibid., pp150-2.
3. *Daily Mail*, 8 June 1909.
4. Biographical information on Lord Northcliffe is mainly from A.P. Ryan, *Lord Northcliffe*, 1953.
5. Lord Northcliffe, in *5,000 miles in a Balloon*, by F. Hedges Butler, 1907, p14.
6. Panel at the Blériot Exhibition, Selfridges, London, 1989.
7. *Daily Mail*, 29 June 1909.
8. Ibid., 8 July 1909.
9. Ibid., 9 July 1909.
10. Ibid., 10 July 1909.
11. Ibid., 12 July 1909.
12. Ibid., 13 July 1909.
13. Ibid., 20 July 1909.
14. H. Latham, in the *Daily Mail*, 20 July 1909.
15. R. Gastambide, *L'Envol op cit*, p174.
16. *Daily Mail*, 22 June 1909.
17. R. Labouchère, in letter to M. Lhospice, quoted in *Icare* No.89, p55.
18. *Daily Mail*, 20 July 1909.

CHAPTER 8

1. *Mémoires d'Alicia Blériot, op cit.*

2. *l'Aérophile*, 15 June, 1 July, 15 July, 1 August 1909.

3. F. Collin, *Parmi les Précurseurs, op cit*, pp57-8.

4. Ibid., pp59-60.

5. *l'Aérophile*, 1 August 1909, pp344-5.

6. *Daily Mail*, 20 July 1909.

7. Ibid., 22 July 1909.

8. *Mémoires d'Alicia Blériot, op cit.*

9. M. Lhospice, *Match pour La Manche*, 1964, p129.

10. F. Collin, *Parmi les Précurseurs, op cit*, p69.

11. Text of naval orders in BA.

12. F. Collin, *Contribution de Souvenirs Personnels pour l'élaboration de notes et anecdotes à l'occasion du vingtième anniversaire de la Traversée de la Manche*, typescript, 1929, in BA.

13. C. Fontaine, *Comment Blériot a traversé La Manche*, 1909, pp18-21.

14. *Daily Mail*, 21 July 1909.

15. Ibid. 23 July 1909.

16. M. Lhospice, *Match pour la Manche, op cit*, p150.

CHAPTER 9

1. C. Fontaine, *Comment Blériot a traversé La Manche, op cit*, p26.

2. *Le Matin*, 26 July 1909.

3. *Mémoires d'Alicia Blériot, op cit.*

4. F. Collin, *Parmi les Précurseurs, op cit*, p70.

5. *Le Matin*, 26 July 1909.

6. C. Fontaine, *Comment Blériot a traversé La Manche, op cit*, pp27-8.

7. *Le Matin* 26 July 1909.

8. F. Collin, *Contribution de Souvenirs Personnels, op cit.*

9. Ibid. and *Parmi les Précurseurs op cit*, pp77-8.

10. *Daily Mail*, 26 July 1909.

11. C. Fontaine, *Comment Blériot a traversé La Manche, op cit*, pp22, 32-34.

12. *Le Matin*, 25 July 1909.

13. *Daily Mail*, 26 July 1909.

14. *Mémoires d'Alicia Blériot, op cit.*

15. Copy of Certificate of 'Pratique' in BA.

16. Copies of correspondence in BA.

17. F. Collin, *Parmi les Précurseurs, op cit*, p82.

18. M. Lhospice, *Match pour La Manche, op cit*, p210.

19. *Daily Mail*, 26 July 1909.

20. Ibid.

21. Ibid.

22. F. Collin, *Parmi les Précurseurs, op cit*, pp84-5.

23. *Flight*, 7 August 1909, p474.

CHAPTER 10

1. H. Harper, in *Flight*, 21 July 1949, p72.
2. Simone Rubel-Blériot in *Icare* No.89, p99.
3. *Mémoires d'Alicia Blériot, op cit.*
4. H. G. Wells in the *Daily Mail*, 27 July 1909.
5. *The Times*, 26 July 1909.
6. Ibid., 27 July 1909.
7. Ibid.
8. Letter in BA.
9. C. Dollfus, in *Icare* No.89, p95.
10. *The Times*, 28 July 1909.
11. Ibid.
12. R. Labouchère in letter to M. Lhospice, quoted in *Icare* No.89, p55.
13. R. Gastambide, *l'Envol, op cit,* p179.
14. *Mémoires d'Alicia Blériot, op cit.*
15. C. Fontaine, *Comment Blériot a traversé La Manche, op cit,* p58.
16. Ibid., p64.

CHAPTER 11

1. H.S. Villard, *Contact! The Story of the Early Birds* ,1969, p67, and M. Lhospice, *Match pour la Manche, op cit,* pp116, 123.
2. eg R. Moulin, in *Le Pionnier* No.2, p19.
3. *Flight*, 1 August 1929, p831.
4. Anzani catalogue, 1911.
5. Louis Blériot in *Le Matin*, quoted by him *in La Gloire des Ailes, op cit,* pp96-7.
6. T.D. Crouch, *Blériot XI: The Story of a Classic Aircraft,* Washington, 1982, p45.
7. F. T. Jane *All the World's Aircraft*, 1912, *op cit*, p111.
8. J.G. Robins, *Wooden Wonder: a short history of the wooden aeroplane,* 1975, p6.
9. Details of the Calais-Dover Blériot XI are based on a general examination of the aircraft, supplemented by several published sources, notably R. Tessier in an unidentified press-cutting conserved in BA; *l'Aérophile*; M. Calderara and P. Banet-Rivet, *Manuel de l'Aviateur Constructeur*; and J.Devaux and M. Marani in *Pégase* No.54.
10. eg D.A. Jolly in *RAF Flying Review*, 7 August 1959.
11. Correspondence in BA.
12. *The Times*, 16 September 1909.
13. E. Chadeau, *L'industrie aéronautique, op cit,* p41.

CHAPTER 12

1. F. Ferber, in *l'Aérophile*, 15 September 1909, pp415-8.
2. P.Rousseau, in 'L'Aviation triomphante' in *Conciliation Internationale* No.11, November 1909, pp108-115. See also S. Nicolaou, *Reims – 1909: Le Premier Meeting Aérien International,* 1999 for a good account of the meeting.

3. *Flight*, 4 September 1909, p540.

4. Details of the Gnome engine are mainly from A. Nahum, *The Rotary Aero Engine,* 1987.

5. P. Rousseau, in 'L'Aviation triomphante', *op cit.*

6. F.W. Lanchester, in the *Aeronautical Journal*, January 1909, pp9-10.

7. C.H. Gibbs-Smith, *Aviation: an historical survey from its origins to the end of World War II*, 2nd. Ed. 1985, p145.

8. P. Rousseau, in 'L'Aviation triomphante', *op cit,* pp164-5.

9. *l'Aérophile*, 15 December 1909, p557, and F. Collin, *Parmi les Précurseurs*, p114.

CHAPTER 13

1.Records data is from C.H. Gibbs-Smith, *Aviation*, and from L. Blériot and E. Ramond, *La Gloire des Ailes.*

2. E. Chadeau, *L'industrie aéronautique*, *op cit,* pp32-3.

3. *Flight*, 9 April 1910, pp272-3.

4. Ibid., 5 November 1910, p908.

5. F. Collin, *Parmi les Précurseurs*, *op cit,* pp133-4.

6. Report by Lt R.A. Cammell, July 1910, Public Records Office, Kew, AIR1/1612/204/87/31.

7. *Flight*, 1 June 1912, pp494-5.

8. Lt Cammell's report, *op cit.*

9. *Flight*, 9 April 1910, pp272-3.

10. Ibid., 1 June 1912, pp494-5.

11. Ibid., 4 March 1911, p184.

12. J. Liron, 'Louis Blériot: L'homme de La Manche', serialised in twenty-three parts in *Aviation Magazine International* (France) from No.666, 15 September 1975 to No.690, 16 September 1976, pt23.

13. *Flight*, 8 June 1912, p521.

14. British Patent No.29785. See also No.28638.

15. List in BA.

16. Lt Cammell's report, *op cit.*

17. *Flight*, 30 March 1912, p284.

18. T.D. Crouch, Blériot XI, *op cit,* p78.

19. *Flight*, 30 March 1912, p284.

20. R. Dallas Brett, *History of British Aviation 1908-14,* 1933, p123.

CHAPTER 14

1. P. Vergnamo, *Origin of Aviation in Italy 1783-1918,* Genoa, 1964, p101.

2. Ibid., pp101-2.

3. Information on Pégoud is mainly from G. L'Herbier-Montagnon, *Un héros dauphinois roi de l'air: Adolphe Pégoud (1889-1915)*, 1980.

4. F.Collin, *Parmi les Précurseurs*, *op cit,* pp178-9.

5. J.Lucas, *The Big Umbrella: the history of the parachute from Davinci to Apollo,* 1973, p46.

6. L. Blériot and E. Ramond, *La Gloire des Ailes, op cit*, p169.

7. *Icare* No.89, pp97-8.

8. Ibid.

9. R. Dallas Brett, *History of British Aviation, op cit*, p245.

10. *Flight*, 13 September 1913, p1008.

11. R. Dallas Brett, *History of British Aviation, op cit,* p246.

12. Ibid.

13. Letter from N. Chéreau to L. Blériot dated 4 October 1913, in BA.

14. Letter from M. O'Gorman to L. Blériot dated 26 October 1913, in BA.

15. L. Blériot, Note pour le Ministère des Finances dated 4 June 1932, in BA.

16. R. Dallas Brett, *History of British Aviation, op cit,* p41.

17. L. Blériot, Note pour le Ministère des Finances, *op cit*.

18. J. Liron, 'Louis Blériot', *op cit,* part 9.

19. E. Chadeau, *L'industrie aéronautique, op cit*, p74.

20. C.C. Turner, *The old flying days,* 1927, p235.

21. Ibid.

22. E. Chadeau, *L'industrie aéronautique, op cit,* pp75-6.

CHAPTER 15

1. *Mémoires d'Alicia Blériot, op cit.*

2. L. Blériot and E. Ramond, *La Gloire des Ailes, op cit,* pp177-8.

3. *Pégase* No.50, p15.

4. S. Pesquiès-Courbier, in *Icare* No.85, 1978, p16.

5. A. E. Insoll, The Blériot Monoplane (memorandum) Public Records Office, Kew, AIR1/727/152/6.

6. Ibid.

7. E. Chadeau, *L'industrie aéronautique, op cit*, p83.

8. J. M. Laux, 'The Rise and Fall of Armand Deperdussin', in French Historical Studies, 1973.

9. Manuscript note, undated and unsigned but attributed to F. Max Richard by the author on the evidence of the handwriting, in BA.

10. Ibid.

11. Ibid.

12. Letter from F. Max Richard to Alicia Blériot, dated 31 July 1939, in BA.

13. S. Pesquiès-Courbier, in *Icare* No.85, pp152-3.

14. J. M. Bruce, *The Aeroplanes of the Royal Flying Corps (Military Wing)*, 1982, p553.

15. Count S. Hallwyl, Marc Birkigt – Father of the Hispano-Suiza, in *Flying Review International*, March 1964, pp48-9.

16. R. Stein, *The Automobile Book,* 1961, p123.

17. E. Chadeau, *L'industrie aéronautique, op cit,* pp90, 105, 138, 193.

18. S.D. Heron, *History of the Aircraft Piston Engine,* Detroit, 1961, pp15, 105.

19. S. Pasquiès-Courbier, in *Icare* No.85, pp154-5.

20. *Pégase* No.50, p16.

21. A.E. Berriman, memorandum dated August 1915, in Library of the Royal Aeronautical Society, Box 5e, Power Plants.

22. Public Records Office, Kew, AIR1/1139/204/5/2305.

23. J. M. Bruce, *The Aeroplanes of the Royal Flying Corps, op cit,* pp556-8.

24. S. Pesquiès-Courbier, in *Icare* No.85, pp58 et seq.

25. *Pégase* No.47, p8.

26. Ibid p6.

27. J. M. Bruce, *The Aeroplanes of the Royal Flying Corps, op cit,* p561.

28. L. Blériot and E. Ramond, *La Gloire des Ailes, op cit,* p180.

29. Text of address by Jean Blériot (1972), in BA.

30. E. Chadeau, *L'industrie aéronautique, op cit,* pp100, 86.

31. D. Wragg, *Flight with Power,* 1978, p153.

32. J. M. Bruce, *British Aeroplanes 1914-18,* 1957, foreword.

33. S. Pesquiès-Courbier, *Icare* No.88, 1979, pp105-6.

34. Data in *Flight,* 7 February 1924, p74.

CHAPTER 16

1. E. Chadeau, *L'industrie aéronautique, op cit,* pp147, 155.

2. M. Lhospice, *Match pour La Manche, op cit,* p306.

3. Statuts de Blériot-Aéronautique S. A., 1922, in BA.

4. E. Petit, *La vie quotidienne dans l'Aviation en France au début du XXe siècle 1900-1935,* 1977, p179.

5. J. Liron, 'Les SPAD d'André Herbemont', serialised in nineteen parts in *Aviation Magazine International* (France) from No.558, 31 March 1971 to No.581, 1 March 1972, part 1.

6. J. Liron, 'Louis Blériot', part 10. See also L. Blériot, *Blériot: l'envol du xxe siècle,* 1994, pp293-6.

7. J. Liron, 'Les SPADS d'André Herbemont', part 4.

8. Ibid. Part 7.

9. Letter from J. Brun to L. Blériot dated 26 May 1923, in BA.

10. Blériot motorcycle catalogue, undated, in BA.

11. J. Brun's letter to Blériot.

12. Unidentified press-cutting in BA.

13. Catalogue of Blériot - Aéronautique, 1920.

14. J. Brun's letter to Blériot.

15. *Mémoires d'Alicia Blériot, op cit.*

16. L. Blériot, Note pour le Ministère des Finances, dated 4 June 1932, in BA.

17. Ibid.

18. *Flight,* 23 January 1919, p126.

19. Letter from J.B. Antelme in London to Blériot, dated 12 January 1921, in BA.

20. L. Blèriot, Note pour le Ministère des Finances.

21. Ibid.

22. M. Lhospice, *Match pour La Manche, op cit,* p306.

23. Publicity leaflets of Blériot-Aéronautique and J. Liron, 'Les SPAD d'André Herbemont', parts 7-8.

24. Statuts of Blériot-Aéronautique S. A.

25. J. Brun's letter to Blériot.

CHAPTER 17

1. J. Liron, 'Les SPAD d'André Herbemont', parts 15-16.

2. Ibid. part 16.

3. L. Blériot, *Blériot: L'Envol du xxe siècle, op cit,* pp414-25.

4. *Icare* No.89, p102.

5. Text of Blériot's speech at his luncheon in honour of Charles Lindberg, 22 May 1927, in BA.

6. *Icare* No.89, p99.

7. Author's conversation with Louis Blériot, Blériot's grandson, in December 1987.

8. J. Liron, Louis Blériot, part 20.

9. Text of speech by Jean Blériot (1972) in BA.

10. L. Blériot, *Blériot: l'Envol du xxe siècle, op cit,* pp530-31.

11. J. Liron, 'Louis Blériot', part 14.

12. Letter from Lucien Bossoutrot in Oran to Blériot, undated, in BA.

13. Ibid.

14. J. Liron, 'Louis Blériot', part 14.

15. L. Blériot and E. Ramond, *La Gloire des Ailes, op cit,* p210.

16. J. Liron, 'Louis Blériot', part 15.

17. Ibid. parts 19-20.

18. Letter from Jacques Breguet to Blériot, dated 16 August 1933.

19. Note, undated, in BA.

20. Internal memorandum, Blériot-Aéronautique, dated 7 March 1936, in BA.

21. J. Liron, 'Louis Blériot', part 22.

22. L. Blériot, 'Are landing places necessary for the commercial aerial crossing of the North Atlantic?', in *The Smithsonian Report for 1935,* Washington, 1936, pp453-62, tr. from l'*Aérophile*, 3 March 1935.

23. Ibid.

24. Internal Memorandum, Blériot-Aéronautique, dated 7 March 1936, in BA.

25. Ibid., and two other such memoranda, one of 7 April 1936, the other undated.

26. Copy of extract from a letter by Blériot to his parents, undated, in BA.

EPILOGUE

1. Letter from Ministère de l'Air to Blériot-Aéronautique, dated 20 March 1940, in BA.

2. Brochure published by the Syndicat d'Initiative Sangatte Blériot-Plage, undated.

Index